Louis Sockalexis

ALSO BY DAVID L. FLEITZ

Shoeless: The Life and Times of Joe Jackson
(McFarland, 2001)

Louis Sockalexis

The First Cleveland Indian

DAVID L. FLEITZ

McFarland & Company, Inc., Publishers
Jefferson, North Carolina, and London

Library of Congress Cataloguing-in-Publication Data

Fleitz, David L., 1955–
    Louis Sockalexis : the first Cleveland Indian / David L. Fleitz.
       p.   cm.
    Includes bibliographical references and index.

    ISBN 0-7864-1383-2 (softcover : 50# alkaline paper) ∞

    1. Sockalexis, Louis, 1871–1913. 2. Baseball players—United States—Biography. 3. Cleveland Indians (Baseball team)—History. I. Title.
GV865.S588F54   2002
796.357′092—dc21   2002010468

British Library cataloguing data are available

©2002 David L. Fleitz. All rights reserved

No part of this book may be reproduced or transmitted in any form or by any means, electronic or mechanical, including photocopying or recording, or by any information storage and retrieval system, without permission in writing from the publisher.

Cover photograph: Louis Sockalexis (National Baseball Hall of Fame Library, Cooperstown, NY)

Manufactured in the United States of America

McFarland & Company, Inc., Publishers
   Box 611, Jefferson, North Carolina 28640
      www.mcfarlandpub.com

For Deborah

Acknowledgments

I would like to thank a few people without whom this book would not have been possible.

I received a great deal of kind assistance from Carole Binette, the census coordinator and rights protection researcher for the Penobscot Indian Nation in Maine. She provided information on the family tree of Louis Sockalexis, and articles and clippings from the tribal files that proved very useful.

The archivists at the College of the Holy Cross, in Worcester, Massachusetts, also made available many useful items on Sockalexis' college career, and enabled me to clear up some of the myths surrounding the feats of this great Penobscot athlete. Archivists Jo Ann Carr and Lois Hamill were generous with their assistance.

As always, Bill Burdick at the National Baseball Library in Cooperstown, New York, offered helpful assistance in rounding up photographs for this book, and the Eugene C. Murdock collection of baseball books and materials at the Cleveland Public Library was invaluable. So was the SABR (Society for American Baseball Research) Lending Library, my source for microfilmed copies of *The Sporting News* and *Sporting Life* for the 1897–1899 period.

I would also like to thank my wife Deborah for her editing skills and her moral support.

Table of Contents

Acknowledgments — vii
Introduction — 1

1. Where the River Broadens Out — 5
2. The College of the Holy Cross — 20
3. From Worcester to Notre Dame — 34
4. The National League — 46
5. Tebeau's Indians — 54
6. "He's the Stuff and He's the People" — 68
7. The Polo Grounds — 82
8. Fall from Grace — 95
9. The 1898 Season — 110
10. Sitting the Bench — 119
11. "The Sorriest Shell of a Team Ever Seen…" — 129
12. "A Sorrowful Spectacle…" — 142
13. Bender, Meyers, and Andrew Sockalexis — 157
14. The End of the Line — 168
15. Louis Sockalexis and the Cleveland Indians — 180
16. Epilogue — 192

Appendix 1: William J. Fox Letter	197
Appendix 2: Sockalexis Statistics	199
Notes	201
Bibliography	213
Index	217

Introduction

I was not a Cleveland Indians fan growing up.

I was a Detroit Tigers fan. My family lived in northwest Ohio, about eight miles south of Toledo, right on the border between Tiger country and Indian country. Everything west of us belonged to the Tigers, while territory to the east was loyal to the Indians.

However, some of my cousins living ten miles east of us were Cleveland fans through and through. I therefore followed the Indians as well as the Tigers, because my cousins did, and listened to Cleveland Indians games on the radio. My cousins even ventured to Cleveland's Municipal Stadium and saw games every now and then.

In all that time, as familiar as I was with the Cleveland Indians, I never questioned where the team nickname came from. I knew that scattered tribes of Indians used to live in northern Ohio, though there weren't any remaining, all of them having been driven westward by settlers and armies nearly two centuries before I was born. I figured that the team was called the Indians after the Ottawa, Wyandot, and other tribes that once made their home in the area of northern Ohio called the Western Reserve.

It wasn't until the 1970s that I heard about a long-ago player named Louis Sockalexis.

Sockalexis, according to the Cleveland Indians media guide, was nothing less than "the original Cleveland Indian." He came from an Indian reservation in Maine, where he was not only a member in full standing of the Penobscot tribe, but also happened to be the son of the chief. Sockalexis was an outstanding student athlete at the College of the Holy Cross, excelling in football and track as well as baseball, and when he joined the Cleveland National League team in 1897, he became the first recognized Native American to play in the major leagues. He was a well-spoken and highly intelligent young man, and within days of his arrival in Cleveland, he became the most popular player on the Cleveland team. He was a nearly perfect physical specimen, handsome and athletic, and showed his prodigious athletic talent by belting line drives and making circus catches in the outfield.

The sportswriters, dazzled by this Indian athlete, called Sockalexis the "Chief of Sockem" and wrote reams of poetry in the sports pages about their exciting new player:

> This is bounding Sockalexis,
> Fielder of the mighty Clevelands.
> Like the catapult in action,
> For the plate he throws the baseball,
> Till the rooter, blithely rooting,
> Shouts until he shakes the bleachers,
> "Sockalexis, Sockalexis,
> Sock it to them, Sockalexis!"

In the 1890s, the Cleveland team was known as the Spiders, but Louis Sockalexis made such an immediate impression that the local sportswriters began referring to the team as the Indians. The ballparks echoed with war whoops whenever Sockalexis took the field, and the young ballplayer, almost single-handedly, brought much-needed excitement and energy to Cleveland baseball.

Sockalexis, by all accounts, was a good enough player to merit all this attention. He posted a lifetime batting average of .313, and he batted .338 as a rookie in 1897. He owned a powerful and accurate throwing arm, the best in the game, and his teammates claimed that he could run 100 yards in near world-record time, even in full baseball uniform. Sockalexis was so physically talented that Hugh Jennings, a Hall of Fame player and manager, once stated that he "had the most brilliant career of any man who ever played the game.... He should have been the greatest player of all time — greater than Cobb, Wagner, Lajoie, Hornsby and any of the other men who have made history for the game." Jennings knew what he was talking about, for he played against Sockalexis as a member of the Baltimore Orioles in the 1890s.

Though Louis Sockalexis disappeared from the major leagues only two years later, and played only 94 major league games in all, he must have made a strong impression on those who saw him. When the Cleveland American League club needed a new nickname in 1915, according to the team's media guide, the ballclub chose the name "Indians" to honor Sockalexis.

For many years, the memory of Sockalexis slowly faded away, though the name "Indians" lived on and became the identity of the Cleveland baseball team. It may or may not have been a coincidence that the Cleveland Indians revived the memory of Louis Sockalexis in the early 1970s, at the same time that the team came under attack for their employment of Native American symbols and images. "Chief Wahoo," the red-faced cartoon character that has appeared on the team uniforms since 1950, draws much negative comment from activist groups. Many of those same critics would like to see the team get rid of Chief Wahoo, and some would also prefer that the team drop the name Indians, as many high school and college athletic programs have already done.

So, with the team's nickname and identity under attack, the Cleveland ballclub points to Louis Sockalexis as its inspiration and claims that their Indians nickname — and, by extension, Chief Wahoo and all the other Indian imagery employed by the team — is intended to honor Sockalexis, the legendary Indian athlete. In 1978, Cuyahoga County (which contains the city of Cleveland) proclaimed a "Louis Sockalexis Day" to further honor the man they called "the father of the Cleveland Indians." One of the county commissioners, despairing over the poor performance of the team, went one step further. He wrote a letter to the governor of the Penobscot Indian Nation in Maine and asked if the tribe could develop another Sockalexis that they could send to Cleveland to play ball for the Indians.

Who was Louis Sockalexis, and why do people remember him more than 80 years after his death? I was surprised to learn that there are no full-length biographies of this man, though I also discovered how difficult it would be to tell his story with accuracy and fairness. Much of the information available is anecdotal, contradictory, and colored by cultural perceptions of Native Americans by mostly white writers and journalists. Sockalexis played major league baseball more than a hundred years ago, when sportswriting and baseball were both in their infancy, and a great deal of myth has grown up around the memory of this impressive ballplayer.

I decided to set out to find the real Louis Sockalexis. All "politically correct" considerations aside, the story of Louis Sockalexis is a most interesting one. Not only was Sockalexis the first Native American to play in the major leagues, but he was also the first minority athlete of any kind to play in the National League. As such, he was a Native American who tried to make a name for himself in a white world, in an environment that turned out to be implacably hostile to his efforts. He was a baseball meteor, who burned brightly but flamed out too quickly, and the more I learned about Sockalexis, the more I wanted to tell his story.

Whether or not he was the "father" of the Cleveland Indians, Sockalexis was certainly the Native American version of Jackie Robinson. This Penobscot from Maine was the first recognized member of his race to play major league ball, a full 50 years before Robinson broke the African-American racial barrier, and the parallels are many between these two great ballplayers and athletes. Though the tragic tale of Louis Sockalexis ended differently than the triumphant story of Jackie Robinson, Sockalexis is remembered today when almost all of the other great players of the 1890s are long forgotten.

There are now 30 major league baseball teams. Some are named after colors (Reds, Red Sox, White Sox), animals (Tigers, Diamondbacks, Cubs) and birds (Cardinals, Orioles, Blue Jays). Some are named after nonspecific groups of people, like the Giants, the Pirates, and the Brewers. However, the Cleveland team of the American League is the only major league club that can trace the inspiration of its nickname back to one specific individual. That man was Louis Sockalexis, and this is his story.

David L. Fleitz
August 2002

CHAPTER 1

Where the River Broadens Out

Brother, the Good Spirit who made and placed the red men here, before the white men came, gave us all the land from whence the waters run into the Penobscot. He caused the forests to abound with game, and the river with fish, for our use and subsistence. We then were contented and happy.
— Captain Francis, Penobscot delegate to Maine treaty conference, 1820[1]

On Indian Island in the middle of the Penobscot River in central Maine, about 12 miles north of Bangor, lies a town that was already flourishing when the European settlers arrived in the early 17th century. This village was the oldest settlement, as well as the tribal capital, of the powerful Penobscot Indian Nation, so the Europeans called the village Indian Old Town. The village, known today as Old Town, is now a small city of nearly 8,000 people. Over the years, the town has expanded to the opposite bank of the Penobscot River, growing ever outward, and today the greatest share of Old Town's population is made up of whites, not Indians. Many of the remaining members of the Penobscot tribe live on the Indian Island part of Old Town, which is now contained within the boundaries of the Penobscot Indian Reservation and still serves as the seat of government of the tribe.

The Penobscot tribe once occupied most of the state of Maine, but the Europeans brought diseases that wiped out a sizable portion of the state's indigenous population in the 1600s. Over the next two centuries, constant warfare and a series of disadvantageous peace treaties reduced the tribe's holdings to a small reservation, comprising only 4,481 acres on Indian Island and a few other islands in the river. This formerly powerful tribe, with a population that once numbered in the tens of thousands, began the 21st century with fewer than 2,100 people on its rolls. Indian Island itself is home to about 500 tribal members, while many other Penobscot live in cities like Bangor, where work is more plentiful than in the economically disadvantaged area around the reservation.

The tribal seal tells some of the history of the Penobscot Nation. In the center of the seal is an image of a Penobscot man; above him is the English name of the tribe, and below him is spelled *Bur-nur-wurb-skek*, the name of the tribe in the native tongue. There are three crosses on the outside of the seal, and below the crosses are the words "Purity," "Faith," and "Valor," the motto of the tribe. The crosses themselves symbolize the Roman Catholic religious identification of the Penobscot, and the dates 1669 and 1749 commemorate the end of a bloody conflict with the Mohawk and the final peace treaty with the English colonists.

Some say that the image in the center of the tribal seal is the profile of Louis Sockalexis. Sockalexis was not a warrior, as he was born in 1871, long after the defeated tribe had been relegated to its tiny reservation in central Maine. He was not a chief, though his father once served as the Penobscot tribal governor and some of his ancestors held the title of chief. Some Native Americans have earned renown as politicians, writers, business leaders, and artists, but Sockalexis was none of these.

Louis Sockalexis, instead, was an athlete, and as such he became more famous than any of the greatest warriors and chiefs in the long and honored history of the Penobscot tribe.

The Penobscot Indian Nation of 1871, the year of Louis Sockalexis' birth, was only a shell of what it had been 400 years before. In the 15th century, there were more than 20,000 indigenous people living in what is now Maine. The Maine Indians were called the Wabenaki, the "people of the dawn," since they lived on the eastern part of the North American continent where the sun rose over the ocean. Those in central Maine, called the Abenaki,[2] lived in a place that they called *Pa-na-wap-skek*, or *Bur-nur-wurb-skek* (as written on the tribal seal), variously translated as "the place of the white rocks," or "the place where the river broadens out." This word became the name of the people as well and evolved into the name Penobscot.

Before the white man came, the settlements and hunting grounds of the Penobscot stretched all along the Penobscot River valley, from the Atlantic Ocean to the mountains and pine forests in the northern part of the state. In the middle of the Penobscot land rose Katahdin, the "Great Mountain" which figured prominently in many of the tribe's spiritual legends. In olden times, many young Penobscot men traveled to Katahdin for spiritual guidance. They climbed the Great Mountain and fasted upon it for four days as a rite of passage.³

To the east lived the smaller Maliseet, Passamaquoddy, and Micmac tribes, related Algonquian groups with similar language and customs, against whom the Penobscot made war in the early 1600s for control of the fur trade. Other tribes lived to the west, providing a barrier between the Penobscot and the expanding Mohawk from what is now New York State, but in the late 1600s those tribes moved north to Canada. When they withdrew, they left the Penobscot undefended against the Mohawk, and the two tribes battled in a series of bitterly fought wars filled with massacres and atrocities on both sides.

The tribal seal of the Penobscot Indian Nation. Some say that the figure in the center is a profile of Louis Sockalexis. (Penobscot Indian Nation)

The tribal capital was Old Town, a village on Indian Island some 30 miles north of the place where the river empties into Penobscot Bay, and the Penobscot people wintered there in wigwams made from birch bark. In the spring, the Penobscot left Old Town and moved toward the Atlantic, hunting seal and gathering crab and lobster, before spreading out into their traditional hunting and fishing grounds. They took salmon, shad, and eels from the rivers and beaver, rabbit, and other small game from the forests. The Penobscot then journeyed back to Old Town, where they planted some corn and vegetables, hunted and fished along the river banks, and held celebrations and ceremonies until the fall. The fall hunt began in September, and the families proceeded to their hunting territories where they tracked and killed moose, deer, and caribou for their meat and hides. When the rivers and lakes froze in December, the Penobscot returned to Indian Island and hunkered down for the winter with the meat and supplies gathered in the hunting season, though they also tracked and killed caribou and moose in the deep New England snow. When the ice thawed again in April, the Penobscot left Old Town for another season's hunting and fishing.

The Penobscot were great hunters, by necessity, as the very survival of the tribe depended on the success of the fall hunt. They were also courageous warriors, famous as the only tribe to hold their own against the fearsome Mohawk, and were also known as quiet, serious, and industrious people. They could not afford to be loud and boisterous, because their western frontier was undefended. Instead, the Penobscot were admired for their stoicism, because they raised their children to be that way. They quickly shushed boisterous children at play, because they did not want to scare away the local game and make life more difficult for the hunters of the tribe. They also did not want to give away the location of their camp to bands of Mohawk attackers who lurked in the area. For this reason, the Penobscot became known for their courage and their stoicism in roughly equal measure.

The Penobscot Indian Nation holds the distinction of having the longest continuously operating government on the North American continent, with an unbroken line of tribal chiefs dating back to at least the year 1568. The tribal chief was called the *sagama*, or "strong man," but the tribe was only weakly governed, and in peacetime the *sagama* served more as a representative in negotiations and tribal ceremonies than as a ruler. Mostly because of the depredations of the Mohawk, the Penobscot found it useful to govern their tribe as a loose confederation, without a single powerful central government. This organizational style made it possible for a band of Penobscot warriors to disappear quickly and regroup in another location for a counterattack, without waiting for one powerful leader to make decisions.

The day-to-day decisions for the tribe were made within the tribal families. The Penobscot were divided into 22 or 23 family groups, each with their own traditional hunting ground along the rivers and lakes of Maine. Each family took an aquatic or land animal as its symbol, and the family name came from the Penobscot word for that symbol. The Crab and Raven families were respected for their hunting and fishing prowess, and others, like the Water Nymph family, were known as fine warriors. The highest-ranking families were the Frog and Squirrel, and for many years the chief of the tribe was chosen from these two groups, although the most famous Penobscot chief, Joseph Orono, who died in 1801, was a Beaver.

The Penobscot spent most of their time and effort in their hunting. "No other regular activity occupied spirit, mind, and body so incessantly,"[4] wrote cultural anthropologist Frank G. Speck, because the hunt provided food, clothing, and many other basic necessities of the tribe. Ethnologists state that the tribal identity of the Penobscot was strongly defined by the hunt. However, they still made time for sports and games. Many of the favorite Penobscot sports, like wrestling and running for speed and for distance, had the additional aim of preparing young men for physically demanding tasks such as chasing game and battling enemies.

They ran races on a three-mile path around the perimeter of Indian Island, either in groups or as individuals, to build endurance and stamina that would prove useful in the fall hunting season. In wintertime a game similar to ice hockey was played with a piece of wood batted around with green sticks along the frozen rivers. They wrestled enthusiastically, and practiced ice skating and sledding in the winter months. The tribal members also played a ball-and-bat game remarkably similar to baseball, possibly adapted from or suggested by the Europeans:

> The field had four posts at the corners. There was a pitcher, batter, and catcher. When the batter hit the ball, which was a large, soft one, he ran around outside the posts. If the pitcher stopped the ball short or caught it on the bounce four times, the man was out, until which time he could keep on batting and scoring runs.[5]

Sports and games, in Native American culture, were no mere pastimes or entertainments. They were an important facet of tribal culture and were contested for ritual and ceremonial purposes. Games involving the entire tribe, such as lacrosse and "shinny," a kind of field hockey, were played to appeal for an abundant harvest in the spring, or to give thanks for one in the fall. The Indians organized games to celebrate victory in war, to bring favorable weather, or to stop the spread of disease or suffering. In most native cultures, the games were preceded by dances, music, and speeches, and the entire process might last for an entire day or more.

Native Americans treated games and sports much differently than the whites that came later to the American continent. Indian games were given great social and religious significance, and the participants spent much time in spiritual preparation and self-purification before the games began. Judges and referees prayed for wisdom and fairness, while athletes asked for strength and good fortune. Players liked to win, of course, but the "win at all costs" philosophy was foreign to the Native American experience before the arrival of the white man.

In his famous poem, "The Song of Hiawatha," Henry Wadsworth Longfellow referred to the importance of athletic endeavor, especially running, in the Native American culture:

> Out of childhood into manhood,
> Now had grown my Hiawatha,
> Skilled in the craft of hunters,

> Learned in all the lore of old men.
> In all youthful sports and pastimes,
> In all manly arts and labors,
> Swift of foot was Hiawatha.
> He could shoot an arrow from him,
> And run forward with such fleetness,
> That the arrow fell behind him.

Because the Native Americans organized games for ceremonial or religious reasons, a high level of sportsmanship and fair play was demanded of the participants. Displays of temper, arguing with officials, and cheating were not tolerated, and indeed such incidents were so rare as to be almost nonexistent. Team members took it upon themselves to punish a participant's loss of decorum with scorn and ridicule. The participants, not the referees, kept order, especially since there may have been a hundred or more players on a side for large tribal contests. In addition, the Indians did not adhere strictly to any standardized body of rules in their sports, preferring to adapt rules to the conditions at hand, and they usually did not keep individual records or statistics of any kind. The ceremony and ritual surrounding the game itself, not the end result of winning or losing, were the most important aspects of athletic participation for the Penobscot and for most North American tribes.[6]

The Europeans arrived in the Penobscot River valley in the early 1600s and brought with them steel tools and cloth, as well as firearms, tobacco, and alcohol, which they traded for beaver furs. The French and the English also brought their rivalry to the new world, and it didn't take long for the Wabenaki tribes to become involved in conflicts between the English Protestants of New England and the French Catholics of Quebec. The French reached the area first and called it Maine after an ancient French province, and by the mid–1600s the Penobscot converted to Catholicism and allied themselves with the French. In 1687 the first Catholic church was built on Indian Island, and the Indians learned French, took French surnames, and used the names of heroic French kings like Louis and Francis for their children. The French influence in Maine drew the ire of the English Puritans of Massachusetts, who offered bounties for Penobscot scalps and induced the Mohawk to commit acts of aggression.

The Europeans also brought the deadliest weapon of all: diseases such as plague, smallpox, and cholera. In the middle of the 17th century, pandemics wiped out more than 80 percent of the indigenous population. Some of the Penobscot family groups disappeared entirely, and others fled up the Penobscot River to the central part of the state to escape the deadly illnesses ravishing the coastal areas. Frank G. Speck, a professor of ethnology who studied the Penobscot for more than three decades and wrote up his findings in his seminal work, *Penobscot Man*, described a Native American way of life that was lost forever. "Theirs," wrote Speck, "was a cultural destiny thwarted by the interruptions of an alien civilization—the end of a primitive Utopia."[7]

This "Great Dying" severely affected all the Wabenaki tribes, and a series of wars with the better-equipped English and their Mohawk allies weakened these native peoples further. The Penobscot warred several times against their Maliseet, Passamequoddy, and Micmac neighbors to the east, but in the 1700s the four decimated tribes joined in a Wabenaki Confederation to protect themselves against their common enemies, the Mohawk and the English. An old Passamaquoddy narrative explains:

> Long ago, the Indians were always fighting against each other. They struck one another bloodily. There were many men, women and children who alike were tormented by these constant battles.... It seemed as if all were tired of how they had lived wrongly. The great chiefs said to the others, "Looking back from here the way we have come, we see that we have left bloody tracks. We see many wrongs. And as for these bloody hatchets, and bows, arrows, they must be buried forever." Then they all set about deciding to join with one another in a confederacy.[8]

The Wabenaki confederacy fought fiercely, but in 1723 the English defeated the Penobscot and destroyed Old Town. A few more conflicts followed, especially during the French and Indian War between the English and the French for control of North America. The Penobscot allied themselves with the French once again, and in 1756 King George II of England issued a proclamation, offering bounties for the scalps of Penobscot tribesmen.[9] By 1763, the French were thoroughly defeated and the Indian wars of Maine were over. The victorious English annexed Catholic Maine to an uneasy union with their former enemies of Protestant Massachusetts.

English rule lasted until the American colonists rebelled and declared independence. The French-influenced Penobscot, no great friends of the English, fought for the revolutionists in the conflict, and after the war the Penobscot received tracts of land from the new American government. However, this land was only a fraction of the original Penobscot homeland, and treaties in the next few decades reduced their holdings even further. By the 1820s Maine, now separated from Massachusetts, became the newest member of the United States, and the Penobscot Nation, such as it was, numbered only about 270 people living as wards of the state. The defeated tribe lived on a reservation consisting of 146 islands in the Penobscot River north of Bangor, the new state's largest city. The center of the

Penobscot Nation was Old Town, on Indian Island, the largest of the islands in the river.

By the mid–1800s the family groups were mostly a memory, and the hunting and fishing grounds, which no longer belonged to the Penobscot, were now congested with settlers, loggers, and sportsmen. The Penobscot lived in wooden shacks instead of their traditional wigwams, and eventually turned their knowledge of the Maine woods into new occupations as river guides, loggers, and river drivers. They intermarried with other tribes and with white settlers, and such mixed marriages are recorded in the generation of Louis Sockalexis' grandfather. Some researchers say that the last full-blooded Penobscot died in 1853.

The state and federal governments took little notice of Indian concerns in the 19th century, being more focused on expanding white settlements and colonizing the former Native American lands. In addition, many Americans of European descent looked down upon the Native Americans of the Penobscot and other tribes, considering them still "savage" and unable to intelligently govern themselves. The Maine Supreme Court, in an 1824 decision on land boundaries, wrote: "[I]mbecility on their [the Indians'] part and the dictates of humanity on ours, have necessarily prescribed to them their subjugation to our paternal control; in disregard of some, at least, of abstract principles of the rights of man." Maine's Indian agent, an official named Purinton, wrote of the Penobscot in 1861, "There are unmistakable indications that the people to which this tribe belongs do not possess the high order of intellect that distinguish the European race."[10]

Fortunately, the Penobscot were nothing if not resourceful. By 1850 members of the tribe followed new professions, earning money as loggers and woodland guides. They also made and sold jewelry, baskets, and souvenirs to the tourists who came to the woods each summer. The older tribal members were dying, taking their knowledge of the traditional Penobscot culture with them, but the population of the tribe continued to increase throughout this period. However, the Penobscot were still considered to be second-class citizens of the United States—they were not allowed to vote in national elections until 1954—and the United States government officially designated the reservations as "enclaves of disenfranchised citizens bereft of any special status." Louis Francis Sockalexis was one of those "disenfranchised citizens" from the moment of his birth on Indian Island on October 24, 1871.

The Sockalexis family enjoyed a high standing in the Penobscot tribe. Their mark was the Sturgeon, and in former generations the family carried the surname Kabahse, the word for sturgeon in the Penobscot language.

1. Where the River Broadens Out

When the French missionaries converted the Penobscot to Catholicism, the families took new French-themed names; Sockalexis, sometimes written as Sock-Alexis, is most likely a corruption of the French name Jacques-Alexis.

The hunting grounds of the Sockalexis family, centuries ago, lay between Ragged Lake and the much larger Moosehead Lake in the mountainous north-central pine forests of what is now Maine. They fished in the rivers and lakes, paddling around in birch-bark or moosehide canoes, spearing sturgeon, salmon, and other varieties. They also set traps and used bows and arrows to hunt the game that was plentiful in the area. Moose, deer, beaver, caribou, and many other forms of wildlife abounded in Maine at the time and provided more than enough to keep the family prosperous. The Sockalexis family also owned the rights to a forest of maple trees from which they gathered sap, which was made into candy and syrup in the fall. They performed some types of agriculture, planting corn and squash, but for the most part the members of the Sockalexis family, like the tribe as a whole, were hunters and gatherers, not farmers.

The Sockalexis men gained fame within the tribe for their athletic ability, which was highly prized among the Penobscot. In early times, a group of the most athletic young Penobscot men were separated from the rest of the tribe and designated as "pure men" or "pure runners." The pure men lived separately, swearing off tobacco, liquor, and sexual relations, because their assigned task in the tribe was an important one. They were the designated hunters of the tribe. They were trained to run fast, so fast that they could capture and kill moose, and even deer, by running them down in the forest and slicing their throats with a knife, the only weapon they carried.

The winters in Maine were incredibly cold. The lakes and rivers froze over from January until April, and the game hibernated or hid deep in the forests. The Penobscot designated the month of January as *angelosamwesit*, or "hard times." If the hunters did not gather enough meat and fish to last the winter, the weaker members of the tribe starved. The pure men, then, played a vitally important role, for the survival of the tribe depended on their hunting skills.

When the pure man lost his speed, or aged, he gave up his position gracefully and allowed a younger man to take over, often accepting a position as a trainer for the next generation of pure men. The pure man was held in high esteem, during and after his service, and status as a pure man was a source of pride in a Penobscot's later years. The Sockalexis family produced its share of pure men, and for many generations the Penobscot celebrated the athletic accomplishments of the Sockalexis men.

The Sockalexis family members were also vitally interested in the well-being of the tribe as a whole. In the 1800s, after the tribe had been defeated and relegated to their newly reduced state, members of the former Sturgeon family came forward and became involved in the governance of the tribe. During these decades, several Sockalexis men held high office within the tribal government. Tomar (Thomas) Sockalexis, Louis' great-uncle, served two terms as tribal governor in the years immediately following the Civil War, and a cousin, Joseph, served three terms as governor in the 1870s.

Francis Peol Sockalexis, Louis' father, was born on Indian Island in the summer of 1841. A strong, intelligent man and a great athlete, in former times he might have earned a place as a pure man. He was tall, handsome, and fast of foot, like so many of the Sockalexis men, and many claimed that Francis once threw a coin from the eastern bank of the Penobscot River all the way to Indian Island on the other side, a distance of more than 600 feet. Surely his admirers exaggerated the stories of his athletic feats, but Francis Sockalexis was certainly an imposing figure. He was the son of the head of the Sockalexis family and a nephew of Governor Tomar Sockalexis, and worked as a logger and river guide. Francis, too, involved himself in tribal matters and voiced his opinions in tribal councils.

Louis' mother, Frances Sockbeson, was also born in 1841, and married Francis Sockalexis at about the start of the Civil War. Sockbeson, a corruption of the French "Jacques-Sebastian," is not one of the Penobscot family names and probably comes from the Passamaquoddy people. It appears, therefore, that Louis Sockalexis was part Penobscot and part Passamaquoddy, with some white blood mixed in from his grandfather's generation.[11]

Francis and Frances Sockalexis had three children. Their first son was Soluice, born in 1862. No further information appears about him in tribal records, and it is likely that Soluice died in infancy. Louis Francis was born in the fall of 1871, and a daughter, Tellus (or Alice), was born six years later.

For a young Penobscot like Louis, growing up on Indian Island in the 1870s and 1880s, the world must have looked like a confusing place. The Penobscot, owners of a long and honorable history, now lived in rude wooden shacks on their tiny reservation and no longer owned title to the ancient Penobscot hunting grounds, taken away by treaties in the early 1800s. Some families still spoke the old Penobscot language in their homes, but many others now spoke only English and wore American-style clothing instead of Indian dress.

Many Penobscot, including Francis Sockalexis, continued to teach the ways of the forest to their children, though they must have wondered if such skills as canoe building and moose-calling had any relevance to the world as it now existed. The Penobscot were still avid fishermen, but in the late 1800s a series of lumber and textile mills sprang up along the Penobscot River. These mills polluted the air and land, diverted the flow of water, and diminished the once-plentiful supply of fish and game, so important to the traditional Penobscot way of life. The hunting prowess of the young Penobscot men, once a great source of pride within the tribe, was no longer needed, and their physical courage was no longer required of them. Some Penobscot accepted the passing of the old ways, but too many others succumbed to despair. Poverty and alcoholism took their toll on the reservation, and many young people left Indian Island to find work in factories in Bangor and other New England cities.

In the 1880s the Indian wars on the western American plains came to an end, corresponding to a national surge of interest in all things Indian. The Penobscot ventured to the seaside resorts of Maine and sold baskets and jewelry to the tourists, though they modified many of their traditional arts to conform to the popular "Injun" images that were fostered in the dime novels and newspapers of the period. They also performed in traveling medicine shows, which became a popular form of entertainment in Maine at that time. The Penobscot, in order to show the tourists what they hoped to see, built teepees and wore fringed buckskins in imitation of Indians from the Wild West. Tribes east of the Mississippi did not use teepees or dress in fringed buckskins, but the Penobscot did their best to accommodate the expectations of white tourists, at the cost of submerging their own culture.

Having few other outlets for their competitive energies, the Penobscot turned their attentions to organized sports, especially baseball. Baseball mania had spread through the entire nation following the Civil War, and before long the hotels where the Penobscot sold their wares and performed for the tourists put together baseball teams. Athletic young Penobscot men, no longer required to hunt and fish for the tribe's survival, quickly adapted their skills to baseball. They also participated in boxing and track meets, but baseball represented the best way to earn money and, perhaps, the admiration of other members of the tribe.

It was apparent early on that Louis Sockalexis would grow up to resemble his father. Like Francis, Louis was handsome and intelligent and grew to be tall and athletic as well. Louis, at a young age, was one of the best young athletes on the reservation, a standout in a tribe in which young men were encouraged to be athletic. He defeated his fellow Penobscot in races on the three-mile path around Indian Island and excelled in wrestling and games of shinny. Young Louis also learned the traditional Penobscot skills such as basketry and canoe building, but enjoyed athletic activities most of all. And, like his father, Louis was talented enough to have earned a place as a pure man.

According to legend, the teen-aged Louis Sockalexis left the reservation one day and observed some college boys playing a game of baseball, which the young Penobscot had never seen before, and asked to join the game. The college boys sent Louis to the outfield to shag some fly balls and were quickly impressed with the young Indian's grace and speed in the field. He ran down and caught fly balls with ease and quickly learned how to hit the fastest pitches from the strongest-armed older boys. Louis fell in love with baseball and spent most of his days practicing the new game.

Many Indian children in the late 1800s left the reservation at a young age and enrolled in white schools, but Louis began his education on Indian Island. He attended high schools in and around Old Town until he won a scholarship to Houlton Academy, a private school in northern Maine near the Canadian border. Houlton Academy, which became Ricker Classical Institute in the early 1890s, existed as a preparatory high school, charged with preparing young men for enrollment in Maine's Colby College. Louis became the athletic star of the school. He participated in baseball, football, track, and other sports, winning praise for his athletic prowess. It is not known if Louis received a high school diploma, because a fire in 1944 wiped out nearly all of the institution's records. Some Penobscot tribal sources insist that Louis was the first member of the tribe to graduate from high school.

Louis' stay at Houlton gave him a taste of the world outside of Indian Island, an exposure that his father had never experienced. Louis liked this glimpse of the dominant white culture, although his father was deeply suspicious of this world and shied away from contact with its inhabitants. This caused friction between father and son. Louis did not enjoy life on the reservation, and though Francis Sockalexis cautioned his son about "mingling with the whites," Louis did not live at home after his early teen-age years. "They [his parents] did not want to see me leaving my people ... after I received an education, I found no more pleasure at my home,"[12] said Louis in an interview a few years later. He returned to the reservation only infrequently for visits, and he lived away from his parents for the remainder of his life.

Intelligent and well-spoken, Louis retained the traditional Penobscot stoicism in his demeanor in his early years. He was nearly six feet tall, with straight black hair and copper-colored skin, as muscular as his father, and a highly talented athlete. He spoke English, Penobscot, and, because the local churches were still French in character, some French. Exposure to white culture led Louis to lose his stoicism and assume some of the traits of those with whom he mingled; he became an outgoing young man, fond of telling stories and quick with a joke. He learned to make friends easily in the white world that his father so mistrusted.

There is little documentation of Louis' late teen-age years. He appears in the records of the St. Joseph Catholic Church in Old Town, signing in as a witness to baptisms and funerals. He worked as a logger alongside his father, cutting down huge trees in the pine forest and hauling them to the river. Legend says that for the entertainment of their fellow loggers, father and son would enjoy a game of catch across an impossibly long distance, throwing baseballs more than 400 feet and catching them on the fly. Another oft-repeated story says that they once visited the horse-racing track at the state fairgrounds in Bangor and astounded the onlookers with a game of catch that spanned the entire length of the oval.

The muscular Louis was in his early twenties when he began receiving offers to play baseball for college and professional teams. Louis stated in a later interview that he played a few games in the early 1890s for St. Mary's College in Van Buren, Maine, though no statistics still exist for that college team, and it is not known if Louis attended classes there.[13] Records show that young Louis returned to the former Houlton Academy and played for the baseball team at Ricker Classical Institute in the spring and early summer of 1894. It appears that he attended classes at Ricker, since the institution had added a fifth year of courses in 1891, and it seems logical that Louis continued his education in this extended program. However, Louis showed no discernible interest in attending college, because he was more interested in pursuing athletics than in obtaining a degree. Louis also spent his summers in the early 1890s playing semiprofessional baseball for several teams in the state of Maine.

Semiprofessional baseball in 1890s Maine was a loosely organized enterprise in which young ballplayers competed and earned small amounts of money during the short summer season. Many college players adopted false names and played for pay in these leagues to earn a few extra dollars, while young Indian men played ball as an outlet for their athletic energies. Many leagues became intensely competitive, with hot rivalries between the sponsoring towns or businesses, replete with heavy wagering on the outcomes of the games. This heated competition appealed to the traditional athletic interest of the Penobscot. Louis Sockalexis, now a young man in his early twenties, stood out among all the other players in these leagues.

Sockalexis at Poland Spring, Maine, in the summer of 1894. (National Baseball Hall of Fame Library, Cooperstown, NY)

Francis Sockalexis was not pleased with the direction, or lack thereof, that his son's life was taking. Francis, who in 1891 gained election to a two-year term as lieutenant governor of the Penobscot tribe, believed that Louis' talents and intelligence were wasted playing a game. Louis already was better educated than almost all other members of the tribe, and Francis preferred that Louis return to the reservation and employ his gifts in the service of his people, as Francis himself was doing. Such disapproval increased the level of friction between father and son and made Louis even more determined to play the game that he enjoyed so much.

Louis did not appear to have any career goal in mind at the time; he enjoyed playing ball and making money in doing so, and that is how he occupied himself in his early manhood. From contemporary accounts, it also appears that Louis played football in the fall, although baseball was his favorite sport. Louis loved athletics more than felling trees in the forest or guiding sportsmen up the rivers of Maine, and for the moment, he saw no need to settle down and begin a steady job on the reservation, as most other young Penobscot his age were doing.

Louis planned to return to Ricker Classical Institute in the fall of 1894, but fate intervened. In July of that year, he accepted a position as an outfielder for a new baseball team operated by the Poland Spring Hotel in Poland Spring, Maine. His play at Poland Spring exposed the young Penobscot's talent to a wider audience and put Louis Sockalexis on the road to a career in major league baseball.

CHAPTER 2

The College of the Holy Cross

> *The air of this city [Worcester] was full of enthusiasm, last evening, which was inspired by the students of Holy Cross college. They were celebrating a victory of their ball team over the crack Harvard University club. A bon fire of large dimensions on the hill illuminated the southern section of the city, while groups of students paraded the streets, cheering and blowing horns while their breath lasted.*
>
> — Holy Cross house diary, 1891[1]

The Poland Spring Hotel was one of the leading resorts in the state of Maine, and the hotel's management assembled a baseball team in the summer of 1894. Although the team was ostensibly an amateur nine, the players were well paid, and the hotel could afford to hire some of the best semi-pros in the state. One of those players was Louis Sockalexis, who was already making a name for himself in Maine baseball circles.

Sockalexis, the 22-year-old Penobscot, made a strong impression almost immediately. Poland Spring won its first game by a score of 11–1 and defeated its second opponent by a 15–5 count. Sockalexis belted a triple and stole two bases in the first game and whacked a single and a home run in the second. Before long, he gained even more attention for his prodigious throwing in the outfield. "Sockalexis is the best thrower in New England," boasted the resort's weekly newspaper in late July.

Poland Spring lost two games in early August to the Lewiston professional team of the New England League, but Sockalexis dazzled the resort crowds with his hitting and batting. He didn't shine in every game, however. "Our star fielder had a decided off-day," stated the resort newspaper after a loss in late July. "Never mind, Louie, we all have 'em. The people are still with you, and the next game we shall expect you to make three home runs."[2] One week later Louis redeemed himself with a homer against the same opponent and led Poland Spring to another win, and in the next game he whacked a triple and homer, scoring four runs in a 22–11 win against the local YMCA squad. Later in the season, the Poland Spring club battered a pickup team from Lewiston, as Louis Sockalexis belted two home runs in the first inning.

Other players and spectators recognized this prodigious talent. One day someone challenged Louis to throw a baseball as far as he could in front of the Poland Spring Hotel. He wound up and let fly, and the onlookers measured the throw at an incredible 408 feet, a few feet farther than the existing major league record at the time. Louis' talent compelled people to tell tall tales about him, as they had told stories about his father a generation before. Some claimed that Louis once stood on Oak Hill on Indian Island and threw a baseball that hit the smokestack on the Jordan Lumber Mill, nearly three-quarters of a mile away! Another legend states that young Louis once hit a baseball the entire length of Indian Island. Sockalexis was so physically impressive that such Bunyanesque feats seemed possible to those who saw him in action.

Louis, the best athlete from a tribe of fine athletes, ran faster and hit the ball farther than anyone in his sphere and played like a man among boys at Poland Spring. Though no Penobscot had ever advanced to play in the highest classifications of professional baseball, Louis Sockalexis was much too gifted to remain in Maine's semipro leagues and small colleges. Francis Sockalexis still disapproved of his son's ball playing and preferred that Louis stay on the reservation, but Louis wanted to be a ballplayer, and when the summer of 1894 ended he cast about for new challenges and faster competition.

One of Louis' teammates at Poland Spring was the team's catcher, Michael "Mike" Powers. Powers also served as the captain of the baseball team at the College of the Holy Cross, a Roman Catholic institution in Worcester, Massachusetts, run by the Jesuit order. The more Mike Powers watched Sockalexis, the more he envisioned the Indian in a Holy Cross uniform. Louis was a Catholic, and though he was a few years older than most incoming college students, the Jesuits had a long-standing interest in educating the Catholic Indians of New England, especially the French-influenced ones in Maine. In addition, Louis was an intelligent young man, and it appeared that he could handle the demanding course work that Holy Cross offered. Powers was certain that he could convince the Holy Cross administration to accept this incredible athlete as a student.

Despite his father's displeasure, the 23-year-old Penobscot accepted the challenge. Holy Cross fielded one of the most powerful college teams in New England and played regularly against excellent college nines from

Harvard, Yale, and Brown. This was definitely the higher level of competition that he was looking for, so Louis decided to join Mike Powers at Holy Cross that fall. Although the Holy Cross team would not play a game until the following spring, Louis Sockalexis traveled to Worcester and enrolled as a student in the fall of 1894.

Mike Powers, the catcher and captain of the Holy Cross baseball team, directed the action on the field and served as what we would now call a playing manager. The team employed a coach, but in those days a college coach was usually a professional

Sockalexis in his Holy Cross uniform in 1895. (College of the Holy Cross Archives)

player who taught strategy and skills in the winter months, then left the team to continue his own career in the spring. The Holy Cross coach in 1895 was James "Chippy" McGarr, a Worcester resident who played third base for the Cleveland Spiders of the National League. McGarr left the Holy Cross nine in mid–March to attend the Cleveland team spring training, leaving the ballclub in the capable hands of Powers.

Mike Powers was one year older than Sockalexis and was an astute and intelligent individual who excelled in the classroom as well as the baseball diamond. They called him "Doc" because he wanted to become a doctor when his baseball career was finished, and in fact Powers did obtain his medical degree several years later. He is identified in Holy Cross records as a "free scholar," and since those same records indicate that only one athlete at Holy Cross was on a full scholarship at the time, it stands to reason that Powers was that athlete.

The captain worked with the student manager, G. E. Kerrigan, in setting up practices and games with little input or interference from the Holy Cross faculty and administration. The college gave Powers a great deal of latitude in scheduling games and obtaining players, and it appears that Powers encountered no difficulty in convincing the school to accept Louis Sockalexis as a student in the 1894-95 term.

The College of the Holy Cross was founded in 1843, and at the time of its creation was the only Roman Catholic college in predominantly Protestant New England. The college weathered much anti–Catholic sentiment and outright bigotry in its early years, but an influx of Irish immigrants to Massachusetts after the Civil War increased the Catholic presence in New England and smoothed the path of success for the college. By 1894 Holy Cross was firmly established as an institution of classical learning. It was one of several Jesuit colleges in the eastern part of the nation; the others included Georgetown, Fordham, and Boston College.

The college was controlled and sponsored by the Society of Jesus, also known as the Jesuits, the educational and service order created by St. Ignatius Loyola in the mid–1500s. In consequence, the seven-year curriculum of the College of the Holy Cross closely followed the *Ratio Studiorum*, the course of study set forth by the Society in the late 16th century. The college clung to the traditional emphasis on classical literature and languages that the Ratio had emphasized for more than 400 years in European Jesuit schools. The college also frowned upon "electivism," the ability of the student to choose among different courses of study, in the belief that the *Ratio Studiorum* provided the correct education for every Catholic student, regardless of interest or background.

The 1895 Holy Cross catalog described the mission of the college this way:

> The student at the end of his college course will not have mastered any special profession, but his mind will be so disciplined as to enable him to pursue a professional or business career with a more vigorous mental activity, with more painstaking care, order, method, energy, and perseverance and therefore with greater ease and more pronounced success, than if he had spent his years without any systematic training whatever, or in pursuing a course other than the one here prescribed.[3]

Students at Holy Cross spent more than half of their class time studying Latin and Greek, mostly through the traditional style of rote memorization. Second-year college-level Holy Cross students were expected to memorize 1,860 lines of Latin and 1,185 lines of Greek for their grueling year-end oral examinations. The school still used the traditional European names for classes; instead of labeling the four highest classes as Freshman, Sophomore, Junior, and Senior, they were known as First Humanities,

Poetry, Rhetoric, and Philosophy respectively. Because of its strong commitment to classical education, the College of the Holy Cross was already flirting with anachronism as the 19th century drew to a close.

In its early years, the college accepted students as young as eight years old, and many students spent nearly a decade there. By the 1870s, the college stopped accepting students younger than fourteen, and the administration divided the Holy Cross curriculum into seven years of study. Qualified high school graduates could be admitted directly into the fourth-year class, the First Humanities, but younger students and those who did not meet the academic requirements for First Humanities entered one of three lower levels. These were called Rudiments, Third Humanities, and Second Humanities, roughly corresponding to the last three years of high school. These three classes were called, as a group, the Holy Cross Preparatory Department, and they were specially designed for students deficient in Latin, Greek, and mathematics.[4]

Louis Sockalexis gained admission to Holy Cross Preparatory in the fall of 1894. He had received a high school education, but his classes in and around Old Town did not prepare him for the rigorous classical training that Holy Cross demanded of its students. In addition, Louis had attended Ricker Classical Institute more as an athlete than as a scholar, and although he was an intelligent young man, he apparently needed some remedial help to tackle the demanding Greek and Latin requirements. He wasn't alone, because about 30 percent of Holy Cross' enrollment in the 1890s was made up of students in the Preparatory program. However, Louis was one of the oldest students, if not the oldest, in Holy Cross Preparatory at the time. He turned 23 in October of 1894, and many of the other students in his classes were younger teen-agers.

The students in the Preparatory program studied the basics of Latin and Greek, including Caesar's *Commentaries*, Cicero's *Letters*, and a great deal of grammar in both languages. They also were required to memorize 10 to 12 lines of literature or poetry each day, by Caesar, Ovid, or Longfellow, among others, and studied mathematics, ancient history, mythology, and religious catechism, with one hour of declamation or elocution per week. Holy Cross taught some of the sciences, such as chemistry and physics, to upper-level students, but the college had no science laboratories and taught the material by memorization instead of laboratory experimentation. Students were required to complete rigorous oral and written examinations at the end of the school year to pass into the next level. Students who failed were held back for another term until the deficiencies in each subject were made up.

The Jesuits demanded strict adherence to standards of behavior. The students were required to attend Mass every morning, without fail, and could not leave campus, or even walk in certain areas of the campus itself, without the permission of the college. In those rare occasions when the students left campus for outside activities, they were closely monitored and regulated. Most of the lower-level students were not even allowed to go home for holidays, and the college routinely opened and read the incoming and outgoing mail of the students. The college exercised no flexibility in matters of alcohol; if a student left campus and returned in an inebriated state, that student was immediately expelled and put on a train out of town as quickly as possible.

Holy Cross saw itself as an island of classical education in a hostile world and did its best to stay aloof from the Worcester community at large. The college administrators wrestled with the question of holding meetings or lectures on campus, open to the general public, because they feared that girls and young women from town would attend "and thus students [would] become acquainted with them."[5] The school charged admission to many of its public functions, to keep out the "rough element" and to hold down the numbers of females in attendance. The original mission of the college was to train future candidates for priestly vocations, and the standards of conduct at Holy Cross still adhered to the traditionally strict Jesuit separation of the sexes.

However, the highly restrictive atmosphere of the school was already changing, in no small part because of the phenomenon of intercollegiate sports. The Jesuits traditionally believed in physical activities as beneficial to their students, and the students of Holy Cross embraced baseball after the Civil War. By the late 1880s Holy Cross adopted the nickname "Crusaders" for its baseball team and began playing other college teams on a regular basis. The success of the baseball program brought much attention to Holy Cross, and after a win against Harvard in June 1891 the students "went wild. They threw their hats in the air and yelled until they were black in the face,"[6] as recorded in the Holy Cross house diary. College sports helped to bridge the long-standing gap between school and community, and the people of Worcester began to take pride in the Crusader baseball team. By the time Louis enrolled in 1894, the Holy Cross baseball team regularly drew crowds numbering in the thousands in the city of Worcester.

Colleges gave athletic scholarships to baseball players as early as the 1870s on other campuses, and by the 1890s Holy Cross awarded some as well. Archives at Holy Cross state that 21 individuals received reduced tuition from 1880 to 1899, and at least some of those were probably athletes.[7] Louis Sockalexis, a poor Native American from a reservation in Maine, was almost certainly one of those 21 recipients.

The 1895 Holy Cross Crusaders. Sockalexis is at the top, second from left, and the man seated in the middle is captain Mike Powers. (College of the Holy Cross Archives)

Some leaders of the Society of Jesus frowned on special admissions policies for athletes, especially older ones like Louis. In 1892, Jesuit provincial Thomas Campbell, head of the Maryland–New York Province that included Holy Cross, cautioned Jesuit schools like Holy Cross and Boston College against the practice. Campbell opposed admitting students "merely for the purpose of helping athletic sports especially those who although well on in age, are compelled on account of their backwardness to enter the classes of the younger students.... It destroys the name of the College and in reality injures the sports." In 1896 one of Campbell's successors, Edward Purbrick, warned the Jesuits against offering athletes "more than their share of interest and time."[8]

Sockalexis, called Sock by his teammates, was by no means the only good player on the Holy Cross squad. The team's star pitcher, a curveballing right-hander named John Pappalau, was one of the best pitchers in college ball at the time. The slick-fielding Walter Curley played second base next to two players named William Fox, one (William J. Fox) played shortstop and the other (William H. Fox) played third. Both were fine players, and William H. Fox was almost as fast afoot as Sockalexis. Mike Powers was an excellent defensive catcher and respected field captain, while outfielder William Maroney was a hard hitter who also drew a few assignments as a starting pitcher. Five members of the 1895 Holy Cross squad—

Pappalau, Powers, Curley, Sockalexis, and William H. Fox — eventually played major league baseball.

By all accounts, the students and the faculty at Holy Cross held Louis Sockalexis in high regard. Shortstop William J. Fox, who became the Right Reverend Monsignor Fox later in life, wrote a letter in 1949 that resides today in the Holy Cross archives. "Sock was a good, sober, likable fellow," wrote Reverend Fox, "and very popular with all the boys on the team with him."[9] The Indian's behavior was also exemplary. The prefect of discipline kept strict records on student behavior in a "discipline diary" that also rests in the college archives. According to the archivists, the name of Louis Sockalexis does not appear even once in the diary for the period in which Louis attended the college.[10]

The multitalented Louis also ran track for Holy Cross. The track season began in March, when the baseball players were still playing practice games for the upcoming season, so Louis participated in track meets whenever he could get an afternoon free from classes and baseball practice. The Penobscot, who in his younger days built up his running skill in races around the three-mile path on Indian Island, excelled in several events at Holy Cross. Louis ran dashes and distances of varying lengths, performed in the broad jump, and also excelled in the hop, skip, and jump.[11] The college track records from that era are sketchy, but one source states that Louis once won five events in a single meet, which was held in the spring of 1895. He was an expert runner, especially at the medium and long distances. He also played basketball, a sport invented only a few years earlier at Springfield College by Dr. James Naismith. The basketball court in the campus gymnasium featured two rows of steel pillars in bounds; one alumnus remembered that "one played basketball at the risk of breaking one's bones."[12]

According to legend, Sockalexis did not begin his college baseball career in the starting lineup. An undated newspaper clipping at the National Baseball Hall of Fame states that the Indian was taking a nap on the sidelines at one early-season game when second baseman Curley suffered an injury. "Powers saw the lazy looking Indian," said the clipping, "and designated him as Curley's replacement."[13] However, according to records of the era, Sock never played second base in college and played all the 1895 season in left field for the Crusaders. It's also highly unlikely that the businesslike Powers would allow one of his players to sleep on the sidelines during a game.

In reality, Sockalexis emerged almost instantly as the star of the Holy Cross team. The 1895 season opened on April 10 with a win against Lyceum, a local high school team, and then the Crusaders defeated a professional team from Springfield by a 3–2 score. Springfield's pitcher, Jimmy Callahan, was an outstanding hurler who later pitched for and managed the Chicago White Sox, but the Indian belted three doubles off Callahan's deliveries.

Sockalexis also saved the game with a great defensive play. The Holy Cross nine was ahead by one run late in the game when the Springfield team put a man on third. The next batter walloped a long fly ball far over Sockalexis' head in left field. The Indian ran back, caught the ball over his shoulder, then whirled around and fired a perfect throw to the catcher, Powers, nailing the runner at the plate to preserve the victory.

The Crusaders, with Sockalexis batting nearly .450, won their first nine games before losing a match against the professional Fall River club. The Holy Cross men put this defeat behind them with a 13–3 trouncing of Dartmouth and then, best of all, a 4–3 win over Harvard for the first-ever Holy Cross victory at Cambridge.

In the Harvard game, Sockalexis made one of the greatest throws in the history of college baseball. A Harvard batter whacked a ball far over the Indian's head in left-center field. Harvard's diamond had no outfield fence, and the ball rolled between some trees and onto a tennis court before Sockalexis could catch up to it. Sockalexis picked up the ball and fired it to the plate. The ball bounced once near the pitcher's mound and settled in Mike Powers' glove, and the base runner wisely held up at third rather than try for an inside-the-park home run. This incredible throw saved the game for the Crusaders, and after the game two Harvard professors marked the place where the Indian threw the ball and measured the throw. The ball, according to their measurement, carried 414 feet on the fly, setting a new unofficial distance record. When the Crusader players returned by train from Cambridge, the Holy Cross students celebrated the victory with a bonfire and fireworks.

The upstarts from Holy Cross began to draw attention from the outstanding teams of college baseball. Brown University was one of the college baseball powers of the age, and in early April of that year Brown battled the National League's New York Giants to a standstill before dropping a 9–7 decision. However, Holy Cross shocked Brown by a 13–4 score on April 19. Sockalexis played left field in that game, belted two homers, and stole six bases as Pappalau pitched a complete game win.[14] Legend states that one of Sockalexis' home runs smashed a fourth-floor window in one of the dormitories behind the right-field fence.

The baseball nine generated so much enthusiasm on campus that the college administration moved classes ahead several hours on April 27 in order to allow as many students as possible to attend the game against

Dartmouth that afternoon. The Crusaders rewarded their followers by walloping the strong Dartmouth team, 13–3, in a game that featured a long homer by Sockalexis over a high net fence in right field. Only Fred Tenney, a former Brown athlete who later starred in the National League, had previously belted a ball over the net. The Jesuit provincial, William Pardow, watched the game that day in Worcester with more than 4,000 other fans.

On May 15, Harvard came to Worcester to avenge their earlier defeat, but John Pappalau pitched the Crusaders to an easy 7–1 victory, in which all seven Holy Cross runs were unearned. "Harvard played a wretched game from start to finish,"[15] sniffed *The New York Times*, but now the national sporting press began to take notice of Holy Cross.

The Holy Cross team was popular in town before Louis Sockalexis arrived, but now the students of the college and the people of Worcester erupted in an explosion of enthusiasm for the Crusaders. Some home games drew crowds of more than 4,000 people, so many that in the next few years the college found it expedient to add nearly 2,000 seats to the baseball stands. Students celebrated wildly when the Crusaders won, and many left campus without permission to greet the returning baseball stars from victorious road games, parading with torches and blowing horns. The college president confined erring students to campus and took away town privileges for a few weeks, but before long the same students would leave campus again to celebrate more victories.

The 1895 season was not a perfect one for Holy Cross. On May 23, a hotly contested game against Brown University in Providence, Rhode Island, ended with a huge argument between the Crusaders and the umpire. The score was 9–8 in Holy Cross' favor in the bottom of the ninth, but the umpire called a Brown runner safe on a play at the plate to tie the score. Catcher and captain Mike Powers argued loud and long, then removed the Crusaders from the field and forced the umpire to forfeit the game to Brown by a score of 9–0, though Holy Cross records list the final score as a 9–9 tie.

Nine days later, the most anticipated game of the year, against the powerful Yale squad at New Haven, Connecticut, ended in an 11–3 defeat for Holy Cross. The Crusaders arrived in New Haven after a long train ride from Worcester, and it took them a few innings to get their bearings against one of the strongest teams in college baseball. The score was close until John Pappalau, the pitching star of Holy Cross, suffered an injury and left the game. William Maroney replaced Pappalau, but gave up several runs late in the game as Yale put the contest out of reach.

The Crusaders also suffered through eight rainouts that season but ended the campaign on a high note with a 12–3 win over Worcester Tech and a 12–0 walloping of Tufts. Holy Cross also split two games against the New York Cuban Giants, one of the outstanding traveling African-American teams of the era. The college rewarded the ballplayers with a "grand banquet" at season's end, attended by reporters from the local papers as well as members of the college administration.

Louis Sockalexis made one more splash in the national press that year. Before one game, the Crusaders engaged in a field day, competing against each other in foot races, throwing contests, and the like. Many people were surprised that Sockalexis did not win the foot race around the bases, won by William H. Fox in a time of 13.4 seconds. However, no one could match Sockalexis in the baseball throw. He heaved the baseball 393 feet and 8 inches for a new national amateur record. The existing professional record was only a few feet longer, and the Indian had unofficially thrown a ball farther than that in the Harvard game. Now it was official that Louis Sockalexis owned the most powerful throwing arm in college baseball.

The Crusaders ended the 1895 season with a 17–5–2 record, and much of the credit for the team's success belonged to the Penobscot. Official Holy Cross records state that Sockalexis played all 24 games, scoring 31 runs and making 41 hits for a .436 average. Other sources credit Sockalexis with 9 doubles, 11 triples, and 3 home runs, which, if correct, gives Sockalexis a phenomenal .862 slugging percentage. It seems strange that Powers kept Sockalexis in the sixth spot in the lineup all season, and as a result, some of the Holy Cross batters went to bat 10 to 15 more times than Sockalexis did that year.

However, Sock's fielding left much to be desired. He made spectacular catches and throws all season, but he also committed 11 errors for a fielding percentage of .784. Still, Louis Sockalexis ended the season as one of the biggest stars in college baseball, and if there was a College Player of the Year trophy available at the time, the Penobscot from Maine might well have won it.

The Holy Cross baseball season ended in June, but Louis Sockalexis was not finished playing ball. He participated in one game for Lewiston in the New England League in the summer of 1895. He went to bat four times in the game, with one hit, a double, and handled all his chances in the outfield cleanly.[16] Playing professional ball might have threatened the Indian's college eligibility if anyone from Holy Cross had found out about it, although the rules regarding amateur status were only loosely enforced at the time. No one knows why Louis played only one game, or whether he used his own name or an assumed one.

He played semiprofessional ball that summer as well, for the Warren town team in Warren, Maine. While playing for Warren in the summer of 1895, Sockalexis received several offers to leave Holy Cross and play ball in the higher minor league ranks. Louis was a highly sought-after free agent, and several teams in the Eastern League, one step below the majors, made offers to the Indian. However, Louis had his eye on the only existing major league, the National, which played in the nation's largest cities and, consequently, paid the highest salaries. Louis knew that another good season at Holy Cross would bring offers from National League ballclubs, so he chose to play college ball for at least one more season. In September of 1895, he returned to his classes at Holy Cross.

There were big changes back at the Penobscot reservation, however. Francis Sockalexis, who served as lieutenant governor of the tribe from 1891 to 1893, won election as tribal governor of the Penobscot Indian Nation for a two-year term beginning in 1895. Francis was still disappointed in his son's decision to live away from the reservation, but Louis was now an adult, making his own decisions. Francis Sockalexis busied himself with tribal matters, though he continued to hope that one day Louis would leave the white world behind and return to live among his tribesmen.

Holy Cross archives list no coach for the spring of 1896, but two Worcester residents who played for Cleveland of the National League advised the Crusaders that spring. James "Chippy" McGarr, who coached the squad in 1895, was one, and the other was the reigning National League batting champion, Jesse Burkett. Burkett, then the premier left-handed batter in the game, pounded the ball for an astounding .423 average in 1895. He also scored 149 runs and led the major league with 235 hits in only 132 games. He offered some hitting pointers to Louis Sockalexis, who turned out to be an appreciative and attentive pupil. McGarr and Burkett left for spring training in March, once again leaving the management of the club to Mike Powers.

The Holy Cross ballclub, with almost the same personnel as the year before, exploded from the gate in 1896. They opened the season on April 11 with a 7–0 drubbing of Worcester Tech, then followed with a 10–4 win over St. Anne's, a 23–8 win over Lyceum, and a 23–5 shellacking of the professional Pawtucket team. Unfortunately, John Pappalau, the star Crusader pitcher, came down with a sore arm in April, leaving some of the hurling chores to second-stringer William Maroney.[17]

These lopsided wins led up to a game against powerful Brown, played in Worcester on April 20 in front of more than 3,000 fans. The Crusaders fought hard with Maroney on the mound but lost by a 7–6 score. Two days later, rain washed out the long-anticipated rematch with Yale. Holy Cross was anxious to avenge the 11–3 defeat handed to them by the Elis in 1895, but the grounds were too wet to play on that day, and the two schools could not find a mutually acceptable date on which to reschedule the contest.

Louis Sockalexis, the fastest man in college baseball, played center field for the Crusaders in 1896 after playing in left the year before. He made eight errors in 1896 for a fielding percentage of .888, an improvement over his .784 mark of 1895 but still rather low for an outfielder. However, he also made his share of spectacular catches and throws. Since he was already famous for his powerful throwing arm, the best in college baseball, other teams learned not to try and take an extra base on any ball hit to Sockalexis. Still, Louis threw out nine runners from center field that season. In recognition of his superior hitting the previous season, Powers usually placed Louis in the second or third spot in the lineup.

The Crusaders lost their next game to the professional Fall River team in a rare two-game losing streak, but they regained their momentum once Pappalau's arm returned to normal. They defeated several teams by lopsided scores, including Wesleyan (10–2), Boston College (22–5) and Trinity (20–4) before they met Brown again on May 19 at Providence. Pappalau, healthy now, pitched a complete game as Holy Cross won by a 4–1 score, and the Holy Cross campus exploded with celebration when news of the victory arrived in Worcester. The house diary reported that 79 students, nearly half of the on-campus student body, left campus to "parade in nightshirts" and welcome the returning players at the Worcester train station.[18]

Sockalexis earned as much attention for his magnificent throwing arm as for his batting skill. In a game against Georgetown on May 26 of that year, the *Worcester Telegraph* remarked on one of Sock's amazing throws. "The crowd went into ecstasies over many plays," reported the paper, "but there was one which raised their hair. It was a throw by Sockalexis from center field which cut off a run at the plate. It was a magnificent liner from the shoulder passing through the air like a cannon ball and reaching home plate in plenty of time."[19] Holy Cross defeated its fellow Jesuit institution, Georgetown, that day by a score of 8–1.

The team from Williams College, one of the strongest in the eastern part of the nation, was steamrolled by Holy Cross twice in 1896 by scores of 8–4 and 12–1, and the most impressive player on the field was Louis Sockalexis. The *Williams Weekly* paid tribute to the Penobscot after the second game, which was played on May 16. Sock, reported the paper, "played a phenomenal game, catching and batting balls, whenever and wherever he pleased."[20]

The Crusaders played Brown three more times that season but lost all three games to the most powerful team in college baseball. Still, the

Holy Cross nine won 19 games in 1896, losing only seven and tying one, with three rainouts. All the other losses came against pro teams, and Holy Cross shellacked all of the rest of their collegiate competition. Included in those wins were victories over Wesleyan (23–4), Vermont (17–1) and Tufts (14–2).

For the second year in a row, Louis Sockalexis led the team with a .444 average, with 38 runs and 56 hits in the 26 games in which he played. Sock batted nearly 100 points ahead of the club's second-best hitter, Mike Powers, though Powers scored one more run than Sock. The Penobscot also batted 25 more times than Powers in the same number of games, reflecting the wisdom of moving Sockalexis to a higher spot in the lineup so that he could bat more often.

The Penobscot was now recognized as the hardest hitter in the college game, and more professional offers came his way in the summer of 1896. John Montgomery Ward, the former captain of the New York Giants, publicly called Sockalexis "a wonder," and the Boston papers reported that the highly respected Ward advised one of the National League teams, most probably the Giants, to sign the Indian without delay. Sockalexis also received a slew of offers from the Eastern League and the lower-level New England League, but he decided to play a waiting game.

Louis was in no hurry. He had deeply impressed both Chippy McGarr and Jesse Burkett of the Cleveland Spiders, and Louis knew that both men were plying the Cleveland manager, Pat Tebeau, with tales of the Indian's feats on the diamond. Louis knew that he would almost certainly receive an offer from Cleveland, so he elected to re-enroll that fall at Holy Cross, where he could spend the next few months weighing his options for the following spring.

CHAPTER 3

From Worcester to Notre Dame

> *During the latter part of the morning we were treated to a delightful discourse on the advantage of base-ball by our professor. He pictured to us the many advantages which were derived from this game, and said we were improved by it, both intellectually and physically, and that proficiency in the science of base-ball was absolutely necessary in order to become a "Sport."*
> — Dennis J. Murphy, Holy Cross student, 1894[1]

Gilbert Patten, a resident of Maine, wrote pulp stories in the 1890s under the pen name of Burt L. Standish. Patten was an enthusiastic college baseball and football fan, and in April of 1896 he introduced the character of an athletic college man in Street and Smith's *Tip Top Weekly*. This creation was Frank Merriwell, star athlete and campus hero of Yale University. Frank Merriwell was a new kind of dime-novel hero, one who used intelligence as well as strength to overcome adversity and triumph in the end. Merriwell possessed "a body like Tarzan's and a head like Einstein's," wrote one admiring writer, and thus represented "the perfect union of brain and brawn."

Patten's Merriwell stories became so popular that the sales of *Tip Top Weekly* boomed, and before long Street and Smith sold more than 200,000 copies of the magazine every week. Patten became one of the most widely read writers in the nation, and before the Merriwell series ended in 1913, Patten wrote the equivalent of more than 200 full-length novels based on the exploits of his handsome sports hero.

Patten saw Louis Sockalexis play many times for the Holy Cross nine, and many of the Penobscot's admirers claim that Sockalexis served as the model for the heroic Frank Merriwell. Patten, who lived until 1945, never revealed the identity of the model for Merriwell, and it is most likely that Merriwell was a composite of many college athletes of the era. Perhaps Merriwell was not Sockalexis, but it is very likely that Patten drew at least a part of Merriwell's persona from the star Indian athlete from Holy Cross.[2]

Later in the Frank Merriwell series, Patten introduced another athletic character to the story line. This person was named Joe Crowfoot, and he was an intelligent, talented Indian athlete who joined Merriwell at Yale. It seems possible that Patten created the character of Crowfoot, not Merriwell, as a thinly veiled homage to a fellow resident of Maine, Louis Sockalexis.

By 1896, Holy Cross, flush with success on the baseball diamond, decided to embrace the other major college sport of the era. The college fielded a football team in the early 1890s, but the Holy Cross president at the time, Father Edward McGurk, disbanded the team in 1894 rather than let it play outside the city of Worcester. Father John Lehy became president in 1895 and reinstated the sport, with former Penn State player Dr. A. C. N. Peterson as coach, student John Finn as captain, and Louis Sockalexis, the best athlete on campus, as the star of the team. Lehy gave his permission for Peterson to organize a six-game schedule for the fall of 1896.

At that time, football was an incredibly rough sport, much more akin to rugby than to the modern game. The forward pass, which eventually opened up the game, was not legalized until 1906, so in 1896 most football games resembled a series of on-field brawls. They called it "mass play," and the object of the game was to gather as many of the team's players as possible in a mass formation and bull the ball over the goal line for a touchdown, which was worth only four points in 1896.

Players took the field with little, if any, protective equipment. Louis Sockalexis and the other 16 Holy Cross gridders grew their hair long, since football players in that era did not yet wear helmets, and the added locks provided some semblance of natural padding for the players' heads. The Penn football team caused a sensation that fall when they appeared on the field wearing leather helmets, but it took a few years for other schools to follow suit.

Thomas Trenchard, a star end for Princeton in 1892–94, described football of the 1890s many years later. "Force was the thing then," explained Trenchard, "and smashing, battering plays were depended upon solely.... We had no great strategy to speak of. We relied mainly on being in superb physical condition and getting the jump on our opponents at the outset of the game."[3] There were many serious injuries in college football then, and a proposal to ban mass formations like the "flying wedge" caused a rift among the major Eastern football schools. Yale and Princeton supported

Three members of the 1895-96 Holy Cross team. Sockalexis and second baseman Walter Curley are standing, while catcher Mike Powers is seated in front of them. All three of these men later played in the major leagues. (National Baseball Hall of Fame Library, Cooperstown, NY)

the ban, while Harvard and Penn opposed it, and the resulting controversy kept Yale and Harvard from playing each other for two years.[4]

A team's best athlete carried the ball and absorbed the brunt of the punishment, but Louis Sockalexis didn't mind. He was by far the best athlete at Holy Cross, if not in the entire nation, and he enthusiastically carried the ball on offense and blocked and tackled on defense. He was especially talented at breaking through flying wedges and other mass formations and tackling the opposing ball carrier.

Louis, like many Penobscot a skilled wrestler and runner, was tailor-made for this new Holy Cross sport. Young Indian men were no longer required to prove themselves in battle or, like the Penobscot pure men of old, run down game on foot in the forest. Football, the rough and tumble variety of the 1890s, served as a substitute. Chasing after a ball carrier appeared to be the closest way that a young Indian athlete could replicate the physical activity of the hunt, and tackling an opponent brought the traditional Indian interest in wrestling into play. The brawling nature of football also filled the void left by the cessation of the legendary Penobscot battles against the Mohawk and other invading tribes, and the cheering of the students replaced the esteem of the tribe. Perhaps it was no coincidence that the Carlisle Indian School, which produced Jim Thorpe and many other great Native American athletes, fielded one of the most successful football teams of the era.

After a tune-up game against a local high school team, Holy Cross played its first football game on October 17, 1896, against Worcester Polytech. Sockalexis, a perfectly proportioned 185-pounder, was the only member of the baseball team to earn a position on the football squad. The Penobscot played halfback on offense and defensive back on defense against Polytech and saved a touchdown early in the game. The Polytech running back burst through a hole in the line and steamed toward the end zone, but Sockalexis caught him and threw him to the ground just a few yards from the goal line. Polytech fumbled on its next play, and the Crusaders relieved the pressure by booting the ball downfield.

The inexperienced Holy Cross squad held Polytech off the board in the first half but gave up two touchdowns and a field goal in the second. The Crusaders lost their first football game by a 10–0 score, mostly because Sockalexis was thrown out of the game by the referees early in the second half. There is no official record explaining what happened, but there was a lot of pushing, shoving, and general roughness in football at the time. Most likely, an on-field row involving the Indian got out of hand, and the referees ejected Sockalexis to restore order to the contest. "The game was not wholly free from objectionable features," stated the *Worcester Telegram* the next day, "but the slugging and other unfair features were few."

The Crusaders then played two scoreless ties. Sockalexis, for reasons still unknown, did not take the field against Boston University, but he returned to the lineup for a game against the Newton Athletic Club, a squad made up mostly of former college players. The Crusaders then lost by a 6–2 score to Boston College, Holy Cross' rival Catholic school, in a game played in Worcester. On November 14, 1896, the Crusaders played a second game against Boston College on a cold, rainy fall day at the South End Grounds in Boston, and that game still lives in college football annals. It gave birth to the long-standing, intense, sometimes heated rivalry between the athletic teams of Holy Cross and Boston College.

In that game, Sockalexis, according to the *Boston Globe*, "played at halfback for Holy Cross and astonished the spectators by his ability. In many respects he was similar to Little Cayou, the Carlisle warrior. When tackled he squirmed along the ground like a snake, while in defensive work he broke up the interference well, and brought down his man." Louis ran all over the muddy field making plays, and before half-time the Holy Cross squad took a 6–4 lead on a drop-kick field goal by Linehan, the Crusader right end.

Boston College failed to score in the second half, due in large part to the defensive play of the Penobscot from Maine. Sockalexis dropped at least two Boston College running backs behind the line of scrimmage for substantial losses of yardage. At the end of the game, Sock and his Holy Cross teammates celebrated their first-ever win, a 6–4 victory. However, Boston College insisted that the clock had not yet run out, and after a long series of arguments and discussions the Holy Cross team left the field to return to Worcester. The Boston College players then lined up in formation — with no opposition — and carried the ball over the goal line, claiming a four-point touchdown and an 8–6 win.

Father James Gardiner recorded his impressions that evening in the Holy Cross house diary:

> A great row at end of 2nd half: Boston Team acted disgracefully & after our team had left, got the Umpire to reverse his decision ... & declaring game against H. C. by score of 8 to 6. No one, however, doubts the record, i.e. H.C. 6 to 4. In consequence of Boston College uniform dishonest and ungentlemanly conduct — Holy Cross will not, either in Foot or Base, Ball again contend with Boston College.[5]

Though the *Worcester Telegram* praised Sockalexis for his "magnificent all-around work," the Boston papers could not agree on the final score. The *Journal* gave Holy Cross the victory by a score of 6–4, while the *Globe* awarded the game to Boston College, 8–6. To this day, both Holy Cross and Boston College claim victory in their respective official records for that game.

News of the Holy Cross athletic success reached all the way to Spain, where the headquarters of the Society of Jesus was located, and to the general of the Jesuit order, Father Luis Martin. Martin was not impressed with athletic activities in the United States, fearing that intercollegiate athletic competition distracted students and exposed them to the influence of the secular world. In September of 1896, as Holy Cross prepared to revive its football program, Martin wrote a letter to President Lehy. "I have been informed," wrote the general, "that in the College, athletic games are indulged in with too much ardor and that too much time, labor, and money is expended in these games. The minds of the students become too excited; it promotes distractions and students are turned from their studies."[6] A few months later, Martin asked that the matter be debated, "lest a frivolous and worldly spirit should undermine the College."[7]

Mike Powers noticed the changing atmosphere at Holy Cross. He had attended the school for several years, and though he performed well in the classroom, he may have been looking for more satisfying opportunities, especially since Holy Cross was now under pressure to stem the growth of athletics. His answer came in the form of an offer from another Catholic school, the University of Notre Dame, in South Bend, Indiana. On December 16, 1896, the college minister recorded the following in the house diary:

> Michael Powers, the great captain of H.C.C.B.B. Nine for some years past & as a consequence a free scholar, recd. Indirectly ... I believe, a bribe from The Notre Dame University & had too small a spirit to refuse it. He left College at 3 this afternoon. Instead of injuring, as we do not believe was intended, it will rather improve our College nine & the College itself, though indeed other ... small spirits, may imitate ex-Captain Powers.[8]

It surprised no one that one of those "small spirits" was none other than Louis Sockalexis. On December 18, Sockalexis, too, left school and boarded a train for Indiana.

Students and faculty were sorry to see Sockalexis leave, but the Penobscot had nothing left to prove as an athlete at Holy Cross, and he had not made much academic progress. Since Sockalexis was still in the Preparatory program, he would have to attend classes for many more years until he could even come close to earning his degree. Besides, he was already 25 years old and was receiving offers from major league baseball teams. Perhaps the Indian felt bored by Latin and Greek, and maybe he felt that it was time to leave Holy Cross behind and strike out in search of new opportunities.

By early 1897, possibly as a result of the defections of Sockalexis and Powers to Notre Dame, Holy Cross president Lehy started to apply the brakes to the runaway train of collegiate athletics. In late March, Lehy refused to let a track squad attend a meet at Penn because "such a trip would be looked upon unfavorably by the bishop and priests and many of the boys' parents, as it makes us too prominent in athletics, and apt to convey the impression that our discipline is being relaxed and prejudicial to study."[9] Edward Purbrick, the Jesuit provincial of the New York–Maryland province, took the matter one step further and pointedly forbade the admission of students to Jesuit colleges in the province solely on the basis of athletics.

Holy Cross, like almost every other college and university in the nation, eventually accepted athletics as an integral part of the college environment, and the Crusader sports teams became a source of much publicity and pride for the school. In future years, Holy Cross enjoyed great athletic success, and their basketball team, captained by all-time all-star Bob Cousy, won the national collegiate championship in 1947. The college started its own Athletic Hall of Fame in 1956, inducting the six greatest Holy Cross athletes as the charter members of the institution. Louis Sockalexis, star of baseball, football, and track, was one of the first six athletes so honored.

Notre Dame was, and is, a Catholic school, but not a Jesuit-run institution. It was founded by members of the Congregation of the Holy Cross (Sanctus Christi), and the school administration eagerly embraced athletics as a way to publicize the college. By 1897 Notre Dame already sponsored a football team, though its greatest successes were still two decades in the future. During the 1890s, baseball was the main sport at Notre Dame. The university was a midwestern baseball powerhouse, despite a small student body of approximately 200, and to maintain their supremacy they enlisted the services of Mike Powers, who was not only a fine student but also a respected captain. It may have been part of the deal between Powers and Notre Dame that he bring the nation's greatest college athlete, Louis Sockalexis, along for the ride.

Despite the "Fighting Irish" nickname that the school's sports teams carry to this day, the university was founded in 1842 as Notre Dame du Lac (Our Lady of the Lake) by French Catholic missionaries, and a French influence still existed on campus. Sockalexis, who grew up in a French-Catholic environment, certainly felt a measure of familiarity in his new surroundings. In addition, Notre Dame students were not as rigidly policed as those at Holy Cross, and this less restrictive atmosphere afforded Louis a new-found freedom.

However, South Bend's bars and nightlife beckoned, tempting the unwary and the immature. South Bend was a gritty industrial community, much like Worcester, but with comparatively more bars and nightspots, and even the occasional brothel. Some of the South Bend clubs featured gambling as well, and the Notre Dame administration worked hard to keep the students from falling under the seedier influences of the surrounding town.

Mike Powers set to work in the early months of 1897, gathering players and arranging indoor practices with the coach. Notre Dame exercised more institutional control over its athletic programs than Holy Cross, since the coach was not a professional player on temporary assignment, but a faculty member. The coach, a man named Frank E. Hering, was an instructor in athletics and English. He and the team manager, Raymond O'Malley, set up a schedule that included games against the University of Michigan and other outstanding midwestern baseball nines.

The Notre Dame team practiced indoors while waiting for the weather to warm up. Even before the team moved outdoors, the talent of Louis Sockalexis impressed his teammates at Notre Dame every bit as much as it had impressed the fans at Holy Cross. William Hindel, who played second base for the Notre Dame nine in 1897, raved about the Indian's ability more than 50 years later. "He was just as great a ball player as they say he was," said Hindel to the *Detroit News* in 1954. "How he could hit! And how he could run, and throw. I've seen the best of the major leaguers but I cannot recall seeing another player with the foot speed of Sockalexis.... He could throw a ball as fast as any man could hit one with a lacrosse bat and he was accurate. There was never another player like him and, quite likely, there will never be another."[10]

While Sockalexis busied himself with attending class and adjusting to this new environment, agents of the Cleveland Spiders of the National League were trying to locate him. James "Chippy" McGarr, who lived in Worcester and coached the Holy Cross nine in the spring, played third base for the Spiders. For two years McGarr had been telling his manager about the Indian athlete and his marvelous skill. McGarr highly recommended the Penobscot to the Spiders, and the Cleveland management was determined to sign Sockalexis before any rival teams could do so.

In late 1896, Pat Tebeau, the manager of the Spiders, ordered McGarr's teammate Jesse Burkett to find the Indian. Burkett, a hard-hitting outfielder and the reigning National League batting champion, was also a resident of Worcester, and witnessed the Indian's talent first-hand at Holy Cross. In the fall of 1896, Burkett received a telegram that directed him to locate the Indian athlete and make him an offer to play for the Spiders. Burkett wrote back to Tebeau, "He is a wonder, but I don't even know how to spell his name. Just send a blank contract and I'll try to sign him."[11] However, by the time the contract arrived in Worcester, Sockalexis was already off to Notre Dame, and Burkett and Sockalexis were unable to connect.

Tebeau didn't want to give up, especially since Louis Sockalexis was now the most talked-about, and sought-after, college athlete in the nation. If Sockalexis was really as good as McGarr and Burkett said he was, the Indian might be one of those rare athletes who could step into a major league lineup without any minor league experience. Tebeau also knew that other National League teams were following the Penobscot's college career. For that reason, Tebeau traveled to South Bend, contract in hand, to make an offer to the Indian personally.

James (Chippy) McGarr, the Cleveland Spiders third baseman and Holy Cross coach. (Library of Congress)

However, Sockalexis demurred on signing with the Spiders, at least for the moment. The Penobscot was interested in the National League and the chance to make some real money, but wanted to complete the college term first. Sockalexis offered to report when the spring term ended in May, but Tebeau wanted him right away, since Cleveland's spring training would begin on March 22 in Cleveland. Sockalexis stood firm, and on March 9, 1897, according to the *South Bend Tribune*, Sockalexis signed a contract to play for the Spiders. The *Tribune* said that Sockalexis returned to Cleveland with Tebeau, but that report was in error. A correction in the paper on March 12 stated that Sockalexis was still attending classes at Notre Dame and that he would report to Cleveland in May, after the conclusion of the Notre Dame season.

As it turned out, Tebeau got his wish, because Louis left school only a few days later.

William Hindel was a Notre Dame student from 1894 to 1897 and played second base on the baseball team in all three of his years at the college. In later years, Hindel recounted the facts, as he remembered them, to Detroit sportswriter H. G. Salsinger regarding Sockalexis' leave-taking of Notre Dame. Hindel, who worked for the Indiana state fire marshal department in later life, related that one evening Sockalexis and a teammate visited an establishment in the seedier part of South Bend, drank a large amount of alcohol, and proceeded to tear the place apart. As Hindel explained it:

> It was during the college baseball season of 1897 that Sockalexis and another Notre Dame student, whose name I don't recall, decided to paint the town of South Bend. They loaded up on Old Oscar McGroggins and wandered about in search of entertainment. They visited an

establishment conducted by "Popcorn Jennie" and wrecked the place. While they were demolishing furniture, and hurling the broken parts out of windows, the local gendarmes arrived on the scene. They tried to quiet Sockalexis but only annoyed him. He became so provoked that he flattened two of the coppers with perfectly delivered rights to their jaws, but he was finally overpowered and dragged to the bastille.

Sockalexis and his fun-loving pal might have gotten out of this mess if the South Bend Tribune had not gotten hold of the story and plastered it over its front page. This greatly displeased the Reverend Father Andrew Morrissey, then President of Notre Dame, and he expelled both Sockalexis and his companion.

Mike Powers wired the Tebeau brothers in Cleveland and advised them to hurry to South Bend and get their Indian out of hock. The next morning Pat Tebeau arrived, squared Sockalexis with the law, and took him to Cleveland, where his major league career began a few days later.[12]

Most of the story, as Hindel remembered it, was correct, although the college baseball season had not yet begun. On Thursday afternoon, March 18, Sockalexis and another student went to a local watering hole, which was sometimes identified as a "brothel" or a "red-light place," and after a drunken row the South Bend police arrived and arrested the two miscreants. However, there was no way that either Sockalexis or his companion could have "gotten out of this mess." Notre Dame, a strongly religious institution, made a practice of summarily expelling students for alcohol-related offenses, and not even a star athlete like Sockalexis was exempt from the rules.

The story appeared the next day on the front page of the *South Bend Tribune*, the local daily newspaper, but Sockalexis was already long gone by then. On Thursday evening, the same day that the two were arrested, both Sockalexis and the other young man were dismissed from the university and ordered to leave the campus at once. The authorities did not even allow Louis to return to his room and pack his belongings, as the *Tribune* explained in its next issue:

> On hearing of the conduct of the two young men, the university authorities ordered their effects packed and sent to them with the information that their presence at Notre Dame was no longer desired. Both were released last night.... The prompt action of the university authorities in expelling these young men should be a warning to others inclined to overstep the bounds of propriety.[13]

The other expelled student must have been the son of a prominent family, because the university took pains to protect his identity from the public. Accordingly, the paper identified Sockalexis by name, but not his companion:

> The other young man was one of the most popular students at the university, and stood high in social circles in this city. For the sake of what he has been and what he still may be his name is not published.[14]

Notre Dame's archives support the paper's assertion that Sockalexis was summarily dismissed, since expelled students are not listed on the college rolls and Sockalexis' name does not appear there. However, Hindel's last statement above was remembered in error, because Pat Tebeau did not have to return to South Bend. According to the local newspaper, Louis left South Bend that night, catching the 11:42 Lake Shore Railroad train to Cleveland, Ohio.

Louis Sockalexis did not choose the most auspicious way to enter the major leagues, and it certainly was troublesome that he was expelled from Notre Dame for drunkenness after compiling an excellent behavior record at Holy Cross. It appears that Sock was able to behave himself in the severely restrictive atmosphere of Holy Cross, but at Notre Dame he was afforded a greater degree of freedom, and the Penobscot could not handle it. Moreover, it seems in retrospect that Sockalexis could not control his intake of alcohol. He was no social drinker, and once he started drinking, did not stop until he was thoroughly intoxicated.

After Louis left campus, the South Bend paper fired one more salvo at the Indian, stating that the Penobscot was "expelled from Notre Dame in disgrace" and "it is intimated that Tebeau will decline to accept the Indian with his newly acquired record."[15] Nevertheless, the night of March 18–19, 1897, found the 25-year-old Penobscot on a train, chugging across eastern Indiana and northern Ohio on the Lake Shore line. The train carried Louis to a new chapter in his life, to the beginning of his professional baseball career in Cleveland.

Another of the many legends surrounding Louis Sockalexis concerns the difficulty encountered by Pat Tebeau in signing the talented Penobscot to a major league contract. Many sources have repeated a familiar story that Tebeau, unable to convince Sockalexis to leave his studies at Notre Dame, took the Indian to dinner and plied him with alcohol until he relented and signed to play for the Spiders. Tebeau got his man, the story goes, by introducing the Indian to whiskey, at the price of destroying Sock's career and life in so doing.

The tale is not true, but like most stories concerning Sockalexis, has been repeated so often that it has become part of the accepted lore of the Indian ballplayer. Pat Tebeau was not the man who introduced Sockalexis to alcohol. It is not known who did, but the Penobscot was already 25 years old in 1897 and had been away from home long enough to find his way to the bottle somehow. Sockalexis may have entered the major leagues in search of greater challenges, but the ready availability of liquor would turn out to be his greatest challenge of all.

CHAPTER 4

The National League

> *Sockalexis is a most valuable addition to the Cleveland team. His record with the Holy Ghost [sic] nine was remarkably good, and had marked him as a man whom major and minor league managers were alike anxious to get their claws on.*
> — Cleveland Leader, March 10, 1897

Louis Sockalexis began generating interest even before he left Notre Dame. The signing of a Native American player by a major league team was unusual, and *The Sporting News* announced Louis' contract on the front page of its March 13, 1897 issue, in an item titled "Tebeau Signs an Indian." The other main sports weekly of the time, *Sporting Life*, also soon introduced the National League's first minority player to its readers. "Sockalexis never saw the wild West," remarked *Sporting Life*. "To all intents and purposes he is a down East Yankee, and is, moreover, a very fluent, agreeable talker, the characteristic reticence of his race being entirely obliterated in his case."[1]

Indeed, Louis had lost much of the traditional Penobscot stoicism from his demeanor by the time he arrived in Cleveland as a 25-year-old rookie in 1897. He was an open and friendly young man, and the other players found it easy to get along with him. Sockalexis was able to give, as well as take, some good-natured abuse in the sometimes rough-edged bantering that went on in the clubhouse and on the practice field. Though Sock's stay at Holy Cross probably made him the best-educated member of the ballclub almost by default — many of the Spiders never even attended high school — the Penobscot's likeability helped him win over his teammates.

Sockalexis, a Native American with both feet now firmly planted in the white world, took on two of the habits of the majority culture. He smoked cigarettes at Holy Cross, as many college men did at the time, and kept doing so as a member of the Spiders. In addition, to his detriment,

Sockalexis had developed a taste for whiskey, one that flared out of control every so often.

Sock's consumption of liquor certainly did not set him apart from his teammates, many of whom were also enthusiastic drinking men. However, many players of the era found themselves unable to discipline themselves sufficiently where alcohol was concerned, and Sock had already been involved in one serious alcohol-related incident. His success or failure in the National League would depend, not only upon his talent, but on his personal maturity as well.

Louis Sockalexis had spent the past few years playing college baseball against cultured, refined Ivy Leaguers. He would soon discover that the type of individuals that he would encounter in professional ball greatly differed from those he knew in college and the semipro leagues back home in Maine.

Most of the National League players of the 1890s were Catholics like Louis, but they were Irish Catholics, mostly from the immigrant populations of the big cities and the factory towns of the eastern states. There were few college men like Louis in the National League at the time, though more would enter the league in the next few years. In 1897, most professional ballplayers were poorly educated, hard drinking, and prone to settle arguments with their fists. It is no wonder that some of the better hotels in National League cities refused to serve traveling baseball teams, due to the rowdy, violent reputation that ballplayers carried in that era.

The accepted style of play differed from college ball as well. Intercollegiate baseball put a premium on gentlemanly, fair, and honest play, in which players respected the umpires and their opponents. However, National League play was another matter entirely. There was only one major league in 1897, and the lack of competition meant that the team owners felt no need to care much about the product that they put on the field. For the most part, the team owners left the players to police themselves.

Cleveland manager Pat Tebeau, who said, "Show me a team of fighters, and I'll show you a team that has a chance,"[2] epitomized the prevailing style of play. National League infielders routinely argued violently with umpires and tripped base runners, while pitchers threw at the heads of opposing batters and runners tried to injure opposing infielders with their spikes. Vile and vicious chatter was the norm on the playing field. The sportswriters railed against the prevalent rowdyism, but few of the 12 club owners appeared to mind, as Francis Richter, editor of *Baseball* magazine, explained some 20 years later while describing baseball of the 1890s:

> Obscene and indecent language between players and to the umpires reached such a pitch that ... some of the magnates could not stand

Cleveland Spiders manager Pat Tebeau, who signed Louis to a major league contract in March of 1897. (Library of Congress)

the raw work of the players, and protested continually against it. But the larger number of the magnates condoned and excused every act of rowdyism, no matter how flagrant.[3]

The umpires, nominally regarded as authority figures on the field, fared poorly in the 1890s. The job of the umpire was almost impossible to perform, especially since the league employed only one umpire per game to save money on salaries. Players treated the umpires so rudely that in 1895, the league employed 59 umpires due to resignations and abrupt retirements. Respected player-turned-sportswriter Tim Murnane said, "The time will soon come when no person above the rank of garrotter can be secured to umpire a game."[4]

Players punched umpires, and umpires sometimes attacked players in return. Tim Hurst, one of the feistiest umpires of the era, belted several players with his mask over the years, and once threw a heavy beer mug into the stands after a fan threw it at him. As might be expected, the mug hit an innocent bystander on the head, and the local police arrested Hurst and charged him with assault.

Umpiring was a rough way to make a living, and sometimes, in the minor leagues, umpires who made unpopular decisions came uncomfortably close to being lynched by angry mobs. One National League arbiter, Stump Weidman, was attacked after a game in Louisville in 1896 by Pat Tebeau and three other Cleveland players and sustained a severe beating. Initially, the league did not punish the four Spiders, since the altercation happened after the conclusion of the game. Instead, the four offenders were arrested by Louisville police and paid fines and court costs.[5] A few days later, the league belatedly fined Tebeau $200, but did not punish the other three attackers.

Brawls and fan riots occurred in the National League with dismaying regularity. Visiting players could expect a flurry of bricks or rocks from the home fans after a hard-fought contest, and when teams fought each other, fans often joined in the mayhem. Any on-field commotion might result in a shower of vegetables, eggs, clods of dirt, or pop bottles raining down among the players. The local police were often called to escort unruly ballplayers off the field, and one on-field fight between the Orioles and the Boston Beaneaters in 1894 ended when the Boston stadium burned to the ground. Forfeits, almost unknown today, happened with regularity in the 1890s, since visiting teams cared little about the opposing club's fans and would pull their players off the field with the slightest provocation.

The Baltimore Orioles were the main offenders. Some say that Charles Comiskey, manager of the St. Louis Browns in the 1880s, introduced fan violence and umpire intimidation into the major leagues as essential facets of team strategy, but the Orioles of Ned Hanlon and John McGraw refined these strategies to a science. Chicago writer Hugh Fullerton commented that "the Baltimore park reeked with obscenity and profanity," and Tim Murnane once blanched at the antics of the Baltimore team. "Diving into the first baseman long after he has caught the ball," related Murnane, "throwing masks in front of the runners at home plate; catching them by the clothes at the third base and interfering with the catcher, were only a few tricks performed by these young men of the South."[6]

One Southern League reporter, watching an exhibition game between New Orleans and the Orioles, said that Baltimore third baseman John McGraw "has the vilest tongue of any ball player ... he adopts every low and contemptible method that his erratic brain can conceive to win a play by a dirty trick."[7] McGraw wasn't the only one. Catcher Wilbert Robinson was known to shove his large mitt into an umpire's face to keep him from seeing a play, and Oriole base runners cut across the pitcher's mound going from first to third if the lone umpire wasn't looking.

The Orioles were hated around the league, but they won pennants each year from 1894 to 1896, so the other National League teams naturally followed Baltimore's lead. By the late 1890s the national sorting press roundly condemned the on-field violence and umpire baiting, but no other club would eschew the rowdy style of play and risk a competitive disadvantage. By the 1890s "Oriole ball" was accepted and encouraged by the team managers and club owners, and the Oriole style of play spread to the other National League ballclubs.

National League president Nick Young, called "Uncle Nick" by everyone, disciplined the players with fines, but the team owners paid the fines under the table, helping perpetuate the rowdiness and violence. The league president was not assertive enough to issue suspensions, especially to players on the more powerful teams, so he busied himself with press relations and the league statistics. The avuncular Uncle Nick served as a figurehead, spending his time making flowery statements to the press and adding hits to the totals of his favorite players.

Evidently, the 12 club owners cared little about the welfare of the fans or the embattled umpires. Almost every spring, the magnates passed a few new rules aimed at controlling the pervasive rowdiness, more for public relations purposes than for anything else. In 1897, the owners decreed that only the team captain would be allowed to address the umpire during a dispute, and the other players on the team would be required to stand ten feet or more away. This rule was aimed at ending the practice of "mobbing" the lone umpire, intimidating him into changing his decisions through sheer numbers. The owners also passed a new rule, ostensibly restricting the constant flow of obscene invective from the coaching lines toward opposition players, especially pitchers. As usual, the players ignored the new rules, and since no punishments came from the league president, the umpire's life became as miserable as ever in the summer of 1897.

Sporting Life, a leading periodical of the time, decried the on-field behavior of players and umpires. "Magnates, beware!" announced the magazine in 1897. "There are other sports in the world besides base ball. And the best and most permanent patrons of base ball do not attend games for the purpose of witnessing prize fights or heavy slum language."[8]

The life of a ballplayer was a difficult proposition for anyone at the time, although Louis Sockalexis must certainly have heard of the trials of a National League career from Mike Powers and others. Nevertheless, Louis boarded a train in South Bend, heading for Cleveland and the beginning of his professional career.

If Louis could manage to impress Pat Tebeau in spring training well enough to earn a spot on the Cleveland roster, he would become the first Native American to play in the National League. Moreover, he would also be the first recognized member of any minority group to do so. Perhaps Louis did not know that baseball's only previous experience with minority players turned out badly for all involved.

In the early 1880s, a small number of African-American players performed in the higher minor leagues. The most prominent of these players was Moses Fleetwood Walker, a young man who attended Oberlin College and the University of Michigan law school before entering professional ball as a catcher. In 1883 Walker served as the starting catcher for one of the nation's strongest minor league clubs, the Toledo Blue Stockings of the Interstate League. Walker batted only .251 that season, but he solidified the catching position and helped the Blue Stockings to the pennant.

Most of the 1883 season passed without incident until the National League champion Chicago White Stockings, managed by Cap Anson, arrived in Toledo for an exhibition game on August 10 of that year. Anson had made it known to the Toledo management that he objected to playing on the same field with African-American players, and the locals planned to oblige Anson. Walker, suffering from a sore hand, had not been penciled into the lineup. The Chicago team arrived in Toledo that morning and was informed that Walker would be kept on the bench. However, according to the *Toledo Blade*, "not content with this, the visitors during their perambulations of the forenoon declared with the swagger for which they are noted" that they would not step onto the field "with no damned nigger."[9]

Anson, further inflaming a situation that the Toledo management had thought resolved, loudly reiterated this demand upon arriving at the ballpark. Toledo manager Charles Morton was not pleased with the demeanor of the visitors. Walker had not been scheduled to play in the game anyway, but the Toledo manager was so offended by Anson's attitude that he put Walker in right field for the contest. "The order was given, then and there, to play Walker and the beefy bluffer (Anson) was informed that he could play his team or go, just as he blank pleased,"[10] reported the Blade.

When Anson saw Walker in the outfield, he exploded. "Get that nigger off the field!" he shrieked to manager Morton. He threatened to go home to Chicago without playing the game, but soon relented after a period of confusion and the threat of forfeiture of the gate receipts. The *Toledo Blade* quoted Anson as saying, "We'll play this here game, but we won't play never no more with the nigger in."[11] Anson gritted his teeth and played the game, and his Chicago team concluded its stay in Toledo with no further outbursts.

Walker may have won the battle, but Cap Anson eventually won the war. The game on August 10, 1883, attracted national attention and served to crystallize the segregation forces already at work in professional baseball. Anson, the most popular player and most successful manager in the game, led the charge to segregate the sport. Slowly, more teams and leagues began to release black players and refuse to hire new ones.[12]

The pennant-winning 1883 Toledo team remained intact and joined the American Association in 1884. Since the Association was considered a major league then, this move made catcher Moses Walker the first African-American major leaguer. Later that summer, Walker's younger brother

Welday played five games as an outfielder for Toledo and became the second of his race to play in the majors. Cap Anson and his White Stockings returned to Toledo for another exhibition game on July 25, 1884, but this time the two teams managed to avoid controversy. Both Walker brothers, by prior agreement, stayed on the bench that day.

Fans in the American Association treated Moses Walker much more rudely than those in the Interstate League. He was booed and hissed at a game in Louisville, Kentucky, in early May but met with more serious threats in Richmond, Virginia, later in the season. Manager Morton received a letter in early September from a group of Richmond baseball fans, threatening violence if Walker appeared at the park in uniform in the former capital of the Confederacy. "We could mention the names of 75 men who have sworn to mob Walker if he comes on the ground in a suit," said the letter, signed by four Richmond citizens. Morton was forced to leave Walker behind in Toledo that weekend. Two weeks later, when the Richmond club traveled to Toledo for a weekday series, Morton received another threatening letter from the Virginia fans.[13]

Walker also ran into trouble with Toledo's star pitcher Tony Mullane, the celebrated "switch-pitcher" and one of the great hurlers of the era. Mullane once said of Walker, "He was the best catcher I ever worked with, but I disliked a Negro and whenever I had to pitch to him I used anything I wanted without looking at his signals."[14] Such shenanigans added errors and passed balls to Walker's statistics and increased the possibility of injury. Walker batted .263 for the 1884 season, but his sore hands and the growing threats against him caused the Toledo club to release him on September 23, 1884. No man of African ancestry would play in the major leagues again until Jackie Robinson joined the Brooklyn Dodgers in 1947.

Walker played for minor league teams in Cleveland, Newark, and other cities for several more years, and crossed paths with Cap Anson again. In 1887 Anson threatened to cancel an exhibition against the Newark team rather than face pitcher George Stovey, Newark's star African-American hurler. Stovey and his catcher, Walker, both remained on the bench for the duration of the game. Anson's campaign began to have an effect, and after the season ended, Newark released Stovey despite his 33 wins.

If John Montgomery Ward had prevailed, Stovey, not Louis Sockalexis, would have been the first minority player in the National League. Ward, the captain of the New York Giants, wanted to sign Stovey to a contract prior to the 1887 season, but Cap Anson bellowed his objections to the other league managers, club owners, and newspaper reporters. The resulting controversy forced Ward to drop his pursuit of the African-American pitcher.[15] Before long, most of the nation's minor leagues formally banned

African-Americans from their circuits, writing the prohibitions into their bylaws.

By 1889 Walker, still with Newark, was the only minority player remaining in the high minor leagues. "Race prejudice exists in professional base ball ranks to a marked degree," said *The Sporting News* that year, "and the unfortunate son of Africa who makes his living as a member of a team of white professionals has a rocky road to travel."[16] Many white pitchers threw the ball at African-American batters' heads, and many white runners did their best to spike black fielders on the base paths. Bud Fowler, the great African-American second baseman, devised a pair of shin guards that he wore under his uniform pants, a full 20 years before shin guards on catchers appeared in the major leagues. Newark released Walker later in 1889, and by 1890 the color line was firmly in place throughout professional baseball.[17]

In the 1890s, the best African-American players, barred from organized ball, plied their trade on barnstorming teams, often against college competition. Louis Sockalexis had played opposite one of the premier black teams, the New York Cuban Giants, several times during his college career at Holy Cross. However, National League baseball remained a Caucasians-only enterprise from its founding in 1876 until Louis joined the Cleveland Spiders in March of 1897. Fifty years before Jackie Robinson of the Dodgers became the first African-American to play in the National League, Louis Sockalexis became the first minority athlete of any kind to perform in the circuit.

Whether he realized it or not, Louis was a pioneer. As the first non–Caucasian in the National League, he could expect to face the type of attention and scrutiny that no other league player had experienced before. Perhaps Louis had never heard of Moses Fleetwood Walker who, like Sockalexis, was a college man who tried to make a career in baseball as a minority athlete. However, at least Native Americans in that era were not treated as badly as African Americans in similar circumstances. Many observers waited to see if Louis Sockalexis would succeed where Moses Walker had failed.

CHAPTER 5

Tebeau's Indians

> *Sockalexis is making a hit wherever he is seen. He has all the ear marks of a ball player besides being an intelligent young man, and if he does not make a big success in this city, a good many wise critics will miss their guess.*
> — Cleveland Plain Dealer, March 22, 1897

Louis Sockalexis, 25 years old, arrived in Cleveland on March 19, 1897. "The Great Sockalexis Is Here," crowed the *Cleveland Plain Dealer* in a sub-headline, and stated that Louis "arrived unheralded and announced himself ready to work." Tebeau, the Cleveland manager, was surprised to see him so soon, having assumed that Louis would finish the semester at Notre Dame, but welcomed the new Spider warmly. Only three other Spiders had reported for duty, though the rest of the players were expected to arrive in the next few days.

The only negative note in the papers was a news item from LaPorte, Indiana, dated March 19. "The following telegram," said the *Plain Dealer*, "shows at what sacrifice Sockalexis joined the club." "The faculty at Notre Dame university," the report stated, "today took summary action by expelling Sockalexis, the famous Indian ball player, who was enrolled as a student.... He signed a contract [with the Spiders, and] wanted to report at once, but could not make arrangements, so, in the language of the collegian, he 'cut'. The faculty today dismissed him."[1]

Perhaps the Cleveland management did not know that the Notre Dame administration expelled Sockalexis for drinking, not for cutting classes. If such was the case, then the Cleveland ballclub also did not know that the Indian already exhibited the beginnings of alcohol abuse.

They also did not know his exact age. Louis, like many ballplayers from the 19th century to the modern day, shaved a few years off of his true age when he signed his first major league contract. He told the Spiders that he was born in 1873, not 1871, and to this day some biographical sketches of Sockalexis list 1873 as the year of his birth.

So far as anyone knows, Louis had paid little, if any, attention to the National League. He was busy playing college ball, going to classes, taking exams, and playing semipro ball in his summer vacations from Holy Cross. It is not known what Louis knew of the Cleveland Spiders, but he was joining one of the most successful — and troubled — teams in the National League.

Cleveland, the Forest City, was the sixth largest city in America, and in 1887 it gained a franchise in the old American Association (AA). Originally called the Blues, the Cleveland team became the Spiders when the sportswriters noticed that many of the team members were tall, stringy-looking individuals. After two seasons in the Association, the team switched to the National League during the baseball labor turmoil of 1889–90. When the Association died after the 1891 campaign, four AA teams joined the National League, and the Cleveland Spiders remained as a member of a new, 12-team circuit.

The Spiders spent the next few years accumulating talent. Jesse Burkett, a pitcher from Worcester, Massachusetts, moved to left field and became one of the most dangerous left-handed hitters in the league. Another pitcher, Bobby Wallace, switched to the infield and eventually took over third base for the Spiders, replacing Chippy McGarr. A fast-throwing farm boy from Tuscarawas County, Ohio, named Denton True Young, joined the team in August 1890, and in October of that year Young pitched an entire doubleheader, winning both games without relief help. By 1892 "Cy" Young was a 30-game winner and the mainstay of the Spider pitching staff. All three of these players—Burkett, Wallace, and Young—would one day gain election to the Baseball Hall of Fame.

Two other Spiders, catcher Chief Zimmer and shortstop Ed McKean, joined the club during the Association years and in 1897 were both entering their eleventh year in the Cleveland lineup. McKean was a fine defensive shortstop and a hard hitter, who batted .355 and .344 in 1894 and 1895, while Zimmer was a tough, hard-nosed catcher who hit .340 in 1895. McKean rarely spoke to his keystone partner, second baseman Clarence "Cupid" Childs, but the two men turned double plays with precision and provided Cleveland with excellent infield defensive play.

Perhaps the most important member of the Spiders was Oliver Wendell "Patsy" Tebeau, the hard-driving manager who also played first base for the team. Pat Tebeau's ancestry was French, but he grew up in the Irish Catholic area of St. Louis known as the Kerry Patch, a part of town where young men learned to fight, drink, and play baseball. This tough-as-nails

Jesse (The Crab) Burkett, the irascible star of the Spiders and part-time coach at Holy Cross in the 1890s. (Library of Congress)

St. Louis neighborhood turned Frenchmen and Germans into scrappy Irishmen, and produced some the most famous ballplayers of the 1890s.

Tebeau wasn't much of a hitter, with a lifetime average of .280 in that hard-hitting era, but his fielding and on-field leadership made him indispensable, and some called him the most important player on the Cleveland team. In the middle of the 1891 season Tebeau became the manager of the fifth-place ballclub. Tebeau turned the Spiders into a scrappy, battling outfit, and when the Baltimore Orioles rocketed to the top of the league with dirty play and umpire intimidation, Tebeau and the Spiders enthusiastically followed suit. By the mid–1890s the Spiders and Orioles were widely considered to be the dirtiest, rowdiest teams in the National League.

The Cleveland Spiders did their best to emulate the Orioles, the "vile lot of blackguards," in the words of umpire Tom Lynch. The Spiders, under the leadership of Pat Tebeau, battled and brawled their way to the top of the National League. They finished second in 1895 but defeated the Orioles four games to one in the Temple Cup series, a post season "World's Series" between the top two finishers in the league. The Spiders finished second again in 1896 but lost the cup back to the Orioles in four straight games.

Fan rioting and on-field disputes marred each Temple Cup series. The strong rivalry between the two rowdiest teams in the league stirred up the fans in both cities, and the resulting violence rivaled the modern-day European soccer riots. After one game in the 1895 series, the Baltimore fans attacked the Clevelanders as they left the park. "The Cleveland players had

5. Tebeau's Indians

Hard-hitting Cleveland shortstop Ed McKean. (Library of Congress)

to sprawl flat on the floor of the bus to escape injury," reported the *Cleveland Plain Dealer*. "Childs was beamed by a piece of rock, while many players later showed the souvenirs of stones and pieces of steel they had picked up from the floor of the bus."[2] The tumultuous series left a sour taste in the mouths of those who watched. Few players took the Temple Cup championship seriously, and the Spiders won in 1895 largely due to the indifference of the Orioles.

Despite their success in the standings, the Spiders suffered from low attendance. In 1895 and 1896 they finished second in the standings, but only the hapless Washington Senators drew fewer fans among the 12 teams. The city of Cleveland had outlawed Sunday baseball several years before, and since most blue-collar workers toiled six days a week at the time, this law kept many fans away from the ballpark. Cleveland Spiders management wanted the city to overturn the law, but the Spiders' nasty, violent style of play aroused opposition to "breaking the Sabbath" with such a vulgar activity as ball playing.

In addition, Tebeau's constant stream of colorful invective against the umpires could be heard all over League Park and served to keep female fans away. It seems obvious, in retrospect, that the National League was losing fan support with the brand of ball espoused by the Cleveland and Baltimore teams. The Orioles, winner of three pennants in a row from 1894 to 1896, also suffered from low attendance and, like the Spiders, scrambled each year to break even financially.

Frank DeHaas Robison, the owner of the Spiders, was a trolley-car magnate who built his stadium, League Park, in east Cleveland at 66th and Lexington, next to his trolley lines. Robison was a hard-nosed businessman who built a large wall outside the park so that people in neighboring houses could not see the game without paying their way in. Robison also endured several nasty labor disputes with the trolley workers' union, which harmed the popularity of his ballclub in a highly unionized city like Cleveland, and also used non-union labor to do work on the ballpark itself. The Cleveland owner appeared to have no idea of how to cultivate a positive public image for his team, or win the favor of the mostly blue-collar fans. Robison spent much of his time criticizing the ministers of Cleveland for their opposition to Sunday ball, and much of the rest of the time negotiating to move the team to Detroit, Indianapolis, or other more accommodating cities.

The Spiders were a good team, but they were also an old team with a lot of high-salaried veteran players. In 1892, when the rival American Association folded, the National League owners instituted a maximum salary of $2,400 per player. Cleveland had nine men earning the maximum salary; these "limit men" included Young, McKean, Childs, Zimmer, Burkett, and Tebeau, who earned more than $2,400 for his managerial duties. Some other National League teams employed only three or four limit men. The Cleveland payroll, reportedly $38,000 in 1897, was one of the highest in the league that year for a team with disastrously low attendance.

The Spiders finished only three games behind the pennant-winning Orioles in 1895, but although they finished second again in 1896, the Orioles owned a nine-game bulge over the Clevelanders. The Spiders were falling farther behind the Orioles, and key players like McKean and Zimmer were now in their mid–30s and running out of time. If the Spiders could not manage to win the pennant in 1897, they might have to dismantle the team and build a new one. They also might lose even more fans, especially if the ban on Sunday ball continued, and lose the franchise itself to another city. Already, Robison was publicly considering an offer from the Brooklyn club to buy the Spiders for $100,000 and move the cream of Cleveland's players to Brooklyn, leaving a shell of a team behind in Cleveland.

The Spiders wanted to sign Louis Sockalexis, at least initially, for his hitting, not as a gate attraction. The Spiders, throughout the 1890s, suffered from a glaring weakness in the outfield. Left fielder Jesse Burkett was one of the greatest hitters in baseball, winning the batting title in 1895 with a .423 average and again in 1896 with a .410 mark. However, Jimmy McAleer in center and Harry Blake in right batted .288 and .240 respectively in 1896 when the team as a whole, pitchers included, hit for a .301 average. McAleer, the best defensive center fielder in the National League, made up for his weak bat with his fielding, but the Spiders could not afford to carry two such weak-hitting starters in the outfield. If Sockalexis could hit and field as advertised, reasoned Pat Tebeau, the Indian would play right field, Blake could return to the bench, and the club could carry McAleer in the lineup for his glove work.

Tebeau hoped that the Indian from Maine could solve the team's chronic outfield weakness and help the Spiders close the gap on the Orioles. However, Louis was an educated college man, not a hard-driving scrapper like most of his teammates. The Penobscot tribe from which Louis came valued dignity and respectful conduct on the field of play, and undisciplined, rowdy on-field behavior was foreign to the Indian's upbringing and experience. It remained to be seen if Louis Sockalexis, after playing two seasons of gentlemanly college ball against teams like Yale and Harvard, could adjust to the comparatively wild National League.

The Spiders gathered for spring training in March of 1897, not on a ball field, but at the former home of the downtown Cleveland Athletic Club. Pat Tebeau told the papers that such indoor activities as playing handball, running a track, and working with weights would get his players in physical condition much better than a cold game of baseball outside. "Our training," said Tebeau, "will consist of each man taking 20 minutes' work in the handball court, 15 minutes of leg work on the running track, 10 minutes of dumb bell exercise, 15 minutes of calisthenics, and the balance of the training time will be devoted to throwing the ball and catching."[3]

"The teams that have gone south," remarked Tebeau, "are either being drowned out or frozen up ... in the meantime, we are getting limbered up and in good condition."[4] Nonetheless, as the papers pointed out, the sojourn in Cleveland cost much less than a spring training trip to the southern states. The Cleveland Athletic Club had folded more than a year before, and Robison undoubtedly received a good deal in renting the unused building. The Cleveland owner wanted to win, but attendance was poor in 1896, and he cut corners on spring training to save money.

The building was dark and musty after a year of abandonment, and Pat Tebeau put the Spiders to work sweeping out the cobwebs before starting the players on a regimen of handball and calisthenics. Tebeau himself was a fine handball player, the champion of the Cleveland team, and he took a great measure of pride in his prowess at the game. However, the new man, Sockalexis, played several matches against Tebeau and beat the manager almost at will.

The Indian made an immediate impression upon his new teammates, who called him "Sock." "He is a massive man," reported *Sporting Life*, "with gigantic bones and bulging muscles, and looks like a ball player from the ground to the top of his five feet, 11 inches of solid frame work." Despite his size — at the time, he was one of the bigger Spiders — Sockalexis was the fastest runner on the team by a wide margin. "The old players," said the *Plain Dealer*, "size up Sockalexis as a born ball player. A more active man on his feet is seldom seen."[5]

Sockalexis, despite his muscular build, was amazingly limber. He performed feats of acrobatics that made the other players and writers gaze in amazement. "Sockalexis, who is quite a gymnast, occasionally breaks out with some caper that would tear the ordinary man in two,"[6] reported the *Plain Dealer*.

Tebeau was impressed, but wanted the Indian to concentrate on baseball. "Those things are all right in a circus, Louie," said Tebeau, "but you don't need 'em to win ball games."

The sportswriters enjoyed the exotic sight of the handsome Indian, with his copper skin, straight black hair, and high cheekbones, in a Cleveland uniform. So impressed were the writers that soon Sock became "the Cleveland Indian" and within hours of Sock's arrival the writers began referring to the team as "Tebeau's Indians." The main paper in Cleveland, the *Plain Dealer*, used the term "Indians" for the first time in a headline on March 20, 1897, the day after Sockalexis arrived in Cleveland. Within a week, the writers were identifying the team as the Indians on a regular basis. On March 27, the *Plain Dealer* commented on the upcoming slate of outdoor practices. "The Indians," remarked the *Plain Dealer*, "have a spring schedule which is bound to give them good, hard work."[7]

No one much cared for the name "Spiders," which dated from the early 1890s, and in those days team nicknames varied from year to year depending upon the whims of the writers. Within days the name "Indians" had caught the fancy of the Cleveland papers, and the influential national periodical *Sporting Life* offered the following in its March 27, 1897, issue, in an article titled "They're Indians Now":

> There is no feature of the signing of Sockalexis more gratifying than the fact that his presence on the team will result in relegating to obscurity the title of "Spiders," by which the team has been handicapped for several seasons, to give place to the more significant name "Indians." "Spiders" did well enough with men like Jay Faatz, Darby O'Brien, and the like on the team but is particularly inappropriate to the present aggregation of stocky players.

Elmer Bates, the Cleveland correspondent for *Sporting Life*, extended the Indian metaphor as applied to the ballclub when he identified Pat Tebeau in a headline as the "heap big chief" of the Cleveland team. One Cleveland writer, C. A. Conrad, suggested that the new player's name might be too long to fit into the box scores. In the style of the period, he expressed his concern with a bit of poetry:

Said Pat Tebeau to the score-card man,
"Tell me, please sir, if you can,
Is there room on our batting list
for my latest find, Sockalexis?"

The score-card man took his pencil out,
In his fertile mind he had no doubt,
That he readily could with becoming grace,
Compress the name in a very small space.

"Let's see: two, four, six, eight, ten,
Pretty near enough letters for two men:
Suppose we cut out just a few,
And then we'll see what I can do."

Hadn't he done such things before?
Guess he could do it at least once more.
Remembering well that he'd some years back
Transformed "McGillicuddy" into plain "Mack."

He scanned the name and mused awhile,
"How is this?" An artless smile.
He has written it "Sock." Pat grinned a grin,
and said, "You'd better try again."

"Won't do? Well now I do declare,
then why not make an even pair?
So I'll add the s. Now that is it."
He had written it "Socks." Quoth Patsy, "nit."

Neither "Alex" or "Aleck" the captain would suit
and Alexis was thrown in to boot,
Said Pat, "It's a blooming, bleeding shame,
But the fellow will have to change his name."[8]

Sporting Life also reported that John Montgomery Ward, the highly respected former player and manager with the Giants and other teams, sent Cleveland owner Frank Robison a letter that stated, "I congratulate you on securing Sockalexis. I have seen him play perhaps a dozen games, and I unhesitatingly pronounce him a wonder. Why he has not been snapped up before by some League club looking for a sensational player is beyond my comprehension."[9] The Penobscot had not yet played a National League game, but he was already drawing more attention than were all the other Cleveland players combined. The papers reported that DeWolf Hopper, the famous actor and baseball enthusiast who made a career of reciting the popular poem "Casey at the Bat," visited the Cleveland camp and came away impressed with Sockalexis.

Elmer Bates, the *Sporting Life* correspondent, appended an aside in his weekly dispatch to the magazine that proved prophetic. "Sockalexis, the Indian, makes friends fast," wrote Bates in the March 27 issue. "He already knows half the sports in town, and he has only been here three days."

The new enthusiasm surrounding the team was tempered by off-field developments. The Spiders struggled to turn a profit in Cleveland all through the 1890s, and rumors of a franchise shift popped up in print almost every day. In late March, Indianapolis was mentioned as a likely destination for the Spiders; a few days later, Detroit and Milwaukee appeared to be the front-runners. Frank Robison, owner of the Cleveland club, also received a solicitation from Toledo, a city that had failed to support teams in the American Association in 1884 and 1890. Toledo allowed Sunday ball, and the *Toledo Blade* declared that Robison's team would draw many more fans in Toledo than they would in Cleveland.

Sunday ball was the crux of the problem. In 1896, the eastern cities did not allow games to be played on Sunday. In the cities that allowed the practice, including Chicago, St. Louis, and Cincinnati, thousands of fans invaded the parks on Sunday compared to hundreds on the weekdays. It especially rankled Frank Robison that the Cincinnati Reds played ball on Sunday with no interference, because the Queen City authorities simply ignored the Ohio blue law where the Reds were concerned.[10] The Sunday-ball teams enjoyed a great advantage in attendance over their rivals, in an era when attendance brought in almost all of a team's revenue. The Cleveland Spiders operated at a competitive disadvantage, and Frank Robison decided to bring the matter to a head.

On March 24, when the Cleveland management should have been touting the upcoming season, Robison filled the newspaper columns with criticism of Cleveland's ministers. "The outcome of the Sunday ball question," said Robison, "will decide whether the Cleveland team will remain in this city another year or not.... I am no lawbreaker, but if there is a law that is a dead letter and has not been enforced for years I think there is no wrong in ignoring it."

Robison's brother Stanley, the vice president and treasurer of the team, chimed in with a condescending air. "Of course there will be some people who object to Sunday base ball," said the younger Robison, "just the same as there are those who object to Sunday papers, Sunday picnics, and, I might say, Sunday sermons ... a great many people can find worse things to do on Sunday than attend ball games, and I honestly believe that these worthy gentlemen [the ministers] might be directed toward a better purpose."[11]

Soon the news hit the papers that Robison and the National League schedule makers planned eight Sunday games in Cleveland during the 1897 season, and the first one would be played on May 15 against the Washington Senators. The ministers of Cleveland were outraged, and in late March the Reverend A. B. Chalmers met with Pat Tebeau and threatened to have all the players arrested if they played on any Sunday. Robison, in turn, refused to back down, and repeated his threat to move the Spiders out of Cleveland unless the city lifted the restriction on Sunday ball. "President Robison ... says that his men will play in this city on Sunday," said the *Plain Dealer*. "If they do not, he says, Cleveland will have no baseball."[12] While the ministers fumed, Robison traveled in late March to Indianapolis. Robison wanted to demonstrate to the ministers that he was serious about the Indiana city as a possible new home for his team.

In the meantime, the Spiders-turned-Indians prepared to move their activities outdoors. Pitcher Cy Young, the largest Cleveland player at six feet two inches and 210 pounds, spent the winter swinging an ax on his Ohio farm and arrived at camp in excellent shape. Jesse Burkett, the reigning batting champ of the National League, lost a good amount of weight after a battle with the flu, but looked to be regaining his strength, while Pat Tebeau sweated off some extra winter weight with handball. Sock needed no such exercise, since he reported to camp at a solid 185 pounds, without an ounce of fat on him, and had already been through several weeks worth of spring practice at Notre Dame.

The Cleveland team needed another pitcher, since George (Nig) Cuppy, a 25-game winner in 1896, reported to camp with a sore arm. In addition, the versatile Bobby Wallace, 10–7 on the mound in the previous season, was such a good hitter that Pat Tebeau preferred to put him in the everyday lineup. Tebeau, always scouring the colleges for talent, signed Sock's college teammate John Pappalau upon the recommendation of Jesse Burkett, a Worcester native who coached Sockalexis and Pappalau at Holy Cross. Pappalau, a 23-year-old right-hander, showed good speed in early throwing sessions, but Tebeau cautioned him against "cutting loose" too soon. Another right-handed rookie, Jack Powell, looked good in camp, and a battle between Powell and Pappalau for the last spot on the pitching staff drew the interest of the fans.

Nevertheless, most of the attention of the fans and writers fell upon Louis Sockalexis. "His batting eye seems to be all that it has been cracked up to be," the *Plain Dealer* reported. "He fields as fast as his indoor training indicated that he would, and he can run bases as fast as any man on the team."[13] *Sporting Life* reported that Sockalexis "in 24 hours [of his arrival] was the most popular man around the Kennard House," a rooming house in downtown Cleveland where Sock and other players stayed.

Sock stirred an enthusiasm among the fans that drew attention away from the many off-field distractions and controversies. Many felt that Sockalexis' presence could lift Tebeau's team past the Orioles and into the National League pennant.

The writers, in the style of the period, produced poetry of varying quality to celebrate the exotic new ballplayer. One such poem appeared in the *Plain Dealer* four days before Sock arrived in Cleveland:

> Sockalexis, Sockalexis, Sockalexis tall,
> Down to wild and woolly Texas soon will sock the ball;
> And the crank, what e'er the sex is, soon will raise his stock,
> Just to prove spry Sockalexis worthy of his sock.
>
> Soon will he, until he's sore, whoop on the coaching line,
> And the music of his war whoop will be very fine.
> Yea, the glamour of his war paint will delight the crowd,
> Though it be but common store paint, laid on thick and loud.[14]

Though the other National League teams had been working out on outdoor fields for weeks, "Tebeau's Indians" did not play outdoors until March 30. After two more days of workouts, Tebeau divided the 21 players into two teams for an exhibition game, which was played on April 2. Managers usually gave their split squads names like "Regulars" and "Yannigans" in that era, but Tebeau liked the team's new unofficial nickname. He put most of the regulars on one team and the youngsters on the other and called them the "Indians" and the "Papooses." For the first time, a box score appeared in the newspapers with the name "Indians" applied to the Cleveland team.

An unusually large spring crowd of 600 fans watched the contest. Sock batted cleanup for the Indians and lived up to his advance billing with three hits in five trips to the plate. He pounded out a single and two doubles, drew a walk, scored three runs, and threw out a runner from right field. The other Holy Cross product, Pappalau, pitched poorly for the Papooses, who lost to Sock and the Indians by a 17–7 score.

For the first time, the Cleveland fans filled the air with war whoops and "Indian yells" as Sock came to the plate. "Sockalexis was the most observed man on the field," reported the *Plain Dealer*, "and although he had to stand about as much 'kidding' from the bleachers as the average outsider, he made two two-baggers and a single, and got his base on balls once while facing the pitcher six times.... In the field the Indian had only two chances, but on one of them he made a magnificent throw straight to the plate and caught out the runner trying to score."[15]

"Kidding" then may have been what we call taunting today, though it seemed to lack any evil intent. Most likely, the whooping and yelling was more enthusiastic than anything else, coming from a group of fans starved for success and excitement in following the Cleveland team. Besides, the Cleveland fans now saw that Sockalexis was the real thing and that he was, if anything, even better than advertised.

It rained and snowed for the next few days, and the new Indians would only have time for one short exhibition trip before the regular season began on April 15. Though Tebeau's team was in excellent physical condition, due to the indoor workouts, many wondered how well the players would perform on the field when it counted. The weather was

Indians.	A.B.	R.	H.	O.	A.	E.
Burkett, l. f.	5	4	1	4	0	1
Childs, 2b	3	3	1	4	2	1
McKean, s. s.	5	2	2	2	2	0
Sockalexis, r. f.	5	3	3	1	2	0
McAleer, c. f.	4	0	1	1	0	0
O'Connor, 1b	5	2	2	9	0	0
McGarr, 3b	4	0	1	1	1	0
McAllister, c.	5	1	3	5	1	0
Cuppy, p.	2	0	0	0	3	0
Wilson, p.	3	2	2	0	2	0
Gear, p.	0	0	0	0	0	0
Totals	41	17	15	27	13	2
Papooses.	A.B.	R.	H.	O.	A.	E.
Wallace, 3b	4	2	1	3	3	0
Blake, s. s.	3	1	1	4	2	1
Mangan, 2b	4	1	1	3	3	1
Zimmer, 1b	5	2	1	6	2	1
Gear, r. f.	4	1	3	3	0	0
Stokes, r. f.	3	0	1	0	0	0
Powell, c. f. & p.	3	0	2	0	0	1
Creiger, c.	4	0	0	3	2	0
Zump, l. f.	4	0	0	2	1	3
Pappalau, p.	2	0	0	0	1	0
McDermott, p.	1	0	1	1	0	0
Wally, c. f.	1	0	0	0	0	0
Totals	38	7	11	24	14	8
Indians	2 1 0 0 2 5 7 0 *—17					
Papooses	1 0 0 1 0 0 0 5 0— 7					

This box score appeared in the *Cleveland Plain Dealer* on April 3, 1897. For the first time, the name "Indians" was applied to the Cleveland team. (Author's collection)

unusually cold and wet in April of 1897, and Tebeau kept the team busy indoors with handball and running while waiting for the skies to clear.

Finally, on April 10, the team traveled down to Columbus for an exhibition against the local Western League club, managed by Tebeau's brother George. There was snow on the ground, but the two teams played anyway, and battled to a 3–3 tie in the cold and rain as Sockalexis whacked three singles and threw out a runner at second. In Dayton the next day, Sock hit two singles, threw out two more base runners, and made no less than three excellent catches in the outfield. Before each game Tebeau led his players in a new "jollying dodge." "Tebeau lines the Spiders up," explained the *Sporting News*, "and they march in front of the grandstand and give an Apache war whoop in chorus. It made a great hit in Columbus and Dayton."[16]

Sock ran so fast that opposing base runners couldn't believe that he could run down line drives and fly balls from such long distances.

Sockalexis covered great expanses of ground in right field, and some were already calling him the fastest man in baseball. Sock's Cleveland teammates told the reporters that the Penobscot could run the 100-yard dash in 10 seconds flat, a near world record time, in full baseball uniform. Some of the writers were already calling Louis the "Deerfoot of the Diamond," comparing him to the famous Indian marathon runner, Lewis "Deerfoot" Bennett, of the previous generation.[17] Sockalexis could also throw a ball from the deepest part of right field, on a line, all the way to any base with great accuracy. As Sock's fame spread, more and more fans came out to see the new sensation.

Tebeau then took the team to Indianapolis for three games against another Western League club. The first of the three games was rained out, but on the next afternoon Sock made a great running catch in right field. He topped that the next day with a double play from the outfield, catching a long fly ball and throwing to first to double up the runner. In Grand Rapids, Michigan, Sockalexis belted a double as his "antics were watched closely by several Michigan Indians, who occupied positions on the sun bleacher."[18] Sock's bat cooled down in the cold April weather — he put together a string of 1-for-4 and 1-for-5 days — but he thrilled a crowd in Toledo on April 20 with a triple and another spectacular running catch. The rookie outfielder from the Penobscot Nation earned a spot on the Cleveland team, both for his playing prowess and his undeniable value as a gate attraction, and signed a contract at a reported salary of $1,500 for the 1897 season.

Everywhere the Clevelanders played, the fans came out to see Sockalexis. Many of the spectators had never seen a real Indian before, and the sight of Sock in a baseball uniform excited the crowds as no other Cleveland player had ever done. The fans let loose with war whoops and Indian yells wherever he appeared. Louis pretended not to notice, preferring instead to concentrate on his playing, but there was an undeniable electricity around the Cleveland team that had not existed in previous seasons.

Cleveland management hoped that the presence of the muscular Penobscot would attract fan interest and improve attendance at Cleveland's League Park, which in 1896 ranked 11th out of the 12 National League teams. Cleveland writer Charles W. Mears expressed this belief in an article, titled "[A] Good Drawing Card," that appeared in *The Sporting News* at the beginning of the 1897 campaign. "Everybody in Cleveland," suggested Mears, "as well as in other league cities, for that matter, are talking Sockalexis, and if the young Indian isn't the best advertised new man that ever entered the big organization then it will not be the fault of the baseball paragraphers of the press. They have discovered a novelty in it.

The newspaper talk concerning the youngster has stirred up great local interest in the Red Man, and of all the young players on the Cleveland Club's list he is the most talked of, and it will be his appearance that will draw the greatest number of curious people at the opening of the season.

"His presence on the team may be the cause of drawing many new patrons to the game, for if they go just once to see the Indian play they may become interested in the game and go again and again until they may finally become regular patrons."[19]

CHAPTER 6

"He's the Stuff and He's the People"

> *Warrior Louis Sockalexis ... was naturally the center of attraction after the visitors reached the grounds [in Cincinnati]. He was greeted with war whoops and Indian yells, but as the game progressed and Socks began to hit and field, he was given an ovation.*
> —*Cleveland Plain Dealer,* April 27, 1897

We now know that Louis Sockalexis was not the first individual of Native American ancestry to play major league baseball. James Madison Toy, a Pennsylvanian whose father was Native American, played for Cleveland's American Association team in 1887 and for Brooklyn's AA team in 1890. Toy played several positions but mostly served as a first baseman, batting .222 in 1887 and .181 in 1890. Toy's ancestry was not a source of comment, and the newspapers of the period made no reference to his Indian background. Besides, Toy looked Caucasian, sporting a handlebar mustache in the style of the period, and did not ethnically identify himself as a Native American. Not until the mid–1960s did baseball researchers establish that Toy, not Sockalexis, was major league baseball's first part–Indian.

In addition, although most sources claim that Sockalexis was a full-blooded Penobscot, he was not. Ethnological researchers say that the last full-blooded member of the Penobscot nation died in 1853, 18 years before Louis Sockalexis was born.[1] It appears that some French-Canadian ancestry, on both his mother's and his father's sides of the family, shows itself in Louis' lineage. Though several other part–Indians played in the majors within a few years after Louis arrived in Cleveland, it took more than two decades for a full-blooded Native American to appear in the major leagues. Moses Yellowhorse, a Pawnee from Oklahoma, became the first full-blooded Indian in baseball when he pitched for the Pittsburgh Pirates from 1921 to 1922.

Today, many researchers reject the concept of "full-bloodedness" as outdated and look more to self-identity as a key to ethnicity. Sockalexis, unlike Jim Toy, grew up in a Native American environment and aligned himself socially and ethnically as a member of the Penobscot Nation. Though Louis may not have been 100 percent Indian genetically, he certainly was baseball's first self-identified Native American, as well as the first minority athlete to play in the National League.

However, Sockalexis was not the first player, or even the first Cleveland player, to be called "Chief." Catcher Charles Zimmer joined the Cleveland Association team in 1887 as a teammate of Jim Toy. Zimmer's ancestry was German, but he had once coached a team in Poughkeepsie, New York, called the Indians, which made him the "chief" of the Indian players. Zimmer, one of Cleveland's most popular players, would now share the "Chief" appellation with a real member of the Penobscot tribe.

The Cleveland team began its pursuit of the 1897 pennant in Louisville against the Colonels on April 23. The pennant-winning Baltimore Orioles had strengthened their team with the addition of outfielder Jake Stenzel, but their star third baseman, John McGraw, struggled with a sprained ankle and arm problems after battling typhoid fever the year before. McGraw's injuries and Oriole team discord cast doubt upon Baltimore's chances for a fourth straight pennant. The Spiders, second in 1896, now possessed the most exciting young player in baseball in Louis Sockalexis, closing their weakness in the outfield and adding a dangerous bat to the middle of their lineup. While team owner Frank Robison sputtered and fumed at the Cleveland ministers over Sunday ball, the Spiders prepared to seek their first National League flag.

On a windy, overcast day in Louisville, Kentucky, Louis Sockalexis made his major league debut for the Cleveland team, now known far and wide as the "Indians." The city of Louisville held a parade to celebrate the opening of the season, and about 10,000 fans filled Exposition Park, partly to cheer the Colonels and partly to see the man whom the papers were calling "Chief" Sockalexis. The mayor of Louisville gave a short speech from home plate, then turned the game over to the umpires.

Cy Young struck out two in the first inning, but the Colonels scored three times in the sixth to take a 3–1 lead, which they held to the end of the game. Young allowed only eight hits, but Louisville's Chick Fraser held Sock hitless and gave only four safeties to the rest of the Cleveland batters. "Sockalexis showed up weak at the bat," said the *Plain Dealer* the next day, "and seemed in poor form on ground balls." Sock committed no errors but bobbled a few balls in the outfield, though the Colonels could not take advantage.

Sock performed better the next day, though Louisville defeated the Indians by a 9–3 score. The Penobscot singled twice, driving in two of the Cleveland runs, and a good play by Louisville left fielder Fred Clarke robbed the Indian of another hit. "The batting, running, and fielding of Sockalexis was one of the features of the game," according to the *Plain Dealer*. "Hits that went to his territory were handled fast and with accuracy." It was a contentious game, with Burkett ejected in the first inning for disputing balls and strikes, and the Clevelanders delayed the game with arguments all afternoon. The Colonels' left-hander Still Bill Hill allowed only four hits, two by Sockalexis, for the win.

The Louisville crowd hated the Spiders, but they liked Louis Sockalexis, and they whooped and hollered whenever the Indian came to bat. "Sockalexis was cheered at every move he made," reported the Louisville paper. "He caught a long fly very prettily and the spectators remarked at his grace. The crowd tried to have fun with Sockalexis' name and imitated war whoops, to all of which the handsome Indian smiled good-naturedly."[2]

Tebeau's Indians then traveled to Cincinnati, losing 6–3 to the Reds, but once again Louis Sockalexis was the star of the game. The Cincinnati crowd let out a stream of whoops and yells whenever the Indian came to the plate, and Sock answered with two singles and a double. One single drove in two of the three Cleveland runs, and Louis handled three difficult plays easily in the outfield. By the end of the game, the Cincinnati fans were cheering Sock as if he were one of their own players.

However, the Reds found Sock's weakness the next day. Ted Breitenstein was a veteran left-handed pitcher with a confusing array of curve balls, and Louis had not yet learned to hit the low, slow curve. Breitenstein struck out Louis three times and induced the Indian to hit a weak grounder on his other trip to the plate, as the Clevelanders lost the game 7–3. The next day, another Cincinnati lefty, Willie Damman, held Sock hitless again, shutting out Cleveland on six hits.

By now the Indians were 0–5, in last place in the National League, and some of the writers were criticizing Tebeau's unorthodox spring training regimen of handball and indoor track work. Tebeau, for his part, admitted that the team could have used two more weeks of outdoor training, especially since the Cleveland team had opened the last few seasons with poor starts. It wasn't yet time to panic, but by the second week of the season, the Indians were already four and a half games behind the league-leading Philadelphia Phillies.

In their next outing, against the Browns in St. Louis, Sock saved the game in the ninth inning. The Indians didn't win the game, but thanks to Louis they didn't lose it either. Cy Young took a 6–4 lead into the ninth, but the Browns scored twice to tie the game and managed to load the bases with two out. Eddie McFarland then smashed a rocket to right field, but Sock ran the ball down and made a spectacular leaping catch to end the inning. The umpires then called the game on account of darkness, and the Clevelanders escaped with a 6–6 tie.

Sockalexis gave another exhibition against the Browns the next afternoon, as Tebeau's men finally broke into the win column. Sock belted a homer, his first in the major leagues, far over the right field fence as the Indians defeated the Browns for their first win of the 1897 season. Only 900 fans were present, but some observers called Sock's home run the longest they had ever seen in St. Louis. "The Indians hang one little scalp at their belts," said a sub-headline in the *Plain Dealer*.

The batting and fielding of Sockalexis started the Indians on a march up the standings. They defeated St. Louis on May 1 when Sock pounded a bases-loaded triple to break up a tie game in the ninth inning. Sock also belted three singles and stole two bases. The Indians won again the next day; although Sock went hitless, he started a double play in the outfield and stole another base.

Cincinnati's Ted Breitenstein handcuffed Sock again on May 3, but the Indians won their home opener against the Reds in front of 4,200 fans on a cold, windy day. The weather kept the crowd small for an opening day, but the fans made up for it with loud pseudo–Indian noise-making whenever Sockalexis stepped to the plate. No Cleveland player — neither 30-game winner Cy Young, nor batting champ Jesse Burkett — had ever excited the fans as much as this Penobscot Indian from the pine forests of Maine.

The enthusiastic papers celebrated their newest star with another round of poetry. It didn't take long for an unnamed Cleveland writer to employ the eight-syllable cadence of Henry Wadsworth Longfellow's "The Song of Hiawatha" as a model for "The Song of Sockalexis":

> "Honor be to Sockalexis!"
> Cried the rooters, cried the ball fans,
> When he came triumphant homeward,
> With his scalps from Vonderahedom,
> In the region of St. Louis,
> From the home of dark Brown baseball,
> In the land of Cross and Connor.
> He had swiped the curving spheroid
> From the hand of Titan "Donnie,"

> From the reach of Dowd and Turner,
> From the lot, to the next county,
> As the Browns stood mute and spellbound
> In their flood-bedraggled ballfield,
> On the banks of Mississippi.
> Up spoke mighty Patsy Tebeau,
> "Henceforth he shall be our right field,
> Somewhere else will play young Blakie,
> 'Ansome' Arry is a good one,
> But he surely is not in it
> When it comes to clearing bases,
> When it comes to swiping home runs,
> And hereafter and forever
> Sox shall hold supreme dominion
> 'Till he shows a streak of yellow,
> 'Till his batting eye deserts him,
> He's the stuff and he's the people."[3]

To date, no one had yet suggested that the whoops and yells for Sockalexis were malign in intent or racist in tone. The fans in Cincinnati and Cleveland reacted enthusiastically to the presence of this exotic new player, and the enthusiasm that Sock generated appeared to be positive in nature. However, the sporting press was already beginning to take note of Sockalexis, and the eastern writers took a closer look at Cleveland's newest star. The *Washington Post* sounded perhaps the first negative tone about the Indian. "Sockalexis, who is doing a medicine dance at the expense of the twirlers in the western teams, has yet to demonstrate that he is not a cigar sign on the bases," suggested the *Post*. "...the critics still insist that a child of the forest is slower to think than the white man."[4]

Some of the compliments paid to the Penobscot in the press smacked of condescension. "One would hardly believe that Socks was the offspring of half-civilized parents," stated *The Sporting News*. "There is not a more gentlemanly player on the Cleveland team than Sockalexis. He has an excellent education, and there is nothing about his actions or his talking calculated to remind one of Wild West shows, tomahawks, and all that sort of thing. The young man is a fluent conversationalist, who can tell many interesting stories."[5]

Despite a few fielding lapses in right field, Sockalexis kept banging the ball. He belted his second over-the-fence homer against the Reds on May 5, and topped himself with a spectacular fielding play late in the game. "The 'Big-Man-Not-Afraid-Of-His-Job'," said the *Plain Dealer*, "after shooting in the air like a skyrocket to pull down an awful line drive far out in right field, he threw the ball like a shot to the plate and cut off a runner trying to score from third. The play was a remarkable one and will not be soon forgotten." Sockalexis was "the real thing," the paper said, but the two batters ahead of Sock in the lineup, Burkett and McKean, each went 0 for 5 that day, and the Clevelanders lost by a 3–2 score.

The Penobscot dazzled the Cleveland fans again in a 6–5 win over the Chicago Colts (now called the Cubs) on May 7. Louis gave perhaps his best performance in a Cleveland uniform and saved the game with a running, one-handed catch in right field in the seventh inning. The Chicagoans had the bases loaded with two outs at the time, and Sock's catch prevented the Colts from taking the lead. Sock, according to the *Plain Dealer*, also "cover[ed] himself with all kinds of glory" at the plate. "Three singles and a three-bagger," announced the paper, "a total of six bases, and a base on balls ... five chances in the outfield without an error ... two runs and two stolen bases. Will the Indian do?" Louis was "the best Indian that ever wandered down the pike."[6]

Sock nearly smashed another homer against Brooklyn on May 10, when his screaming liner hit the top of the right field fence and bounced back into the outfield. The Dodger fielder held Louis to a triple. Louis had two of the five Cleveland hits that day, and, with the Indians down by one run, Sock led off

Cartoon of Sockalexis in the *Cleveland Plain Dealer*, May 4, 1897. (Author's collection)

the bottom of the ninth inning with a double. Jack O'Connor sacrificed him to third, but both Harry Blake and Chief Zimmer failed to get Sock home, and the Clevelanders lost to the Dodgers 3–2.

By now Tebeau's band of Indians had fought their way back to the middle of the standings after their 0–5 start, but the Cleveland brand of feisty, battling play reared its head again. In the first week of the season, Pat Tebeau challenged umpire Sandy McDermott to a fist-fight under the stands after the game. Jesse Burkett and Jack O'Connor were ejected from games for calling umpires names like "robber" and "lobster," popular pejoratives of the era. According to the *Philadelphia Press*, "Tebeau's Indians are said to be members of the Kickapoo tribe, with accent on the 'kick'."[7]

Louis, however, rarely spoke to the umpires and refrained from protesting calls even if they were obviously blown. In Native American cultures, it was almost unheard of for players to argue with or threaten referees, and those few Indian athletes who did so were quickly scorned by their own teammates for an egregious breach of proper behavior. Louis' attitudes, formed by his upbringing on Indian Island, set him apart from many of the battling Irishmen on Cleveland's "Hibernian Indians." Sportswriters remarked that Louis did not "do a war dance" for the umpires or "spring the medicine man act" on a bad call. Several other Cleveland players did, however, and many observers believed that the Cleveland team had finally surpassed the Baltimore Orioles as the rowdiest club in baseball.

The Spiders played their style of roughneck baseball because Pat Tebeau expected them to do so. He believed that the patrons of the game wanted to see a scrappy, hard-fought affair, and that if two clubs brawled on the field, the attendance would increase the next day as fans lusted for a renewal of hostilities. Tebeau firmly believed that rowdy ball kept attendance up, not down, despite all evidence to the contrary. *The Sporting News*, long an advocate of clean baseball, refuted Tebeau's belief on its editorial page. "Base ball should not depend for its popularity upon its worst features, and reform is demanded," declared the paper, though the National League magnates did not appear to be listening.[8]

Pat Tebeau probably didn't notice right away, but the era of battling baseball was already drawing to a close. In mid–May Arthur Soden, the president of the Boston Beaneaters, told his players that the team management would no longer pay their fines to the league for abusing umpires. The Boston players improved their on-field behavior almost instantly, and within days they began a winning streak that brought them to the top of the standings. By June the Beaneaters had taken first place from the Orioles, who were torn apart by internal conflicts and postgame fist-fights in the locker room.

When the Brooklyn and Boston teams traveled to Cleveland in mid–May, the eastern players and sportswriters finally got a look at Louis Sockalexis. On May 13, Sock belted a double and a triple off Boston's 30-game winner, Kid Nichols, but the rest of the Indians managed only two singles in a 4–1 loss to the Beaneaters. Sock still couldn't figure out how to hit slow curves from left-handers, as Boston's southpaw Fred Klobedanz struck him out twice on May 15, but the easterners saw enough to come away impressed. "Sockalexis is chipping off doubles and triples for Tebeau's Cleveland braves with the regularity of a man filling a contract," remarked the *Boston Globe*.[9] Perennial stars Jesse Burkett and Ed McKean were slumping, but Sock's average was the second highest on the team. After 20 games, the Indian's batting average stood at .372, one of the highest in the league behind Bobby Wallace's .402 mark.

Sock, however, was still a rookie, and an unpolished one at that. He had trouble judging liners hit directly at him, as many young outfielders do on their first tour around the league. Pat Tebeau promised to hit balls to him in practice, as he had done with Harry Blake when Blake joined the team in 1894. In addition, Louis was a wild swinger at the plate. Some of his hits came off pitches above the bill of his cap, or even bouncing in the dirt. The pitchers certainly noticed that they didn't have to throw the ball across the plate for Louis to swing at it, and the Indian would have to become more selective in order to keep his batting average in the high .300s. Pat Tebeau was convinced that Louis would have no problems adjusting. "He is a sensible fellow and sees his weakness," said Tebeau, "which is a good trait in a young player."[10]

Sock's presence in the lineup helped improve the attendance figures for Frank Robison's team early in the season. A crowd of 7,000, a healthy number for Cleveland in May, saw the Indians split a doubleheader against Boston on Saturday, May 15, and some of the weekday attendances passed the 2,500 mark. However, a Sunday game between the Colts and Reds in Chicago drew 16,700 in early May, and the envious Robison decided to press the Sunday ball issue once again.

The Cleveland owner announced his intention to defy the Cleveland ministers and play a game against Washington on Sunday, May 16, while the ministers were every bit as determined to arrest the players if they dared take the field. Robison put placards around the city, advertising the game and promising to refund tickets if five full innings were not played. He also ordered hundreds of dollars worth of halves and quarters from local banks to expedite the refunding process.

That Sunday, the faithful fans and the merely curious filled League Park to the rafters, and Robison ordered the gates closed after 9,500 passed through the turnstiles. Thousands more milled around outside, and the police department feared that the interruption of the game would cause rioting. Nevertheless, the police informed Robison that the players on the field would be arrested after one inning of play.

The Clevelanders batted first — in those days, the home team could elect to bat first — and three men went out without scoring, including Louis, who flied out to right field. The Senators managed a single against third-string Cleveland pitcher Zeke Wilson; then the police came in and stopped the game. Robison gave a brief speech at home plate, promising to battle the law in the courts. The police then proceeded to round up umpire Tim Hurst and the 18 players on the field, including Louis, load them into wagons, and transport them to the central police station.

Hundreds of fans gathered around Robison to shake his hand, and his speech seemed to have a calming effect on the crowd. There was plenty of booing of the police action, but no rioting. Robison, for one day, was hailed as a hero in Cleveland, and he promised to battle the ministers, whom he called "a lot of unheard-of divines anxious to secure free advertising in the newspapers." In the meantime, Robison paid $100 for bail, and Louis and the other players were released pending further legal action.

At first, the authorities declared that they would try all 19 of the arrested men, but Robison and his attorneys publicly demanded 19 separate jury trials, after which the two sides met and hammered out a compromise. The authorities decided to try only one player for violating the prohibition on Sunday ball, and Jack Powell, the rookie pitcher, would be the legal guinea pig. Powell played first base in the game on Tebeau's orders, and the little-used Powell could be left behind in Cleveland without harming the team on the road. The other Indians were so relieved that they would not have to stand trial that they won the next three in a row against the Senators and climbed into fifth place.

Louis went on a tear against the Senators, pounding six hits in the next three days. He still had problems with the slow curve, but he belted out three hits against the slow-ball artist Win Mercer. Mercer's "slow ball," which did not rotate on the way to the plate, was almost certainly an early instance of what is now called a knuckle ball. Tim Keefe, the star pitcher of the Giants in the 1880s, was the first hurler to experiment with a knuckler, and by 1897 the slow ball was something of a rage in the National League. Some of baseball's most feared sluggers, including Ed Delahanty of the Phillies, could not touch the quick-breaking knuckler, but Sock moved up in the batter's box and pounded Mercer's slow ball with little difficulty.

Sock also became more comfortable speaking to the reporters. "I have seen all the good outfielders of the League," said Sock to the *Washington Post* on May 20, "and I am just as good as any of them." Sock was "on excellent terms with himself," mentioned the *Post*.

Pat Tebeau helpfully suggested to the *Post* that Sock's amazing throwing came naturally to Indians, since in their youthful games, especially lacrosse, the participants strengthen their arms by throwing the "primitive boomerang and cestus." Elmer Bates of *Sporting Life* also offered a theory on Sock's talent. Bates commented that Sockalexis' sensational throwing, marked by both consistency and sureness of aim, was attributable to "characteristics of his race in handling the bow and arrow."[11]

Tom Brown, the captain of the Senators, marveled at Louis' unusual running style. "Sockalexis, the redskin of Tebeau's Erin-go-bragh Indians, has the flatfooted glide that betrays his origin," said Brown. "Watch him closely when he's on the bases and you will discover that he plants the pedals firm on the ground at every step. He probably inherits this flatfooted tread from his forefathers, whose moccasined feet fell firm on the snow. You would think that Sock's emphatic habit of clouting the ground with the soles of his feet would handicap his speed. But he's one of the nimblest sprinters the major League has ever seen."

Brown said that he asked the Penobscot if spiked baseball shoes were a problem for him. "When (Sock) began professional ball playing," said Brown, "he found the spiked shoes clumsy, so he told me, and it took him one full season to accustom himself to spikes. The heels of his shoes are about half an inch thick, almost as flat as moccasins, and are built on a special last for him."[12]

Unfortunately, rumors began appearing in the papers that Sock and left fielder Jesse Burkett, Cleveland's two-time batting champion, were "on the frosts." Burkett, whose nickname was "The Crab," was a particularly irascible individual, and he began the season in a prolonged slump. In late May Burkett, who batted .423 in 1895 and .410 in 1896, hovered slightly above the .240 mark while Sockalexis belted the ball at a .350 clip. Burkett was accustomed to receiving the lion's share of attention, but now Sock drew the biggest cheers from the fans, and from all reports Burkett didn't like it one bit.

One news item stated that Burkett and Sock were "about as popular with each other as a pair of rival tenors in the same opera company." Although Burkett coached Sockalexis at Holy Cross and recommended him to the Cleveland team, Burkett now appeared to feel threatened by the Penobscot's popularity. Charlie Reilly of the Senators claimed that he "guyed," or teased, Burkett about Sock, and Burkett exploded, "Don't ask me about that bead peddler. He's a Jonah [a jinx]. I haven't hit over .100 since he joined the team!" Burkett, according to Reilly, concluded his rant by saying, "Wait till I strike my gait and I will make him go back to the woods and look for a few scalps."[13]

The *Plain Dealer* found it necessary to refute these stories at some length, and Louis also publicly denied the rumors, but the reports of tension between the team's two hitting stars would not go away. Back in early April, *The Sporting News* suggested that the Cleveland players would not be happy to see Sockalexis take the place of the popular veteran Harry Blake in right field. Despite the "hammering" from the veterans, Louis appeared to be getting along well with most of his teammates, but not with the highly-strung Burkett.

Jesse Burkett was not yet hitting, but Pat Tebeau had other problems. Shortstop Ed McKean, a stalwart for the Cleveland team since 1887, was 34-years-old and had gained about 20 pounds in the last few seasons. His range at shortstop was never exceptional, but by 1897 he no longer covered much ground in the infield. Second baseman Cupid Childs was injured and out of the lineup for several weeks, forcing the weak-hitting Tebeau to play second base and alternate utility man Jack O'Connor and catcher Chief Zimmer on first. Cy Young struggled on the mound early in the season, alternating good performances with poor ones, while number two pitcher Nig Cuppy battled a sore arm, and a series of rainouts prevented Tebeau's men from building any momentum. There was good news, as Sockalexis kept stinging the ball and pitcher-turned-third baseman Bobby Wallace developed into a star,[14] but Tebeau's Indians still hovered in fifth place, slightly above the .500 mark.

The Clevelanders swept the Philadelphia Phillies in a three-game set in mid–May but split a doubleheader against the Giants and split two games with the Orioles, sandwiched around several rainouts. Tebeau, trying to shake the team out of its doldrums, moved Sockalexis to the leadoff spot, with mixed results. Burkett and McKean still weren't hitting, and Cy Young struggled to find his form, losing to the Giants by a score of 11–2. The bad weather and the off-field controversies harmed the Cleveland attendance in late May, although Sockalexis energized the fans who did come out to League Park. If not for the popularity of the Penobscot, the Cleveland team would have been in much worse financial shape.

Still, despite the bad publicity and newspaper criticism, Frank Robison plowed ahead with threats to move or sell the team. The eccentric owner of the St. Louis Browns, Chris von der Ahe, offered Robison $60,000 for five players on Cleveland's roster, most likely Young, Burkett, Wallace, Tebeau, and perhaps Sockalexis. Robison countered publicly with an offer to buy the Browns and move Cleveland's best players to St. Louis. In late May, Robison suddenly left Cleveland for a trip to Milwaukee, and rumors abounded that he would move the team to Wisconsin, perhaps before the end of the 1897 season. The constant sniping between Robison and the Cleveland ministers continued unabated, and ministers railed from their pulpits against Robison every Sunday.

The Cleveland team's legal problems also consumed valuable column inches on the sports pages. Pitcher Jack Powell, the designated defendant in the Sunday ball case, waited nervously for his trial to start in June. Powell's dilemma attracted sympathy from the fans, as well as irritation that Robison would pile a legal burden upon a rookie pitcher's shoulders. Most Clevelanders assumed that Robison would pay any fine levied on Powell for playing ball on Sunday, but the possibility existed that Powell would also receive a jail sentence.

Such negative publicity did not endear the Cleveland team to its fan base. Robison, not the team, was the focus of much of the newspaper reporting, and despite the popularity of the exotic Sockalexis, Robison's activities crowded the games themselves off the sports pages. As early as March 23, the *Plain Dealer* reported a conversation between Robison and Tebeau in which the owner asked if "you and the boys would be willing to play for me in St. Louis, Detroit, Brooklyn, Indianapolis, or Louisville?" The Cleveland fans, faced with the imminent threat of losing their team to another city, understandably withheld their support of the Spiders-turned-Indians.

League president "Uncle Nick" Young barely noticed. He delivered a typically flowery oration at the beginning of the season. "Baseball," said Young, "is the best emblem of the American people I can think of. For our nation's game symbolizes the great traits in the disposition of Uncle Sam's children — energy, fair play, and the wistful uncertainty that has marked the work of all Americans who have achieved name and fame in the passing of the day."[15] Perhaps he didn't realize that the fans in Cleveland and throughout the country were tiring of the free-for-all style of ball perfected by the Cleveland and Baltimore teams. Cleveland attendance figures remained disappointing, especially with the Sunday-ball question still unresolved.

As might be expected, newspaper writers employed a great deal of racial imagery to describe the new sensation. Since Louis was the first ballplayer to be identified as Native American, the media of the day based their descriptions on popular Indian stereotypes. It comes as no surprise that the newspapers, especially Eastern ones, called Sockalexis "the savage" or "the aborigine" and referred to his bat as a "war club." Tebeau's Indians were "on the warpath," and when the Cleveland team won a game, they "took the scalps" of the opposition. One Cleveland writer, ecstatic over one of Sock's better games in May, used one of the worst statements ever made against any racial group to express his enthusiasm. "The man who said that there are no good Indians except dead Indians, or words to that effect, surely never saw Louis Sockalexis," he wrote.[16]

The writers also harped upon recent historic events. The massacre of

Little Big Horn, in which the troops of General George Custer were defeated and killed by the Sioux under Sitting Bull, had occurred only 21 years before. Custer, at the time, was considered a national hero, and his widow still traveled the country extolling the memory of her husband's bravery against the "red man." The fate of Custer and his men was also kept fresh in the national memory through dime novels and sensational news reporting, most of which depicted the Indians as bloodthirsty, murdering savages. There were literally hundreds of Indian tribes on the American continent, each with its own history, language, dress, and customs; however, the generic term "Indian" encompassed a limited vision of tom-toms, teepees, feathers, and rain dances, applicable to all native communities.

Even respected newspapers found that they could not avoid using clichés. The *Plain Dealer* printed a drawing of Sockalexis, in full baseball uniform, titled "Sockalexis Breaking for Third." In it, Sock wore feathers on his head instead of a baseball cap and appeared to be sneaking, instead of running, down the base line. The *Washington Post* called Sockalexis "stalwart, erect as the branch of a briar, and built on the architectural lines of an Apollo. He is as swift as the wind on the bases and covers a wide area of ground in the outfield." However, the writer couldn't resist adding this bit of racial overtone. "Robison denies that Sockalexis, the medicine man, tender of his starboard reservation, is to receive a string of beads, a bottle of Kentucky joy juice, and a blanket in consideration of his success this year."[17]

After Louis struck out against pitcher Bill Kennedy in a Cleveland-Brooklyn series in mid–May, the *Brooklyn Eagle* described the action in a bit of poetry modeled after Ernest L. Thayer's "Casey at the Bat":

> There is crepe upon the wigwam,
> There is silence all about;
> Roaring Bill's the one who scalped him,
> Sockalexis has struck out.[18]

Sportswriters often spiced up their columns at that time with invented stories about popular players, but the legends surrounding Louis Sockalexis were often hilariously fabricated. Louis' father, Francis, was credited with throwing a coin across the Penobscot River, a distance of more than 600 feet, but now the sportswriters wrote that Louis once threw a baseball over the same distance. Louis owned the most powerful throwing arm in the game, but the recognized throwing record for distance at the time was slightly over 400 feet. Another exaggerated report stated that Sockalexis, as a teen-ager, once hit a baseball the entire length of Indian Island, and threw a baseball from home plate over the center field fence and over a row of houses across the street. Before long, there were two rows of houses, then three, all cleared by Sock's mighty throw.

Another apocryphal story about Sockalexis that is still repeated today concerns his father Francis, who is identified as the chief of the Penobscot, and his disapproval of Louis becoming a ballplayer. The older Sockalexis feared that his son, the future chief of the tribe, would never return to the reservation, so the elder Sockalexis decided to take matters into his own hands. He paddled a canoe from Maine to Washington, D.C., to appeal the "Great White Father," President Grover Cleveland, to send Louis back to the reservation. How any man, even a fine athlete like Francis Sockalexis, could paddle a canoe that far through the choppy Atlantic is anyone's guess. Besides, the Penobscot no longer used the title of chief for the leader of the tribe, and the tribal governorship, which Francis Sockalexis held at the time, was an elective office, not a hereditary one.

However, there was some racial discord on the Penobscot reservation in the spring of 1897. Members of the Penobscot tribe had been intermarrying with whites for several decades, but tribal governor Francis Sockalexis believed that the operating budget of the tribe, mostly money that the tribe received from land sales, would soon be used up if new white residents kept increasing the population of Indian Island. Therefore, the governor ordered all whites to leave the reservation, causing a furor that reached the papers in Boston and other Eastern cities. Because of Louis Sockalexis' new-found popularity, the controversy even reached the pages of *Sporting Life*, in a story titled "Papa Sox" with the subtitle "The Father of Cleveland's Indian Player Banishes Palefaces."[19]

When the Clevelanders began their 18-game road trip to Brooklyn, Boston, Washington, and Baltimore in late May, the Eastern papers and fans were hungry for a peek at the Penobscot. Though attendance in Cleveland was still disappointing, due to bad weather and the constant off-field turmoil, the fans were ready to storm the gates in the Eastern cities. The papers talked about the "child of the forest" in almost every edition, and baseball fans of the era were infamous for their unfriendly treatment of opposition players, especially the most popular ones. The next few weeks would tell how Louis Sockalexis, the most celebrated player on the most hated and rowdy team in the league, would react to the inevitable crush of attention.

CHAPTER 7

The Polo Grounds

"Will I succeed? Yes, of course I will. You have no idea how anxious I am to learn every point and trick of the game. There are many little things that come up in nearly every game which are new to me, but the white players are good to me, and are always ready to advise me."
— Louis Sockalexis, June 1897[1]

The Penobscot were admired for their sense of humor, and the art of the jest was not lost on Louis Sockalexis. One day in 1897, a group of Indians in full costume, from a local performance of a Wild West show, took in a game at League Park. Frank Robison spied the Indians in the ticket line, ushered them in through the free gates, and personally escorted them to seats in the front row of the grandstand.

Before the game, some of the fans leaned over the dugout roof and asked Pat Tebeau about the costumed Indians in the grandstand. "Why, they're Sox's folks, of course," replied the manager. "Ask him."

The spectators then asked Sockalexis if he knew who the Indians were. Sock didn't even change expression. "Nobody but Mama and Papa Sockalexis," replied Sock, without the hint of a smile.

"In ten minutes," related *The Sporting News*, "it was whispered all over the grounds that Sockalexis' folks have come all the way from Maine to see him play ball."[2]

There was no official rookie of the year award in 1897, since the major leagues did not bestow it until 1947. If there had been one, Louis Sockalexis, in the early part of the season, would have been one of two main contenders, along with Napoleon Lajoie of the Philadelphia Phillies. Lajoie, a French-Canadian from Rhode Island, played first base for the Phillies, and in the next decade he moved to second base and became the most popular player on the Cleveland American League team.

Lajoie played in the major leagues for 21 years, amassed more than 3,400 hits, and was the sixth player elected to the Baseball Hall of Fame, but in early 1897 many observers believed that Louis Sockalexis was a better player. Another future all-time great, Honus Wagner, made his debut with Louisville in July of 1897 but started slowly for the bottom-dwelling Colonels. Wagner eventually joined the 3,000-hit club, won eight batting titles, and became the almost unanimous choice as the greatest shortstop of all time, but Sock gained more attention from the national press at this early stage of their careers.

Sock quickly became the most talked-about young player in baseball, and other players began watching him more closely. Win Mercer, slow-ball pitcher of the Senators, claimed that he found a way to get Sockalexis called out. "I have been watching the Indian Sockalexis closely," said Mercer, "and I believe I have discovered his weakness. Feed him a high one over the outside corner and he will masticate it as though he were going for a plate of Indian corncakes. But get it knee high, about opposite the low water mark of his knickerbockers and you have him guessing. Like Jesse Burkett, he is not stuck on a low curve."[3] However, Sockalexis pounded three hits off Mercer in their previous meeting.

Sock's fielding, though sometimes erratic, won praise as well. "Sockalexis, although a little shaky in judging a ball, is a natural fielder," claimed the *Plain Dealer*. "Perhaps he 'dances about' a little too much to be au fait in the judging of flies, but as long as he gets them there is little fault to find in the way he gets them. Results are what count, and Socks has been in with the best of them in the matter of keeping up his end."[4]

The *Plain Dealer* produced another round of poetry to celebrate the new sensation:

> The afternoon was waning fast,
> When down the city streets there passed
> A group of strong men, good and true,
> It was the band of Pat Tebeau,
> And as they journeyed on their way,
> Way down in their hearts they say,
> "Sockalexis."
>
> The people see them passing by
> And stop to look again. "Oh my!
> Tis he," they say, with one accord,
> And as the mob takes up the word
> Tis passed along from tongue to tongue
> And wide upon the breeze is flung,
> "Sockalexis."

> You'll meet defeat, the cynic said,
> As on their way the Spiders sped,
> But as they reach the grassy plot,
> Each one to tend his garden spot
> The fans set up a crushing yell
> That makes up hope, that augurs well,
>   "Sockalexis."
>
> And when the fans have been appeased
> By sundry drives by "Sox" released,
> And divers pretty starts and throws
> Done by these men of Pat Tebeau's,
> The crowd goes home to cheer again
> For every one of Cleveland's men,
> But high above the mixed-up strain
> Is heard a clear-cut, clear refrain,
>   "Sockalexis."[5]

"Sockalexis," remarked *Sporting Life*, "is responsible for a lot of bad poetry."[6] Nevertheless, R. K. Munkittrick of the *New York Journal* couldn't resist taking his own shot at Longfellow's "Song of Hiawatha":

> This is bounding Sockalexis,
> Fielder of the mighty Clevelands.
> Like the catapult in action,
> For the plate he throws the baseball,
> Till the rooter, blithely rooting,
> Shouts until he shakes the bleachers,
> "Sockalexis, Sockalexis,
> Sock it to them, Sockalexis."[7]

On Memorial Day, May 31, the Spiders faced the Dodgers (or Bridegrooms, as they were also called then) in Brooklyn. Rain washed out the morning game of the doubleheader, but more than 17,000 fans came out for the afternoon contest. The crowd was so large that more than 5,000 people were obliged to stand in the outfield. The size of the crowd broke all the existing Brooklyn attendance records. Most of the fans came to see the sensational Cleveland rookie Sockalexis, and the noisy response that greeted Louis was the loudest heard so far in the 1897 season. The Spiders rarely played before so many people at home or in the Western cities, which explains why the National League magnates liked to schedule holiday games in the East.

Louis took some notice of the fans this time. One newspaper report said that the Indian smiled at the din and "heaved his chest and gave a funny little nod" toward the whooping crowd. After the Indian made a sensational catch in right field, turning a sure triple hit by Billy Shindle into a long out, Sockalexis took off his cap and bowed to the applauding crowd. The Brooklyn fans, appreciative of the Indian's outstanding fielding play, cheered Sockalexis with shouts of "You're a peach!"

He didn't do much at the plate in his Eastern debut, however. Sock, still somewhat confused by left-handed curve balls, went hitless against Brooklyn lefty Harley Payne, and the Clevelanders lost by a 5–2 score. The Brooklyn team battered the struggling Cy Young for five runs in the second and held on for the win. The Dodgers won again the next day, 7–3, on the wet Brooklyn field in front of a crowd of 3,500.

Joe Vila, sportswriter for the *Brooklyn Eagle*, caught up with Sockalexis in late May and managed to persuade the initially reluctant Indian to sit down and discuss his newfound fame. Vila mentioned that the "small boys," or young fans, seemed to be giving the Penobscot a hard time by razzing him from the stands. "If the small and big boys of Brooklyn and other cities find it a pleasure to shout at me," replied Louis, "I have no objections. No matter where we play I go through the same ordeal, and at the present time I am so used to it that at times I forget to smile at my tormentors, believing it to be a part of the game."

Sockalexis denied that friction existed between himself and other team members. "I have seen printed in several papers that the Cleveland players are liable to freeze me out because I am an Indian," said Sockalexis. "That is all bosh, for the white players can't do enough for me, especially Burkett, who is said to be jealous because I lead him in batting. Jesse is proud of me because I have made such a good showing." The Penobscot also displayed some humility amidst all the attention. "Maybe someday I will be a great player, but not yet. I have a good deal to learn and watch every player, some of whom may do something that may be of benefit to me another time."

However, Sock may have inadvertently revealed his true age when Vila asked how old he was. "I think I was born in 1871," replied Sock, "and [I] will be 24 years old next October 24."

"No! No! No! That's a mistake!" said Sockalexis quickly. "I was born in 1873. I have so much to think of that I get things mixed."[8]

The two-game sweep by the Dodgers started Tebeau's Indians on their roughest stretch of the season. The team journeyed to Boston to meet the first-place Beaneaters and lost the first game of the series by an embarrassing 21–3 score. Worst of all, Boston pitcher Fred Klobedanz beamed Jesse Burkett in the first inning, knocking the batting champion unconscious. Jimmy McAleer took Burkett's place in left, but Boston scored a near-record 14 runs in the bottom of the first. Ed McKean made three errors at shortstop that day, and Louis Sockalexis misplayed a line drive for another error. The entire Cleveland team was thoroughly embarrassed in front of 4,000 fans, though pitcher Zeke Wilson managed to pitch a complete game for the Clevelanders.

Pat Tebeau frantically shook up the lineup once again, moving Sock to the second spot and Bobby Wallace to the leadoff slot in the order, but Boston's star right-hander Kid Nichols easily beat Cy Young the next day, 6–1. Tebeau's team was now 17–16 on the season and mired in the middle of the standings by their inability to beat the top two teams in the league, Boston and Baltimore. The Indians cleaned up against bottom-dwellers like St. Louis and Washington, but with Jesse Burkett out and Cy Young struggling, this Eastern trip loomed as a disaster in the making.

The presence of Sockalexis, however, was a boon to the attendance figures in the Eastern cities, though many fans came to jeer Cleveland's newest star. "Columns of silly poetry are written about him, [and] hideous looking cartoons adorn the sporting pages of nearly every paper," commented Elmer Bates in *Sporting Life*. "He is hooted and bawled at by the thimble-brained brigade on the bleachers. Despite all this handicap the red man has played good, steady ball, and has been a factor in nearly every victory thus far won by Tebeau's team."[9]

In Washington, a struggling baseball town, a healthy crowd of 3,400 fans greeted Louis with war cries as he circled the bases in the third inning. Louis beat out a bunt, went to second on an error, took third on a single, and scored on a sacrifice fly. Sock also singled in the first off Win Mercer, who claimed to have found the Indian's weakness several weeks before. The Clevelanders won 10–5 as the embarrassed Mercer stalked off the mound late in the game, leaving the bullpen to finish the contest.

There was no Sunday ball in Washington, so Tebeau's Indians ventured across the Potomac to Alexandria, Virginia, to play an exhibition game against a team put together by a local entrepreneur named Harry Mace. Few of the Cleveland players took such games seriously, but Sockalexis put on a show for the crowd of 700. He belted out three hits, scored four runs, and threw out a runner at the plate from the deepest part of right field as the Indians trounced Mace's club by a score of 12–1. The crowd enjoyed the game immensely, especially the sight of catcher Chief Zimmer pitching the last two innings, and yelled heartily every time the "stalwart child of forest and stream," as the papers called him, came to bat.

The Monday game was rained out, so Sockalexis accepted an invitation to visit the campus of Georgetown University in Washington. Georgetown, like Holy Cross, was a Jesuit institution, and the Jesuits were pleased that one of their own was finding success in the world of athletics.

Cy Young, star pitcher of the Spiders from 1890 to 1898. (National Baseball Hall of Fame Library, Cooperstown, NY)

Sockalexis met and chatted with faculty members, students, and the Georgetown baseball team, against whom he and his Holy Cross teammates had played one year before.

On the day following the rainout, the Indians flattened the Senators 7–0 in a game that featured another outstanding running catch by Sock in right field.[10] Tebeau's men won two in a row against the inept Senators, but the toughest series of the year came next. The Indians journeyed to Baltimore to face the Orioles on the enemy's home field. Tebeau left his best two pitchers, Cy Young and Nig Cuppy, behind to nurse their ailments, so Cleveland would have to battle the Orioles with second-string hurlers.

The result was easy to foresee. The Indians lost the first game, 11–6, to the defending champions. Burkett returned to the lineup with two hits, but rookie pitcher Mike McDermott failed to last through the fourth inning. John Pappalau, Sock's former Holy Cross teammate, entered the game in relief and fared no better. Tebeau quickly sent for Cy Young, who returned by train to Baltimore and pitched the next day. Young held the Orioles to five hits, but the Clevelanders lost again, 4–2, before a crowd of nearly 5,000. The Indians belted nine hits, but Louis Sockalexis went hitless that day.

Tebeau held a special batting practice for Sockalexis before the next game against Baltimore. Sock was in a bit of a slump, especially against left-handers—*Sporting Life* claimed that "the pitchers all around are getting onto Soxie"—and Tebeau ordered reserve pitchers Zeke Wilson and Mike McDermott to throw Sock nothing but low, slow curves. It must have helped, since Sock blasted a triple for two runs against Oriole left-hander Jerry Nops that afternoon. The Indians took a 4–3 lead into the ninth, but three singles and an error by Bobby Wallace gave Baltimore their third win in a row. The Cleveland team was now stuck at the .500 mark with a 19–19 record, struggling to remain in the pennant race.

Sockalexis, baseball's newest star, made a fine impression upon the other players of the National League, though the *Plain Dealer* reported that many opponents "require several days' acquaintance with the Indian to recognize his ability. At first they regard his work as accidental, but when the accidents start occurring with startling regularity they become convinced."[11]

Hugh Duffy, the hard-hitting Boston outfielder, needed no convincing. "The moment I saw that man in practice," said Duffy, "I realized that the stories about him were not exaggerated. He is a wonderful player, and the greatest find in many a day. He is not only wonderful now, but he will keep on improving, and I expect to see him the fastest fielder and one of the greatest batters the game has ever known."[12]

By now, Sockalexis was such a fixture in right field for Cleveland that former starter Harry Blake sat the bench for weeks on end without getting into any games. With a road trip looming, Tebeau saw no need to keep Blake on the roster, so he sent Blake to Connie Mack's Milwaukee Brewers in the Western League. Blake took the demotion well and even expressed sympathy for his rival's treatment at the hands of the fans. "There has been so much talk about Socks," said Blake to the *Plain Dealer*, "that the pitchers are all after him and pitch harder for him than for any man on the team. Then, the rooting he has to stand is something awful."[13]

The sporting press noticed the "rooting" as well. As *Sporting Life* reported on May 8:

> War whoops, yells of derision, [and] a chorus of meaningless "familiarities" greet Sockalexis on every diamond on which he appears. In many cases these demonstrations border on extreme rudeness. In almost every instance they are calculated to disconcert the player new to the unique methods prevailing in some of the cities of the big League. But the big red man of Tebeau's team is not disturbed by these vehement and often grossly discourteous demonstrations.

Sock was hitting well, but fielding still presented a problem for him. He made two more errors against the Phillies in Philadelphia on June 14, though the Clevelanders won the game 10–4 behind Cy Young. Sock still had difficulty in judging line drives hit in front of him, though most young outfielders faced the same difficulty early in their careers. Outfielders judge the flight of a liner based, at least partially, on the sight of the batter's swing and the sound of the ball hitting the bat. In 1897 the umpires kept a ball in play until it was lost or the cover was torn, and by the middle of the game the ball would become soft and darkened with grass stains. The ball was difficult for the batters to see, but perhaps more difficult for the fielders to judge in flight. Experience was the only teacher, and playing time was the only thing that would help Sock in the field.

The Cleveland "Hibernian Indians" traveled next to New York for a four-game series against the Giants. If Tebeau's men were going to make a charge up the standings, it would have to begin immediately against the fourth-place Giants in the Polo Grounds. The New York team was riddled with dissension between players and management, and attendance suffered from off-field controversies much as it did in Cleveland. However, New York fans were some of the most vocal in the National League, and they especially loved to exchange insults with the Cleveland team.

As far as it is known, this was the first trip that the 25-year-old Louis Sockalexis ever made to New York City. The rookie from the forests of Maine, who found the nightlife of South Bend, Indiana, too much to handle only a few months before, would now be exposed to the temptations and distractions of the biggest city in the nation.

Amos Rusie, the "Hoosier Thunderbolt," was the star hurler of the New York Giants and the most fearsome pitcher in baseball. He and Sockalexis were born in the same year, but Rusie began playing in the major leagues while Louis was still attending Houlton Academy. The powerfully built Rusie joined the Giants as a 19-year-old in 1890, armed with the hardest fastball in the National League. He led the league in strikeouts five times in the 1890s, won more than 200 games, and set records for walks allowed. Rusie so overwhelmed the hitters of the League in 1892 that the baseball magnates moved the mound back 10 feet before the 1893 season began to its present distance of 60 feet and 6 inches from home plate.

Rusie threw hard and threw wildly, and despite a season-long holdout in 1896, he was still intimidating batters and winning games. In addition, Rusie was a Notre Dame man like Sockalexis, though Louis stayed at South Bend for a much shorter period than Rusie. The "Hoosier Thunderbolt" had heard of Sockalexis, and one paper reported that the star Giants pitcher boasted that he would "strike that damned Indian out." Some of the less-reputable New York papers, in this age of yellow journalism, cast the upcoming Rusie-Sockalexis contest as a racial grudge match. They compared the light-haired Rusie to the doomed General Custer and openly rooted for the white man to defeat the Indian for a change.

A much-larger-than-usual weekday crowd of 5,200 filled the Polo Grounds on Wednesday, June 16, to cheer the Giants and to catch a glimpse of the much-touted rookie Sockalexis. The crowd was so unexpectedly large that the Giants management constructed a rope barrier in the outfield, and fans were allowed to stand on the outfield grass behind the barrier. A delegation of Penobscot Indians, who made the trip from Old Town to see their tribesman in action, sat in the bleachers and drew a great deal of comment from the local papers. Reporters also noticed that more female fans than usual attended on a weekday to see the handsome young star of the Cleveland nine.

Rusie retired the first two batters, Burkett and Childs, in the top of the first, and then war whoops and Indian yells filled the horseshoe-shaped ballpark as Louis stepped to the plate. No stadium in the National League could match the Polo Grounds for noise, and this crowd created a din the likes of which many observers had never heard before.

Amos Rusie, strikeout king of the 1890s, gave up a memorable home run to Sockalexis in June of 1897. (National Baseball Hall of Fame Library, Cooperstown, NY)

Louis, who appeared to ignore the hostile crowd, wasted no time. He caught hold of one of Rusie's low curve balls and hit a line drive over the head of right fielder Mike Tiernan, over the rope barrier in right field, and into the overflow crowd. The ground rules at the time allowed the fielder to retrieve the ball among the patrons on the field of play, but before Tiernan could recover the ball, Sock sped around the bases for a solo home run. It was Sock's third homer in a Cleveland uniform, in an era when only a handful of players in the National League hit more than nine or ten home runs in an entire season.

Sock's blow startled the crowd, since Rusie was the Giants' best pitcher and rarely surrendered homers. In fact, Sock's homer was one of only six given up by Rusie in the 1897 season in over 320 innings of pitching. However, the Giants answered in the bottom of the first, when Sock misplayed Tiernan's liner for a three-base error, after which a sacrifice fly tied the score. Sock's error brought the crowd back to life, and the war whoops took on a more menacing tone.

Rusie then regained his bearings and held the Clevelanders off the board in the second and third, but two runs in the fourth and two more in the sixth gave Cleveland a 6–1 lead. Tebeau's men made 12 hits in the game, including a single by Sockalexis, and left the park with a 7–2 victory. Nevertheless, Rusie kept the promise that he reportedly made before the game. He struck the Indian out in the fourth inning on four fastballs.

The New York Times expressed its admiration for Cleveland's newest star. "It is quite evident that Sockalexis, the Indian," said the *Times*, "whose phenomenal stick work has been one of the surprises of the season, has been giving the other Cleveland players some of his ideas on how base hits should be made." The paper remarked on Sock's "usual home run," and congratulated the Indians on their "hustling, aggressive, winning game."[14]

However, Tebeau's men spent a great deal of time arguing with umpire Hank O'Day, even after they assumed a five-run lead, and the *New York Herald* took a dim view of the behavior of the Cleveland team. "It is a fine ball team," remarked the Herald, "but not one to engender local pride. The conduct of the nine tells plainly why Cleveland people refuse to support it. Spectators want more than good ball playing. They want sportsmanlike conduct and clean conduct on the diamond. The bulldozing and indifferent action which Tebeau and his men yesterday mixed up was disgusting in the extreme."[15]

The next day saw a different outcome. On a dark, gloomy afternoon, only about 2,000 fans saw the Giants shut out Tebeau's club by a 5–0 score. Jouett Meekin, the Giants' number two pitcher, struck out Sock with two on in the first and again with one on in the ninth. The rest of the Clevelanders hit Meekin freely, but ineffectively, as Meekin completed an 11-hit shutout. Two more losses to the Giants over the next two days plunged the Clevelanders back under the .500 mark and into seventh place.

The team limped back to Cleveland on Sunday, June 20, an off day for the exhausted, demoralized club. Some of the other players around the National League wondered why Tebeau's team, second in the standings in 1896, struggled to stay above .500 in 1897. Giants manager Bill Joyce, who came from Tebeau's old neighborhood in St. Louis, blamed the Cleveland fans. "Tebeau receives no encouragement from the home patrons of the game," suggested Joyce. "...When the team is given the heart of marble by the fans at home, there isn't much stimulant for them for spirit, and sand is entirely knocked out of them. The patronage of the game in Cleveland has been the poorest in the League for the last four years, but it is even worse this season."[16]

Tom Brown, the new manager of the Senators, offered the opinion that the new coaching rules hampered the Cleveland team. "Under the old rule," said Brown, "Tebeau was always after the young pitchers, joshing and abusing from the coach line and roasting any player of the opposition who could possibly be rattled ... many a game won by the Spiders was due in no small measure to the coach line efforts of Tebeau, O'Connor, and Burkett, who took their sting out of the pitchers every day and even rattled some of the old heads with their ribald comments."[17]

However, team owner Frank Robison found some measure of hope for Sunday ball. Pitcher Jack Powell was found guilty as expected for playing on Sunday, May 16, and the young pitcher was fined $5 with $153 in court costs. Robison immediately filed an appeal and hoped that the local Common Pleas judge would overturn Cleveland's municipal statute against Sunday baseball. If not, Robison was already negotiating to move Cleveland's scheduled Sunday games to other cities. Attendance still suffered in Cleveland, and only 600 fans attended the game at League Park on June 21 to see the home team lose to the Louisville Colonels in a game that featured three errors by shortstop Ed McKean.

The finale of Powell's trial had another, unexpected outcome. Powell, free of worry about the verdict, was now available to pitch, and he gave the team a much-needed boost. John Pappalau lost to Louisville by a 14–6 score on June 22 in a sloppily played game (Jimmy McAleer, the best-fielding outfielder in the league, committed two errors), but Powell breezed to an 18–1 victory the next day for his first major league win. Pappalau pitched no more for Cleveland after Tebeau sent him to Detroit of the Western League a week later, but Powell joined the rotation and pitched admirably. In addition, rookie catcher Lou Criger, who threw out six Louisville base runners in Pappalau's loss, appeared ready to lift some of the catching load from the aging Chief Zimmer and Jack O'Connor.

Jack Powell's pitching, and the return to form of Cy Young, helped the Indians to wins in four of their next six games against the Colts and Pirates. They pulled back to the .500 mark in a 14–3 rout of Pittsburgh on June 30 in a game that featured two hits, a stolen base, and a catch-and-throw double play from the outfield by Louis Sockalexis.

The St. Louis Browns arrived in Cleveland on July 1 for a three-game series. The Browns were the worst team in baseball by far in 1897, and the other National League teams loved seeing the Browns come to town. At that time, the St. Louis contingent was buried deep in the league cellar, winning less than 30 percent of their games, and to make matters worse, they played disinterested baseball, especially on the road. *The Sporting News* condemned the Browns as "the Cherry Sisters of baseball," comparing them to an infamously horrible vaudeville act then playing in New York City. The presence of the hapless Browns was made to order, so that a hustling team like Cleveland could pick up a few much-needed wins.

Louis Sockalexis fattened his average against St. Louis pitching. Sock belted five singles on July 1, as the Clevelanders won 6–2 in front of 700 fans, and added two singles and a double in a 13–1 win the next day in front of 800 people. Sock had only one hit, and an error, on July 3, but Jack Powell won his fourth game against no losses as Tebeau's Indians completed a three-game sweep of the helpless Browns. This sweep completed a streak of six wins in seven games and left the Clevelanders in fifth place at 30–27.

Louis broke out of his slump against the Browns, and in the last several games the Indian swatted the ball at a .518 clip, with 11 hits in his last 21 times at bat. Sock was batting above .330 for the season, and now that Jesse Burkett was finally hitting and Young, Wilson, and Powell formed a formidable three-man rotation, the season started looking brighter for Tebeau's Indians.

Unfortunately for the Clevelanders, the Fourth of July fell on a Sunday in 1897, and there was no Sunday ball and no huge holiday crowd to fatten the coffers of Frank DeHaas Robison. Tebeau's men rested in Cleveland on Sunday and proceeded to Pittsburgh the next day to start the second half of the campaign.

The legend of Sockalexis grew, and over the next several decades continued to grow at the expense of accuracy. One oft-repeated story states that Sock's home run at the Polo Grounds on June 16, 1897, occurred during Sock's first time at bat in the major leagues. Baseball record books list all the players in baseball history who managed to belt a homer their first time up, and many people wonder why the name of Louis Sockalexis is not on the list. Louis had been playing for Cleveland for two months when he hit that famous homer off Amos Rusie, but still the story lingers that it happened in his first time at bat.

Other accounts state, with great conviction, that Sock's homer was a grand slam, or that it was the first of two that he hit that day, and the second homer won the game in the ninth inning. Sock belted only one homer that day, a solo shot in the first, but recollections of a game played more than a century ago inflated Sock's heroics to almost unreasonable proportions. The homer in the first inning could not have been a grand slam because Louis was the third batter of the inning. Also, a second homer by Sockalexis could not have ended the game, in what is now called a "walk-off" home run, since the Giants batted in the bottom of the ninth.

One of the most widely stated inaccuracies, however, deals with what happened after the game. Legend says that Sock walloped the game-winning homer in the ninth inning, after which the excited Cleveland players carried the Indian off the field on their shoulders and took him to a nearby bar to celebrate. Louis, so the story goes, had never touched alcohol in his life until June 16, 1897, but the resulting celebration gave Sock a thirst for liquor, which proved his undoing. Another version of the same tale states that it happened in May in Chicago, and when Sock won the game with a bases-loaded triple, his teammates celebrated by introducing the Indian to alcohol.

As it turns out, this is the most inaccurate story of all. Sockalexis became well acquainted with alcohol long before the summer of 1897, and though no one said so publicly, the Cleveland players and management already knew of the Indian's thirst for intoxicants. Alcoholism was a disease that claimed the careers of many major league ballplayers in the 1890s, and it would not take long for Louis Sockalexis to fall under its spell.

Chapter 8

Fall from Grace

> *If anyone catches me playing for a personal record, he is at liberty to bang me in the nose.... I am trying to help Cleveland win the pennant, and I don't care a rap what the figures show in my batting and fielding, if the results show that I played all the time to win.*
>
> —Louis Sockalexis, May 1897[1]

The Pittsburgh Pirates did not play Sunday ball, so they scheduled a doubleheader for Monday, July 5, against the Cleveland team. More than 5,500 fans, a large number for a Monday, showed up for a belated holiday and to see the National League's newest star, Louis Sockalexis, up close.

They were roundly disappointed. Louis did not play in either game.

Pat Tebeau kept a lid on the reasons for Sock's absence as long as he could, but soon the *Cleveland Plain Dealer* revealed part of the story. The paper reported that Sock, somehow, injured a leg over the weekend in Cleveland. Louis said nothing to anyone about how the injury occurred, but merely boarded the train to Pittsburgh as quietly as possible. "His right foot was badly broken," recalled Tebeau years later, "...but he bandaged it up and went with the other players to Pittsburgh that night. I went over the next day and hurried out to Exposition Park, and there in the bus was Sox, his broken foot swollen four or five times its natural size."[2]

The foot was not broken, but it was badly injured nonetheless. When Sock arrived in Pittsburgh, Tebeau found out that Sock's right leg was bruised and swollen, and the Indian could not put any weight on it without a great deal of pain. Tebeau sent Sock back to Cleveland to visit a doctor and have the leg examined. The writers did not know yet what caused the accident, but they knew that it didn't happen in Saturday's game against the Browns.

The papers also remarked upon an ugly surliness among the Cleveland players during the Monday doubleheader. In the second game, the bases were loaded for the Pirates in the sixth when left fielder Jesse Burkett misplayed a line drive that went through his legs and rolled behind him. Burkett, thoroughly disgusted, refused to retrieve the ball. Shortstop Ed McKean ran all the way from the infield to the left field fence to corral the ball, but the batter and all three base runners scored. The Clevelanders made four errors as the Pirates won the second contest 6–1 and salvaged a split of the two games.

With Harry Blake gone to Milwaukee, Sock's injury could not have come at a worse time. The Penobscot's replacement in right field, Lew McAllister, did not manage a hit in either of Monday's games, and now Tebeau would have to audition other right fielders. In addition, McKean's father was gravely ill, and the shortstop prepared to leave the team for a few days. The catchers were getting banged up, though rookie Lou Criger looked like a real find behind the plate. Sockalexis had solidified the Cleveland lineup, though his fielding still left something to be desired, and now he would be out of the lineup for an unspecified length of time.

If the Cleveland writers knew what was really bothering Sock, they kept it to themselves for a few days more. Indeed, the main mention of Sockalexis in the papers that week concerned his popularity with the female fans of Cleveland. Sockalexis, according to the *Washington Post*, received a steady stream of mail at the Kennard House, consisting of "Cupid missives from palpitating maidens who pine for a photo of the shifty copper-tinted tender of Tebeau's outer reservation. Barrymore, Kelcey, or any of the thespian heart-slayers never aroused such an inflammable, consuming, equatorial torridity in the feminine bosom as Sockalexis, child of stream and forest."[3]

Slowly, the real story of Sock's injury came out.

Louis went out on Saturday night, July 3, to celebrate his recent hot streak (it couldn't have been Sunday night, because the bars were not open on Sunday). The Indian was a popular man in Cleveland, and everywhere he went, he was surrounded by fans that wanted to celebrate his outstanding play. Louis, who had spent much of his life tucked away on an Indian reservation on an island in Maine, was now a local celebrity, running around with what would be called, then and now, a "fast crowd."

In one place, in downtown Cleveland's red-light district, Louis downed what onlookers described as a truly prodigious amount of alcohol. At some point in the evening, Louis, in a drunken stupor, either jumped or fell out of a second-story window. This fall resulted in a severely injured right foot and ankle.

Fortunately, despite Tebeau's later recollections, the limb was not broken. From the contemporary descriptions available it was probably a high ankle sprain, the worst kind to have and the slowest to heal. Somehow, the Indian managed to keep his injury a secret from Tebeau and his teammates until just before game time in Pittsburgh on Monday, an act that may explain the sullen behavior of the Cleveland players that day.

It also appears that Louis had been drinking to excess for some time. Although his alcohol consumption had not yet taken its toll on the field, despite the Indian's continuing trouble with judging line drives, Sock's after-hours behavior had concerned team management for at least the past several weeks. *The Sporting News* reported in late July that Sockalexis got into a serious altercation in a bar in Chicago in June, about ten days or so before his injury on the July 4 weekend. "[Sockalexis] tried to clean up a saloon," reported the magazine. "A hanger-on at the place had Socks by the neck with one hand and a big cheese knife in the other when the police interfered."[4]

Louis Sockalexis was not the first major league ballplayer to run into lifestyle problems in his first major league season, nor would he be the last. Many young players find difficulty in adjusting to the major league life, and Louis may have found more trouble than most. Life on the Penobscot reservation, and at Holy Cross, was highly regimented in comparison to the life of the traveling ballplayer. In those days, all games were played during the day and most contests lasted two hours or less, leaving a lot of unencumbered time for a bored young man to fill with pursuits of his own choosing. In addition, Pat Tebeau led one of the loosest teams in baseball, with no curfews or morning practice for road games, because the manager expected his veteran team members to take care of themselves off the field.

Louis was nearly 26 years old, but had not experienced much of life on his own, and appeared to lack the maturity to handle his free time in constructive ways. College life and his previous experience in the Maine leagues had not allowed Louis to develop much of an awareness of the world and the people who inhabited it. In every city in the league, fans wanted to meet the famous Indian, shake his hand, and buy him a drink. Louis did not know how to say no.

It soon became apparent to Pat Tebeau that Louis' problem with alcohol was much more serious than he first suspected. Sixteen years later, Tebeau said in an interview, "I sent him back to his hotel in Cleveland, and a doctor put his foot in a plaster cast and ordered him not even to turn over in bed. But do you know that he would get up during the night and walk a block on his plaster foot to get a drink of whiskey?"[5] While the team played three games in Pittsburgh, Louis rested his foot at the Kennard House by day, and walked down to the bars to drink at night.

Fortunately, Sock's injuries began to heal, and when the team returned to Cleveland Sock began to practice with them again. However, his ankle still hurt, and Louis' speed, his greatest asset on the ball field, was now greatly reduced.

Sockalexis returned to the lineup on Thursday, July 8, against the Senators in Cleveland. He was still limping noticeably, but Lew McAllister could not manage a single hit in the three games against Pittsburgh, so Louis played. Sock couldn't cover much ground in the outfield, but he belted two singles as the Clevelanders beat the Senators 10–5 behind Cy Young. The teams were off on Friday, but McAllister played in Louis' place on Saturday in a 3–1 Cleveland win.

A studio pose of the young Louis Sockalexis. (National Baseball Hall of Fame Library, Cooperstown, NY)

Finally, the Cleveland team received some good news. The Common Pleas judge hearing the Sunday-ball case released his decision and declared Cleveland's Sunday-ball restriction unconstitutional. Cleveland prosecutors promised to appeal the ruling, but the overjoyed Frank Robison immediately announced that his club would play on Sunday, July 11, against the Senators at League Park.

Robison expected 12,000 fans or more to storm the park on Sunday, but torrential rains swept the Cleveland area that morning, no doubt encouraged by the Cleveland ministers railing from their pulpits at morning services. The field was unsuited to play at game time, but after an hour or so the rains stopped and the game got under way with perhaps 1,500 fans in attendance. The weather and the tiny Sunday crowd dealt a bitter blow to Robison, but the game proceeded as scheduled.

Louis was still limping, but he played and pounded out three hits as Tebeau's men won the game by a 15–4 score. Rookie pitcher Jack Powell won his fifth game against one loss, and Wallace and McKean also belted three hits apiece. The Clevelanders, despite all their problems, won three in a row from the inept Senators and maintained their hold on fifth place, five games above .500.

The league-leading Boston Beaneaters came into town on July 12 for three games, and Tebeau wanted Louis, his best hitter, in the lineup. Tebeau gave up on Lew McAllister in right field, and the team was further hobbled when the veteran center fielder, Jimmy McAleer, reacted to some newspaper criticism of his hitting by packing his bags and going home to Youngstown, Ohio. With Harry Blake released to Connie Mack's minor league team in Milwaukee several weeks before, the Cleveland team had only three outfielders on the roster. If Sock couldn't play, one of the reserve pitchers would have to play right field.

The weather cleared overnight, and a fine crowd of 8,000 came to League Park to see a duel between two of baseball's greatest pitchers. Cleveland's Cy Young and Boston's Kid Nichols were the two winningest major league hurlers of the 1890s, and any game between them promised to offer a well-fought, tightly played contest.

Unfortunately, the Monday game against the Beaneaters turned into an unmitigated disaster, for the Cleveland team and for Louis Sockalexis personally.

The game began well for the Hibernian Indians. Louis opened the contest in right field and singled in both the first and third innings, though the Clevelanders could not manage to score. Boston pushed a run across in the second off Young, and the score stood at 1–0 as Boston batted in the fourth.

With a runner on first and two out, Boston's Bobby Lowe lofted an easy pop fly to right field that should have ended the inning. Sock, unaccountably, dropped it and allowed the runner to score for a 2–0 lead. Marty Bergen followed with a single that scored Lowe, and then pitcher Kid Nichols walloped a home run to put Boston ahead by a 5–0 score.

It grew worse in the fifth inning. Boston's Fred Tenney, the former Brown University star, hit a grounder to right that got through the Penobscot's legs for a three-base error, Louis' second of the game. Tenney scored on a single by Hugh Duffy, and with the score 6–0, rookie Henry Clarke came in to relieve Cy Young. Clarke retired Chick Stahl, but Jimmy Collins belted a liner to right that Sock didn't appear to notice right away. By the time Sockalexis belatedly retrieved the ball, Collins had circled the bases for an inside-the-park home run and an 8–0 lead. "It should have been a single," said the *Plain Dealer* the next day, "but Sockalexis was dreaming of his collection of love letters and got to it late enough to let it bound by."[6]

The official scorer could not charge Sockalexis with another error, since Sock didn't touch the ball in flight, but this may have been the worst misplay of all. Tebeau had seen enough, and the frustrated manager sent Lew McAllister to finish the game in Sock's place. Boston won the game by an 8–2 score, and the usual whoops and yells were replaced by boos directed at Sockalexis.

Not only did Sockalexis lose the game almost single-handedly, allowing six of the eight Boston runs to score on misplays, but he did so in front of one the largest crowds of the season. Now the entire city knew that Cleveland's most popular player was significantly impaired. If the fans did not know about Sock's alcohol problem before, they certainly did when the local papers came out the next morning.

The *Plain Dealer* pulled no punches in its game recap, titled "A Wooden Indian." "Had [umpire] Sheridan been at Winchester or anywhere else about twenty miles away," snarled the paper, "it would have been well for Cleveland yesterday, and it would have been still better if Sockalexis had been there with him, enjoying a sociable chat and sipping mint juleps. As it was the two acted as if they had disposed of too many mint juleps previous to the game.... A lame foot is the Indian's excuse, but a Turkish bath and a good rest might be an excellent remedy."[7]

Sock didn't play in the next two games, and the Boston papers reported that the Cleveland players accosted Pat Tebeau after Sock's misadventures in the outfield and demanded that the manager put someone else — anyone else — in the lineup. Tebeau relented, sending Sockalexis to the bench and putting rookie pitcher Henry Clarke in right field against the Beaneaters. Surprisingly, despite Sock's absence, the Clevelanders defeated the first-place Boston club by scores of 8–5 and 18–2. Clarke erred twice in right field, however, and Pat Tebeau took it upon himself to rehabilitate the Penobscot and restore him to the lineup. Tebeau assigned other players to watch Sockalexis in the evenings, especially on the road, to keep him out of trouble and away from the bars. Just in case, however, Tebeau recalled Harry Blake from the minor leagues to reinforce the outfield if Sock couldn't play.

Lew McAllister finally started hitting, and he played right field for the next three games as Cleveland swept three in a row from the Brooklyn team. Once again, dark clouds held the crowd down on a Sunday in Cleveland, but Jack Powell won his seventh game and McAllister chipped in two singles. Sock watched the proceedings from the bench. His manager and teammates were shadowing him at night, but he wasn't yet ready to play, so he remained on the bench as the Clevelanders split two games against the Orioles in front of small crowds.

Despite the constant surveillance, it soon became clear to the Cleveland management that Sock would not, and could not, stop drinking. He was still besieged by admirers, and he would not steer clear of their invitations to dine and drink. He also became adept at shaking free from his handlers and escaping for a night on the town. "It is admitted at headquarters that Cleveland is after a good outfielder and this at once suggests 'how the mighty have fallen,'" said the *Plain Dealer*. "It means that unless a certain young man 'takes a tumble to himself' one of the most promising players of the year will soon have gone wrong. Too much popularity has ruined many a good young ballplayer, but it would seem that a man with brain enough to complete a college course would know too much to be led astray by a little flattery."[8]

The *Plain Dealer* printed the following summary of the problem on July 22, after the third game of the Cleveland-Baltimore series was canceled by rain:

> It is no longer a secret that the local management can no longer control Sockalexis, and when that management once loses control of a player it is likely to be "all off" between said management and said player. This is an unfortunate fact for the team and also for Sockalexis. When the Indian came here he was ambitious and his head was level. He was courted by a pretty lively crowd and then the troubles began. Discipline had no effect. When a player begins to realize that he is the whole thing nothing can stop him.
>
> Manager Tebeau still has hopes that the great Indian will come to his senses, and it is to be hopeds that he will. He is likely to see that his popularity depends upon his ability as a player, and will not last after that ability is gone. If Sockalexis takes proper care of himself, his baseball career is bound to be a most brilliant one. If not, he will soon find that he was a nine-days wonder and that the nine days have passed. It will not take many days to decide the fate of Cleveland's great find.[9]

Many of the writers and fans in other National League cities didn't mind seeing the Clevelanders run into problems with Sockalexis. Tebeau's ballclub was still the most hated team in the league, with the possible exception of the Orioles, and one unidentified scribe wrote this ode for *The Sporting News*:

> Oh, Patsy Tebeau,
> This year you are sleau,
> And nothing you do can now vex us!
> You have troubles and weau,
> And we're sorry to kneau
> That old booze has knocked out Sockalexis.[10]

The Sporting News also turned Sock's name into a verb. The paper reported that Jimmy Donnelly, a New York Giants player who fought his own battle with the bottle, promised manager Bill Joyce "that he would do no more Sockalexing."[11]

Sock wasn't the only young star to run into trouble in 1897. Napoleon Lajoie, the hard-hitting first-year first baseman of the Philadelphia Phillies, also ran afoul of his admirers in the Quaker City. Lajoie, like Sockalexis, enjoyed the nightlife, and as the season wore on he began to miss bed checks. "[Lajoie's] crowning offense," said *The Sporting News,* "was to appear upon the field in uniform in such a decided state of intoxication that every spectator in the stands recognized his condition. He was suspended immediately and fined." As if the National League didn't have enough problems, now both of the league's two newest, most exciting young stars found themselves fined and suspended by their teams for drunkenness.

The Phillies, who reinstated Lajoie only because they were riddled with injuries, then arrived in Cleveland for a three-game set. The Phillies always drew well in Cleveland, because Philadelphia star Ed Delahanty was a Cleveland native and hard-hitting outfielder Elmer Flick lived in Twinsburg, about 10 miles from League Park. Many Clevelanders came out to League Park to cheer Delahanty and Flick, and the atmosphere for Tebeau's men felt more like a road game whenever the Phillies came to town.

After the teams split their first two games, Tebeau decided to give Sock another chance in right. Batting eighth in the lineup, Sock pounded two singles in three trips to the plate, raising his average above the .340 mark. He also booted two more fly balls in the outfield.

Sock's poor fielding had no effect on the outcome of the game. The Phillies fell behind early and trailed 4–3 in the ninth when they became enraged by the ball-and-strike calls of a substitute umpire named McGinty. After Zimmer and Tebeau walked in succession, the Phillies left the field and refused to continue, handing Cleveland a 9–0 forfeit win.

Sockalexis played again the next day as Frank Robison finally got his big Sunday crowd. More than 15,000 people, the largest crowd ever to attend a game in Cleveland, came out to see the locals battle their enemies from Baltimore. The contest went into extra innings, but in the bottom of the 10th Joe Kelley and Jake Stenzel belted doubles off Cy Young to win the game for the Orioles. Louis managed only one hit but played errorless ball in right. His ankle still hurt, however, and after the game Louis asked Tebeau to leave him out of the lineup for a few days in order to allow his ankle to heal.

Tebeau acceded to Sock's request. The manager put Lew McAllister back in right field for Monday's game against the Giants, in which a group of Louis' admirers presented the Penobscot with a wooden Indian doll in the third inning. Such presentations of gifts like watches and flowers were common in baseball at the time, but they were usually made to players who were in the lineup. Louis was warming the bench, and stayed there for the next few days. The teams were rained out on Tuesday—1897 was a wet summer all over the country—but Louis did not play in Cleveland's 14–8 win on Wednesday either. He watched as Cy Young surrendered seven runs in the first inning, after which the Cleveland bats came to life and won the game easily.

Sock's alcohol problem came to a head on July 29. The Cleveland team left town to begin a two-week road trip to Cincinnati, Louisville, and Chicago, but Louis did not accompany the team. A hastily procured minor leaguer named Fred Cooke occupied right field, because team owner Frank Robison suspended Louis without pay. The *Plain Dealer* picked up the story on July 31:

> Sockalexis, Cleveland's sensational right fielder, is on the ragged edge. He did not go to Cincinnati with the team for reasons now apparent. President Robison began an investigation recently and yesterday the result was made known to Mr. Sockalexis. The result was that for four sprees within the past few days the Indian must settle. For the first offense he is fined $25, for the second $50, for the third $75 and for the fourth he is suspended without pay.

The article further stated that Sock would not be returned to the lineup until he promised to take no more alcohol for the balance of the season. "This action," continued the paper, "will not be a surprise to many who have observed the Indian carefully, and the only wonder is that he did not get into trouble with the management of the club before this."

Robison explained the suspension a few days later. "It was reported to me early in the season," said Robison, "soon after Sockalexis had been secured by the Cleveland club, that he had been intoxicated, and I found, on investigation, and on authority which I could not doubt, that the story was correct. I spoke to the Indian about it, and he admitted that he had been in such condition but pleaded extenuating circumstances and promised to abstain from then on. For a time I heard no more stories, but lately it has come to my ears that he has been drinking a good deal, and I received indisputable evidence today that he had been intoxicated two nights this week."[12]

Robison suspended Sockalexis until the team physician could certify that the Indian was free from liquor and in proper condition to play ball. "I think I can truthfully say, " remarked the owner to *The Sporting News*, "that I have done everything I could for Sockalexis, and he has repaid me, and the Cleveland club, by the basest ingratitude. I have waited as long as I could, and have given him every chance to do what is right, and only punished him when I felt that I must do so in justice to myself and the rest of the club."[13]

By now, Tebeau's ballclub was so desperate for outfielders with both Sockalexis and Jimmy McAleer gone that they signed Ollie Pickering, who had been released by Louisville for poor hitting.[14] The light-hitting duo of Pickering and McAllister played center and right, with an occasional appearance by newcomer Fred Cooke, but the Clevelanders suffered a disastrous road trip. They lost 9 of their next 11 games and limped back into Cleveland on August 10, still in fifth place but only two games above .500. With Boston and Baltimore winning at a .650 pace, the Clevelanders fell steadily out of the pennant race.

The fans responded to the losing streak by staying away from League Park. Weekday games against Pittsburgh drew less than 1,000 people, and only 1,200 showed up on a Saturday as Cy Young lost to the Browns by a 10–5 score. There weren't even any more large Sunday crowds, as only 2,500 saw the Cleveland club beat the Browns 13–3 on August 15. The excitement of the early season, mostly caused by the presence and hitting of Louis Sockalexis, was now only a memory for the disappointed fans. By late August, some of the local papers had stopped calling the team the "Indians," referring to Tebeau's men as the Clevelands or, sometimes, employing the old Spiders moniker.

Louis remained in Cleveland while the team went off on its western road trip. He managed to stay out of trouble and convinced Frank Robison and Pat Tebeau to give him another chance. When the Cleveland team returned, Robison reinstated Sock to the active roster, and on August 13 Sock played right field with one hit and no errors. Reported *Sporting Life*, "Sockalexis has shown that he can play great ball. By next season he will probably have laid aside his tendency toward frivolity, settle down and play a great game."[15]

However, the battling Irishmen of the Cleveland team were in a surly mood. They had dropped more than 15 games behind the league-leading Boston team, and by early August even the most hopeful players had to admit that they would not challenge further for the 1897 pennant. Jesse Burkett, crabby as ever, showed his disgust with the whole situation by playing the outfield with less than his usual enthusiasm. "I know that Jesse Burkett loafed on a hit to left field the other day," lamented Tebeau, "but what are you going to do? It's almost a clock that we can finish no higher than fifth notch, and we are certain to remain in that position."[16]

Burkett was not happy for most of the last half of the season. On

August 4 in Louisville, he called umpire William (Bill) Wolf a vile name during the first game of a doubleheader. The umpire threw Burkett out of the game, and when Tebeau refused to send up a pinch-hitter for the Crab, Wolf forfeited the game to the Colonels. One paper reported that "the Indians played as if they did not care whether school kept or not in the second game,"[17] and the Colonels won that game as well. In the ninth inning of the second game, Burkett argued with the umpire again, so forcefully this time that Wolf enlisted two policemen to remove the defending batting champion from the field of play.

Second baseman Cupid Childs, who was not on speaking terms with his keystone partner Ed McKean, summed up the feelings of many of the Cleveland players. "We are no longer the Spiders, nor are we the Indians," grumbled the second baseman. "We are the Quitters, and we've got it up to here."[18]

In retrospect, it seems unusual that the Cleveland team did not mount a more serious challenge for the 1897 pennant. They finished second the year before, and then added four outstanding new players to the ballclub in the same year. Jack Powell pitched for 16 seasons in the major leagues and won 248 games, while Lou Criger lasted until 1912 as a solid, dependable catcher, one of the best defensive backstops in the game. Bobby Wallace, who was a mediocre pitcher before Pat Tebeau shifted him to third base, played until 1918 and wound up in the Baseball Hall of Fame. The other member of Cleveland's noteworthy rookie brigade, and perhaps the most talented of the group, was Louis Sockalexis. In the game's long history, few major league teams have ever managed to find so many outstanding new players in the course of one season.

Some of the players blamed the fall of Louis Sockalexis for their predicament, and Sock's relationships with his teammates took a beating. During a game in Washington in July, Jack O'Connor, an Irishman from Tebeau's neighborhood in St. Louis, shouted to the Senator pitcher, "Give him a slow one opposite across the tops of his golf socks. Lob it up to him and see him make a ... full hook punch at it!"[19] Of course, Louis still had trouble hitting a ball in exactly that place. The papers noted that Burkett and O'Connor, in particular, criticized Sock in full hearing of the fans and the opposition players. Burkett, who took the lion's share of the credit for Sock's success early in the season, now became the Indian's severest critic, and some sources report that Burkett's comments carried an ugly racist edge.

The manager, too, began to lose patience with Sockalexis. One paper reported that Tebeau, disgusted at the sight of Louis dropping and kicking a fly ball, shouted to the Indian, "Just cut that out for a minute till I send you a pair of boxing gloves and you can scrap all you want with it!"[20]

Double play.

BOB WALLACE

ST. LOUIS.

Pitcher-turned-third baseman Bobby Wallace, who played in the major leagues until 1918 and was elected to the Hall of Fame in 1953. (Author's collection)

The fans, even in Cleveland, also made their feelings known. "Take that bat from his mitt and put a bunch of cigars in his hand. He'd look better in front of a cigar store, Tebeau!" was one of the usual outbursts from the League Park box seats.[21]

With Cleveland out of the race, the management turned its focus to 1898. Rumors swirling around the league stated that Ed Delahanty, the slugging outfielder of the Phillies and a Cleveland native, had worn out his welcome in Philadelphia and wanted to play in Cleveland. An outfield of Burkett, Delahanty, and a sober and willing Sockalexis might be the strongest one in the National League. Ollie Pickering would be the extra man; though Louisville cut him loose for failing to hit, Pickering batted .352 in 42 games for Cleveland.

The Delahanty deal was only a rumor, so Tebeau continued to audition new outfielders. All the while, the manager hoped that Sockalexis could pull himself together, quit drinking, and reclaim his stardom. In late August, Tebeau left Sock at home in Cleveland when the club left on another Eastern swing, but he noted that the Indian seemed genuinely repentant and eager to make up for the trouble of the last few months. His ankle was still painful, though, and in early September the Cleveland management sent Sock to a hospital for an x-ray. The doctors found that no bones were broken but advised that Sock stay off the field until the swelling and irritation subsided.

A six-game losing streak ended the road trip, dropping the club below the .500 mark yet again. When the team returned to Cleveland on September 12, Sock played right field and managed a single as the Clevelanders walloped the dreadful Browns 15–4. He played the next two days as well, then retired to the bench to allow Tebeau a look at newcomer Ira Belden in right field. Sock coached, cheered his teammates, rested his ankle, and kept out of trouble for the rest of the home stand.

The Spiders, with the pressure of the pennant race behind them, played their best ball of the 1897 season in September. They won 12 in a row against the Browns, Reds, Colts, and Colonels, a streak highlighted by Cy Young's no-hitter against the Cincinnati Reds on September 18.[22] Crowds were small, however, and only 2,500 fans saw Young's masterpiece on a pleasant Saturday at League Park.

In early October, the Clevelanders lost three games in Pittsburgh, without Sockalexis, to end the season in fifth place with a record of 69–62. They finished the season 19 games behind the pennant-winning Boston Beaneaters, who won the flag in a furious finish against the Orioles.

All in all, it was a disappointing season for Cleveland, though Jesse Burkett batted .383 and Bobby Wallace developed into a star with a .339 average and 112 runs batted in. Ed McKean slumped to a .273 average, and Pat Tebeau fell to a .267 mark. Cy Young, inconsistent all year, won 21 games and lost 19, while Nig Cuppy battled a sore arm and won only 10 games. Zeke Wilson and Jack Powell provided hope for the pitching staff, winning 16 and 15 games respectively, but the team's traditional outfield weaknesses plagued the club once again in 1897.

The team also proved disappointing at the box office. Only 115,000 fans paid their way into League Park, leaving Cleveland in 12th place out of the 12 National League teams in attendance. Tebeau's men drew well on the road, helping the attendance figures of all the other clubs, but disastrously bad weather and the lack of Sunday ball conspired to keep people away from the home ballpark. If attendance did not improve in Cleveland, Robison would have problems paying salaries the next year. The Cleveland owner certainly noticed that the minor league teams in Columbus, Indianapolis, and Milwaukee drew more fans than his Spiders drew in Cleveland.

As for Louis Sockalexis, perhaps no other rookie in the history of baseball burned so brightly and fell so quickly. Louis hit .338 for the season, and in 66 games he scored 43 runs and drove in 42. He showed great speed with 16 stolen bases, and only Bobby Wallace hit more home runs for the Cleveland club than Sock, who belted three of them. On the minus side, Sock's 16 errors gave him a fielding average of .888, a mark that was totally unacceptable for a major league outfielder in that or any other era. Burkett committed only 13 errors in almost twice as many games, and the light-hitting Jimmy McAleer erred only three times all season for a .950 fielding average. Harry Blake, in 24 games, made only one error.

Tebeau believed that Sock's considerable potential was worth saving, and the manager was determined to keep the Indian in Cleveland. When the Cleveland team turned in its reserve list to the league office, Sock was one of the 18 players named as Cleveland property for 1898. Tebeau also included Ira Belden, Lew McAllister, Harry Blake, and Ollie Pickering on the list, providing a measure of competition for starting outfield spots in the 1898 season.

Unfortunately for Frank Robison, an appeals court judge dealt the 1898 Spiders a blow before the 1897 season concluded, reversing the previous favorable Sunday-ball decision. The judge upheld the local Cleveland ordinance against playing baseball on Sunday, declaring that such activity qualified as a "public nuisance" and enjoining the Cleveland team from playing further games on the Christian Sabbath. Robison immediately planned to appeal the decision to the Ohio Supreme Court. The Ohio General Assembly would be required to overrule the local statute and repeal the state blue law if Robison's team hoped to play on Sundays in 1898, but the next legislative session would not begin until the following baseball season was well under way.

This unfortunate legal setback promised the Cleveland fans another spring full of sniping with ministers and threats to move the team, and the long-suffering fans—what few there were that showed up at League Park—faced another unpleasant, controversy-filled baseball campaign.

Sockalexis displayed a great deal of promise in his rookie season, but in future years his 1897 campaign took on almost a mythical aura. *Sports Illustrated*, in a 1973 story about Sockalexis, stated that the Indian "didn't strike out once all season."[23] The league's statistical office, headed by "Uncle Nick" Young, did not record batter's strikeouts in 1897, so it is not known exactly how often Sockalexis struck out, but the box scores and newspaper accounts say that he did, at least a few times. Many sources state that his famous homer off Amos Rusie at the Polo Grounds was a grand slam or that it was the first of two homers that he hit that day. In truth, Sockalexis hit only three homers in 1897, none of which was a grand slam, and each came on different days.

Indeed, despite Sock's undoubtedly excellent play, especially early in the season, it may seem surprising to compare his statistics with another 1897 Cleveland right fielder, Ollie Pickering:

	Sockalexis	*Pickering*
Games	66	42
At Bats	278	182
Runs	43	33
Hits	94	64

	Sockalexis	Pickering
Doubles	9	5
Triples	8	2
Home Runs	3	1
Runs Batted In	42	22
Stolen Bases	16	18
Batting Average	.338	.352
On-Base Average	.385	.392
Slugging Average	.460	.418
Errors	16	6
Fielding Average	.888	.950

Pickering played about two-thirds as many games as Sock, but stole two more bases with a higher batting and on-base average. Sock hit for more power than Pickering, but Pickering fielded much better than the Indian. Pickering performed so well that Tebeau penciled him into the starting center field slot for 1898 after Jimmy McAleer announced his retirement from active play. "Pickering is as good a man as McAleer was, if not better," said Tebeau, "for he is almost as fast a fielder, and a stronger batter, and is improving in both."

The manager also liked what he saw of Ira Belden, who batted .267 in eight games and played errorless ball in the outfield. Tebeau told *The Sporting News* that Belden "shows every sign of becoming a star, and looks like a regular man."[24]

Perhaps Tebeau praised Pickering and Belden so effusively to pressure Sockalexis to take care of himself over the winter. Sock now knew that he didn't have a starting position, or even a roster spot, locked up for the coming campaign. Tebeau still loved the Penobscot's potential, but a battle among Sockalexis, Blake, and Belden for the starting slot in right field promised to be one of the interesting sidelights of the upcoming 1898 spring training season.

CHAPTER 9

The 1898 Season

> *Whenever [Sockalexis] appeared, he was greeted with derisive war whoops, and Cleveland writers began calling the team the "Indians." Thus, whenever Tebeau's rowdy crew stirred up emotions, the most menacing threats were directed at Sockalexis. Although some writers urged fans to lay off the "Ki-Yi's" and war whoops, it is likely that such pleas merely provoked more of the same.*
> — David Voigt, 1966[1]

The spectacular rise and fall of Louis Sockalexis in 1897 grabbed the imagination of the sporting press, and in January of 1898 *The Sporting News* printed a brief article, headlined "Sockalexis' Ancestors," that attempted to describe Sock's heritage. "Sockalexis is an interesting product," the article began, "not only as an Indian but on account of the peculiar brand of Indian to which he belongs." The writer claimed that Sock's forefathers were "as troublesome to the early settlers as he is to the Robisons," and described the Penobscot tribe as follows:

> The Penobscots are a branch of the Abenaki race, a people which gave the early settlers of Maine and New Hampshire more trouble than any other Indians in the land. The Abenaki were never very numerous, but as scalpers and wholesale murderers they had a proud and pre-eminent record. Those who infested Maine were known as Tarratines and were perhaps a trifle less ferocious than those of New Hampshire. The French missionaries Christianized them without trouble and then turned them loose upon English settlements. After peace became the popular thing, the Tarratines found their occupations gone and decided to settle down and do as the white man does.[2]

The Tarratines, or Penobscots, settled down quite successfully, according to *The Sporting News*. The writer claimed that the tribe "refutes all the arguments usually heard in conversation concerning the red man—that the Indian is doomed to pass away, that he will be absorbed by the whites, and that he cannot be civilized."

"Sockalexis has no reason to be ashamed of his people," stated the article, though there is no evidence that Sock ever expressed regret about his Indian ancestry. "Theirs is indeed a proud record and one that the young Indian ball player should bear in mind when the temptations of the big city beset him."[3]

In early 1898, the Cleveland team made arrangements to hold their spring training in Hot Springs, Arkansas, a popular warm-weather resort town. Team owner Frank Robison recognized that the cut-rate spring training of 1897 was a monumental mistake, and, at Tebeau's urging, decided to invest several thousand dollars in a first-rate training trip to warmer surroundings.

The pennant chances of the Cleveland team influenced Robison's decision. The perennial champion Baltimore Orioles failed to win the flag in 1897 for the first time in four years, following a bitter season-long battle with the Boston Beaneaters. The Orioles appeared to be on their way down, while many believed that Boston's narrow victory was a fluke. If Nig Cuppy's arm improved, and Louis Sockalexis stayed on the straight and narrow, Tebeau's team might finally win a National League pennant.

Sock, however, faced a challenge for his job that year. Jimmy McAleer changed his mind about retirement and returned to center field, so the competition for the starting right field slot emerged as a four-way race among Sockalexis, Harry Blake, and late-season acquisitions Ira Belden and Ollie Pickering. Blake and Belden were both steady but unspectacular players. They were solid fielders with low batting averages. Pickering was a better hitter, belting the ball at a .352 clip in the last two months of 1897, but a poor fielder and prone to pull dumb base-running mistakes. Sockalexis was the most talented of the quartet by far, but proved unreliable due to his off-field battle with the bottle. If Sock could control his drinking, he might save his career and lift the Clevelands to the pennant at the same time.

The rest of the league took a wait-and-see attitude concerning the Indian. The local writers, perhaps remembering how the excitement surrounding Sockalexis the previous March was dashed by July, decided to keep their enthusiasm under wraps. *Sporting Life* still referred to the Cleveland team as the Indians, but some of the other papers reverted to the old Spiders nickname in their 1898 spring training dispatches.

Louis Sockalexis told the papers that he kept out of trouble all winter, and that he "turned his glass upside down for several months and communed with nature in the wilds of Maine."[4] Louis looked fit when he and the other players arrived in Cleveland on March 3 for the spring training trip to Arkansas. Louis traveled to Cleveland by train in the company of Burkett, Blake, and McAleer, and people remarked on how clear-eyed and determined the Indian appeared to be.

However, Louis had two days worth of free time on his hands before the train left for Arkansas, and it didn't take him long to find trouble. He ate dinner with other members of the team on Friday, March 4, but when the meal was finished, Sockalexis disappeared. When the time came to board the train for Hot Springs on Saturday afternoon, Sockalexis was nowhere to be found. Pat Tebeau and other Cleveland team officials looked frantically for the Indian, but the manager eventually gave up the search and ordered the train to leave without him. "It's a pity [Sockalexis] doesn't keep straight," sighed Tebeau to the writers on the train. "If I can keep him in line this year he will strengthen us to a great degree. However, it looks as though Blake would start the season covering right field."[5]

Back in Cleveland, the *Plain Dealer* reported that Louis turned up in a "downtown resort" on Saturday night, explaining that he missed the train, but that he would make the trip to Arkansas the following day. Robison, who had already arrived in Hot Springs, ordered team secretary George Muir to wait at the team offices on Sunday, in case Sockalexis made an appearance, but the Indian did not come on Sunday either. Louis finally surfaced at the hotel in Cleveland late Sunday evening but would not say where he had been.

"It is not a very hard matter to conjecture why he is still in the city," remarked the *Plain Dealer*. "He is short of funds, and, as Tebeau took along his transportation with him, it left the Indian in a bad plight, and no doubt he is waiting to receive transportation."[6] Louis finally met with Muir on Monday, then went down to the train station on Monday evening and boarded a train for Hot Springs without incident. Several of Louis' friends in Cleveland sent telegrams to Pat Tebeau, denying that the Penobscot missed the train because of drunkenness, but the truth of the matter was clear. Louis had fallen off the wagon again.

The Penobscot arrived at Hot Springs two days later and immediately went in for a one-on-one talk with a disappointed manager Tebeau. Louis, to his credit, was honest about his behavior. "I did it again, Cap," said Louis to the manager sadly. "A crowd got hold of me and before I knew it they had loaded me. I had not taken a drop in so long that I did not know my capacity, and before I knew it they had me. I am through for good now. My friends in Cleveland are my worst enemies, I fear, even though they don't mean to be. After this I will defy anybody to get me started."[7]

The Indian had promised to stay out of trouble several times before, but with the right field situation unsettled, Tebeau elected to believe him, at least for the moment. However, the *Plain Dealer* commented "it is a known fact that the club will stand no more foolishness from Sockalexis. One more slip and he will be suspended, just as sure as there is a rule to provide for such suspension ... there are too many good outfielders to put the club in any seriously embarrassing position by the suspension of one, and the rest are all conscientious workers."[8]

A spring training trip to Hot Springs was no easy vacation for the Cleveland players. The baseball field was two miles from the hotel, up an incline, and the Spiders ran there each morning for a two-hour practice. They jogged back to the hotel for lunch, and then ran back to the ball field for a three-hour afternoon practice in the sunny Arkansas spring weather. The day ended with another jog back to the hotel for dinner, followed by a session in the hot springs from which the town took its name.

"The violent exercise of muscles long unstrained," reported the *Plain Dealer*, "the loosening up of cords unused and the rattling around of bones that have been for months idle is well calculated to make the human frame feel as if it had been put through a threshing machine."[9] Tebeau kept the players on a 10:30 P.M. curfew, but the men were usually so exhausted by the practicing and running that no one was still up at that hour anyway. It was hotter than usual in Arkansas that spring, and the extra pounds melted away quickly from the frames of the Spider players.

Tebeau put Sock on the field almost immediately after their conference, and he played right field in a split-squad contest on March 9. Sock played sluggishly in the first spring training games, especially in the field, but Tebeau continued to make excuses to the writers. "The first trip south for a man who has lived in an extreme cold climate is bound to make him loggy," explained the manager to the *Plain Dealer*. "I think Sockalexis wants to do well, but is not as energetic as he might be. As soon as this sort of premature spring fever wears off of him he may be as full of life as ever."[10]

Sock explained himself in an April interview with the *Plain Dealer*. "After wintering in the woods of Maine," said Sockalexis, " it takes the life out of me to get down in this warm place. I feel well but can't get ginger enough in my game. I am in good condition again and when I get north again I will play as well as ever. As to my falling by the wayside again there is no chance of it. I made a big fool of myself and know it. Mr. Robison and Mr. Tebeau stuck to me longer than I deserved and I mean to repay them. When I get to Cleveland I intend to get a place near the ball grounds to live in and then I will not go down town all the season. My mind is made up and it is no joke. I have a good future as a ball player and only have to take care of myself to keep in the game."

"All this talk by Sockalexis would have more weight," suggested the

Plain Dealer, "had not the Indian told about the same story before on several occasions."[11]

Sockalexis hit well down South, as always, but he ran poorly and his fielding had improved not a bit, as easy liners and grounders skipped between his legs and rolled for doubles and triples. Louis would simply lose his concentration in the outfield and appeared prone to daydreaming. "When he wakes up in time to get after a fly, he handles it splendidly," said the *Plain Dealer*, "and his throwing is quite as phenomenal as it ever was, but he turns many a single into a double or three-bagger by letting it slip through him."[12]

He stayed out of trouble off the field, probably because he and the other players were too tired to venture out at night. However, Louis appeared to show little interest in his work, and soon the other players criticized the Indian for "shirking" and loafing. "Blake and Pickering are working like nailers," said the papers, but Sock appeared to play with an air of disinterest. To make matters worse, the fans in Hot Springs razzed the Indian sarcastically whenever he touched the ball and taunted him mercilessly about "firewater" and his poor fielding. The sensitive Sockalexis responded with more indifferent playing. "He is very susceptible to flattery," remarked the *Plain Dealer*. "He poses in the field and seems to feel that all eyes are resting upon him; but worst of all, he does not play ball with his old-time vigor."[13] Sock didn't begin to apply himself until Tebeau dropped him from the regular team and sent him to play with the rookies in the split-squad games.

Sockalexis won a place on the opening-day roster, though Blake, Pickering, and Belden were present as well. The starting job, for the moment, went to the steady Blake, while Sockalexis warmed the bench, waiting for another chance. After the first few weeks of the season, Tebeau planned to cut the roster down and carry no more than two, and probably only one, spare outfielder, so Sock, Pickering, and Belden all found themselves on the bubble.

The baseball magnates, as usual, found several new ways to take advantage of the players as the 1898 season began. They unilaterally lengthened the season from 132 games to 154, giving each club an extra 11 home dates without raising the players' salaries in kind. They also passed a new 21-point standard of conduct, applicable only to the players and not the owners, umpires, or fans. Under these "Brush Rules," proposed by Cincinnati owner John T. Brush, a player could be fined and suspended for addressing an opponent or umpire in a "villainously filthy" manner. A three-man disciplinary panel would then hear an accused player's case and could, if it so chose, expel the offender from the National League with no right of appeal.

The players objected to these new rules, especially the expulsion aspect, and they feared that the league was itching to make an example of the first man to cross the line when the season began. When the league distributed copies of the new regulations to each team and ordered all players to sign it, the Spiders refused to do so. Indeed, they publicly considered obtaining legal advice on the matter. However, just in case the league was serious this time about controlling player rowdiness, Tebeau instructed his men to work on controlling their tempers in the spring training games.

Louis Sockalexis in the uniform of a town team in Castine, Maine, in 1908. (College of the Holy Cross Archives)

Sockalexis, of all people, had an answer for the Brush Rules. "I'll cuss the umpire in Penobscot," Sock told his teammates, as related in *The Sporting News*. "And if they call me I'll say that I was telling them they are right and that you fellows are dead wrong in kicking." Sockalexis also offered to teach his teammates Indian words like "hickehowgo" (robber) and "kanylanyee" (green lobster) to use on the umpires. Jesse Burkett, according to the papers, listened enthusiastically to the Indian's impromptu language lessons.[14]

The club owners also discontinued the season-ending Temple Cup series, though the players rightly shared the blame for its demise. The Baltimore Orioles vied for the cup in all four years of its existence and played each series in a lackluster, disinterested manner. In three of the four post season matches, the Orioles arranged to split the winnings with their opponents on a 50–50 basis, removing any incentive for either team to play good baseball. Knowledgeable baseball people commented that the only team that refused to split the pot was the 1895 Cleveland ballclub, which played to win and drubbed the Orioles four games to one.

The magnates were concerned with player behavior and its effect on attendance, but the biggest threat to baseball in 1898 came from the

Spanish-American War. Tension between the United States and Spain over Spanish rule in Cuba came to a head when the battleship U.S.S. *Maine* blew up in Havana harbor on February 15, 1898. The explosion killed more than 200 American sailors. Most Americans believed that Spanish saboteurs destroyed the ship, and on April 25 the United States declared war on Spain.

War fever gripped the nation, and the ensuing news coverage forced the baseball season to the back pages of the nation's newspapers. Attendance suffered throughout the league as thousands of young men left home and signed up for military service. Many of these young men were baseball fans, and their absence from the nation's ballparks slashed attendance drastically. The Baltimore Orioles, who drew more than 25,000 fans for the deciding game against Boston in late 1897, attracted only 6,100 for their 1898 home opener.

In addition, it didn't help baseball's image as the "national pastime" when only one major league player, Baltimore pitcher Arlie Pond, volunteered for military service. Pond, who pitched for the Orioles while attending medical school, earned his degree from the University of Maryland in 1898, then left the Orioles and joined the Army Medical Corps. Pond became a career officer and served with distinction in Cuba and the Philippines for the next 30 years. No other players followed his lead.[15]

One player who declined to serve in Cuba was Louis Sockalexis. In April a newspaper cabled Sockalexis and asked if he would lead a regiment of Penobscots in battle. Though the braves of the Penobscot Nation earned a fine record as warriors in centuries past, Sock demurred. "Sock's patriotism does not seem to be very warm," clucked *The Sporting News* in disapproval, "for he replied that he would [enlist] if he could get command of a regiment ... and draw as much money as he is making out of base ball ... he prefers the ball bat to the war club."[16] The papers expressed disappointment in Sock's attitude, though the Penobscot were merely "disenfranchised citizens bereft of any special status" by law and not really full American citizens.[17]

Baltimore's attendance woes served as an ill omen for the Cleveland franchise, but Frank Robison made a few more of his typically bullheaded moves. He found himself embroiled in a nasty labor dispute with the unionized employees of his trolley lines, and when the workers went on strike, Robison brought in non-union strikebreakers. The Cleveland owner also enlarged League Park by 5,000 seats, bypassing the established construction unions in favor of using cheaper non-union laborers to accomplish the task. This action infuriated the union organizations of Cleveland, the Knights of Labor and the Building Trades Council, which in turn called for a general boycott of Robison's businesses, including the trolley lines and the baseball team. The boycott ensured that Cleveland attendance would fall even further in 1898.

To make matters worse, Robison also publicly considered offers to sell or move the team, apparently learning nothing from the turmoil of 1897. He also believed that he could get the Sunday-ball issue resolved in his favor once and for all, and he and his brother Stanley spent another spring sniping at Cleveland's ministers in the papers over Sunday ball.

On April 15, the Spiders opened the season in Cincinnati, and Harry Blake played right field as the Reds defeated the Clevelanders by a score of 3–2. Sockalexis rode the bench in that game but got his chance the next day when Jesse Burkett left the team to attend to his seriously ill nine-year-old son. Sock played left field and led off against Cincinnati left-hander Still Bill Hill. Louis struck out twice against Hill's slow curve ball but contributed a bunt single as the Spiders beat the Reds 3–1 for their first win of the 1898 season.

Burkett's son died on April 17, and Sockalexis filled in for Burkett in left field for the next several games. Sockalexis managed a single in a 12–1 loss to the Reds that Sunday, in front of a noisy crowd of 15,000 in Cincinnati. Then, after two off-days, the Penobscot went hitless three days later in a 10–5 win at St. Louis. A rainout on April 21 was followed by a 7–0 Cleveland win, played against the Browns in ankle-deep mud, in which Sock hit a single and a double. The next day's game was rained out again, and it was difficult for Sockalexis to build momentum with all the off-days and bad weather.

Burkett rejoined the team on April 24 for a Sunday game at Louisville, and Sock returned to the bench. Sock played well enough in his limited action to survive the first round of the outfield battle, as Tebeau sent Ira Belden down to Robison's Fort Wayne minor league club after the Louisville series. This move left Sock and Pickering to fight for the reserve outfield slot, as backup to starters Burkett, McAleer, and Blake.

Sock watched one of the most unusual plays of the season from the bench on April 25 in Louisville. In the third inning, Honus Wagner, the outstanding young Colonels player, slid hard into Bobby Wallace at third base and jarred the ball loose from Wallace's grip. Wagner then grabbed the ball, heaved it into left field, then trotted home. It took the two umpires 15 minutes to decide that Wagner should be declared out for interference. Wagner, for his part, told the papers that he was merely "fighting the devil with fire" in making such a play against the hated Spiders.[18]

On that same day, April 25, President William McKinley declared war on Spain, and the American people turned their attention from baseball to focus on the war effort. Four days later, the Cleveland Spiders drew only 2,000 fans for their home opener, which they won against the Browns by a 6–2 score. The boycott was partially responsible for the small crowd, but thousands of other potential fans attended a rally in downtown Cleveland that same day, cheering the new Army recruits as they marched off to war, and baseball seemed far from the minds of the people of Cleveland. Only 300 showed up at League Park the next day, on a cold, wet Saturday.

Sockalexis stayed on the bench for several weeks. He didn't get into another game until May 9, when he entered a contest in the sixth inning when Jimmy McAleer was called home to Youngstown by an illness in his family. Sock hit two singles in two trips to the plate that day, and after another rainout, he belted three singles against the Chicago Colts, helping the Clevelanders to a 7–5 win behind Cy Young.

Louis tried to make the most of his chances. He played errorless ball in the outfield, and teams still respected his considerable throwing ability, so much so that opposing runners did not dare to take an extra base on balls hit to the Penobscot. When McAleer returned on May 13 Sock reclaimed his spot to the bench. However, the umpire ejected Pat Tebeau in the first inning that day for arguing, and when Blake came in from the outfield to spell Tebeau at first base, Sockalexis took Blake's place for the rest of the game. Ollie Pickering, on the other hand, played in no games at all for Cleveland, and on May 26 Tebeau sent him to Omaha of the Western League.[19]

The backup outfield job now belonged to Sockalexis. His only chance to play regularly depended on the failure of Harry Blake or Jimmy McAleer, but both men hit and fielded well in the early stretches of the 1898 campaign. Sockalexis had to be content with the occasional pinch-hitting appearance, for the moment, but at least it appeared that Sock was staying out of trouble at night. If Sock had been creating problems with his behavior, Tebeau would have sent him away and kept Pickering or Belden.

The Interstate League club in Youngstown made inquiries about obtaining Sockalexis, but in the end, Tebeau elected to keep the Indian in Cleveland. The hard-charging manager still believed in the Penobscot's talent, and he continued to hope that Louis would straighten out his life and regain the stardom that everyone predicted for him in the first three months of 1897.

Chapter 10

Sitting the Bench

> [Sockalexis] seems more sincere than ever now, however, and may stick to his resolutions. President Robison and Manager Tebeau make no secret of what they will do with Socks at the first outbreak. He will be suspended without pay and will play no more baseball. His contract provides that he will receive his salary only on the condition that he keeps away from the firewater.
> —*Cleveland Plain Dealer*, April 1, 1898

In April of 1898, the Cleveland papers reported that more than 15,000 Cleveland fans had signed petitions asking the Ohio General Assembly to enact a state law allowing baseball to be played on Sunday. The number of signatures, though it sounds impressive, probably had little effect. It did not appear that any state legislator wanted to incur the wrath of the powerful Cleveland Ministerial Association (the "same old crowd of fanatics and nobodies," sneered *Sporting Life*) by introducing a bill to permit Sunday ball, so Robison decided to try another tack. Robison, still fighting the battle that began in May of 1897, prepared to appeal the conviction of pitcher Jack Powell to the Ohio Supreme Court. In the case labeled *Powell v. Ohio*, Robison and his attorneys asked the Court to overturn the local blue laws as unconstitutional, hoping that, in doing so, that the state law would become invalid.

The court acted quickly. On April 19, the justices upheld Cleveland's Sunday statute and ruled against the Cleveland team in *Powell v. Ohio*. Despite the fact that amateur teams had played ball in the city on Sunday for years, often accompanied by wagering and drinking, the Court ruled that the city of Cleveland had the right to ban professional ball playing on Sunday as a public nuisance. The overjoyed Cleveland ministers celebrated their triumph by announcing plans to shut down theaters and movie houses on Sundays as well.

With no other course of action open to him, Robison made plans to bring the Sunday-ball controversy to a head on the field once more. He scheduled a game in Cleveland against St. Louis for Sunday, May 1, and dared the police and ministers to intervene. Both sides harrumphed and blustered for the papers, but bad weather forced the cancellation of the game. On the following Sunday, the local police were prepared to stop a game against Louisville at League Park, but once again, the rains washed out the contest before it began. Robison, undaunted, scheduled the next Sunday game in Cleveland for June 12, and both sides braced for a renewal of hostilities.

The Cleveland team got off to a good start in 1898, and by the end of May was solidly entrenched in second place with a 24–12 record. Cy Young, up and down in 1897, found his form and won 8 of his first 11 games, while Bobby Wallace recovered from a serious early-season beaming and continued his good hitting. Nig Cuppy's arm still bothered him, but Zeke Wilson and Jack Powell picked up the slack with an occasional assist from outfielder-turned-pitcher Lew McAllister.

Louis, though he appeared to be staying sober, found trouble off the field nonetheless. In early May, the Cleveland players shared a train with a contingent of soldiers. A few of the soldiers mistook the copper-skinned Penobscot for a Spaniard, and, according to *Sporting Life*, a brawl on the train was the result.[1] On the field, things were not going much better. The three starting outfielders performed so well that Louis Sockalexis did not appear in a game for weeks at a time, except for the odd pinch-hitting assignment.

One such appearance on May 23 resulted in a protracted argument. In that game, the Spiders trailed the Senators 4–3 in the ninth when Sockalexis pinch-hit with one out and runners Jimmy McAleer and Jack O'Connor on second and third respectively. The Indian hit a sharp liner that Senator left fielder Kip Selbach caught off his shoe tops. O'Connor returned to third, but McAleer strayed off second, and Selbach threw to second to double up McAleer and end the game. However, Tebeau and the other Spiders crowded around the umpire and intimidated him into calling McAleer safe. After a long protest by the Senators, Jesse Burkett, the next batter, drilled a single to score both runners and win the game for Cleveland.

Sock made a more successful appearance on Memorial Day. At the Polo Grounds in New York, a hooting and whooping crowd of 14,000 saw the Spiders and Giants battle into the ninth inning, tied at 4–4. The Spiders loaded the bases with no one out, and Tebeau sent Sockalexis up to bat for pitcher Jack Powell. Sock drove home two runs with a hard single, after which Jesse Burkett drove in another run and Cupid Childs singled to drive in Sockalexis. The Spiders took an 8–4 lead, but the Giants

Jimmy McAleer, who retired from baseball in 1899 rather than play for the decimated Spiders. In 1900 he became the manager of Cleveland's new American League team. (Author's collection)

pounded relief pitcher Cy Young for five runs in the bottom of the ninth and won the game by a 9–8 score.

Despite the fine play of the second-place Spiders, for the second year in a row the fans stayed away from League Park due to the war, the union boycott of the team, and bad weather. Attendance in 1898 was even worse than it had been the prior year, and Robison knew that his team could not survive in Cleveland without Sunday ball. The Cleveland magnate then hatched a plan. He decided to build a temporary ballpark at Euclid Beach Park in the suburb of Collinwood, nine miles outside of Cleveland, and play Sunday games there.[2]

Robison's plan worked, at least for one day. Six thousand fans attended the game at Collinwood on June 12 as the Spiders defeated the Pittsburgh Pirates behind Jack Powell. However, the next Sunday game, played on June 19 in front of 3,000 at Euclid Beach Park, ended differently. A Collinwood minister swore out a complaint against the team, and the police invaded the field in the eighth inning, arrested the Cleveland players (not including Louis, who didn't play that day), and halted the contest. Fortunately for the Spiders, the authorities waited until late in the game to intervene, because the Clevelanders fell behind early and did not retake the lead until the eighth inning. When the police stopped the game, the Spiders received credit for the victory.[3]

The local authorities were not much concerned about the violation of the Sabbath. When the players appeared before a Collinwood judge a few days later, the judge smiled and let each man off with a one-dollar fine. This lenient treatment indicated to Robison that the controversy was over, and that the next scheduled Sunday game in Collinwood, set for June 26, could proceed as scheduled. *Sporting Life* stated that Robison received the assurances of the Collinwood mayor and police chief that the police would not interfere with Sunday ball in the future.

However, the Collinwood ministers, encouraged by the Cleveland Ministerial Association, brought pressure to bear against the mayor and police chief that weekend, and the local authorities changed their minds. On July 26, the police did not allow the game between Cleveland and the New York Giants to begin. The authorities turned away more than 5,000 disappointed fans, dashing Robison's hopes for Sunday ball and ending any possibility that the team could turn a profit for the 1898 season. Two days later, the angry Robison announced that he would move most of the remaining Spiders games to other cities for the last half of the 1898 campaign.[4]

Robison had threatened the people of Cleveland with such a move more than a year before. "I am not in the baseball business for fun, nor for patriotism for my own city," said the owner in the previous spring, "and I do not propose to have a few people in Cleveland run my team to my disadvantage when I can see good money in it elsewhere."[5] The magnate figured that, since the Cleveland team was one of the league's best draws on the road, he could make more money from the visitors' percentage of the gate in other cities than from tiny hometown crowds. The extra income would more than offset the added travel costs for his team.

The league magnates and the sportswriters worried about the "Cleveland situation," but the St. Louis Browns presented a more pressing problem. The woeful Browns, buried in last place since April, teetered on the brink of collapse. Owner Chris von der Ahe was once one of the most wealthy and flamboyant owners in baseball, but a series of bad business decisions sent him to bankruptcy court. To make matters worse, von der Ahe's stadium burned down in April, and he spent the summer of 1898 dodging his creditors and trying to figure out how to pay his players.[6] St. Louis was a fine baseball town, but von der Ahe's mismanagement threatened to ruin baseball in that city, and some of the other owners wanted von der Ahe to surrender the franchise to the National League.

Stanley Robison, treasurer of the Cleveland ballclub, watched the St. Louis situation with great interest and suggested to the papers that the Spider management might do well by shipping the entire Cleveland team to the Missouri city. "What we will do with our franchise hasn't been determined," said Robison. "...We have not been negotiating with Buffalo parties, nor have we considered a bid from Pittsburgh for certain players. Of course, we could make a 10-strike by transferring our best players to St. Louis, shifting the Browns to Cleveland and playing out the season. But that scheme, though it looks feasible, would be almost impossible considering the present state of affairs in St. Louis. The Cleveland issue will not be settled until the fall meeting of the major league."[7]

The Spiders, perhaps distracted by the off-field controversies, went 12–12 in June and fell back to fourth place. Many observers believed that the Spiders would contend for the pennant with even fair home support, but the tiny crowds and the ban on Sunday ball hindered the team. Reds manager Buck Ewing faulted the Cleveland and Baltimore players for their low fan support. "I'm afraid," said Ewing, "[that] the foul tactics of the Orioles in the past have served to kill Baltimore, just as Cleveland was killed by the kicking of the Indians."[8]

Tebeau, among others, blamed the war. "During a close-score game," said Tebeau in July, "[the fans] sit in the bleachers reading war extras. Why, in one of our recent games on the home grounds, Burkett pushed three runs over the plate at once. The program boys and candy butchers gave him a genial hand, but every other pair of palms in the stand were engaged in holding war extras. The war certainly has contributed a dab of rust to the turnstile in Cleveland."[9] No one wanted to mention that Robison's anti-union stance in a heavily unionized town and his constant threats to move the team to another city played the biggest role in keeping the fans away from League Park.

In the meantime, Sockalexis wasn't getting any playing time, and a pinch-hitting assignment against Boston on June 30 (in which he grounded out in the sixth inning of a 10–5 loss) was his first on-field appearance in nearly two weeks. Minor league teams noticed that Sock wasn't playing much, and the Youngstown team of the Interstate League offered pitcher Pete McBride in exchange for the Indian. Tebeau considered, and then rejected, the deal, which suggests that Sock was indeed keeping sober despite his long stretches of enforced idleness. Although Harry Blake and Jimmy McAleer were both hitting near the .250 mark, their good fielding and steady play kept them in the starting nine at Sock's expense.

In early July, Blake was called home by an illness in his family, and Sockalexis finally got a chance to play. "His eyes bulged out with joy when he was ordered out into the field," remarked *Sporting Life*. However, Sock pounded out only two hits in his next 17 times at bat, dropping his batting average into the .220 range. In four games against the Colts in Chicago, Sockalexis hit only two singles, though he threw a Chicago runner out at home plate on a failed sacrifice fly.

Tebeau put the Indian in the lineup in both games of a doubleheader on the Fourth of July in Chicago, but the day turned out badly for Sock. He managed only two hits in nine trips to the plate, and the bleacher fans entertained themselves by throwing firecrackers at Sockalexis in right field.

At several moments during the second game, Sock could barely see the infield through the blue smoke from the fireworks going off at his feet. He went hitless in the next two games, as the Chicago fans taunted the Penobscot about his fondness for "firewater" and made derisive war whoops and yells.

Though Blake returned and sent Sockalexis back to the bench for a series against the Orioles, the Baltimore fans showered the Indian with abuse, with a never-ending stream of insults and yells issuing from the stands. That year, the Baltimore fans taunted visiting players with terms like "Spanish spy" and other war-related insults, as well as the usual unpleasantries. Many fans appeared to be trying to goad opposing players, especially the Clevelanders, into losing their tempers and committing a violation of the Brush Rules.

Sock wasn't the only Cleveland player receiving insults from the fans. In Chicago, Chief Zimmer charged into the stands after a heckler, and the veteran catcher was removed from the field by the local police for his trouble. In a July game in Baltimore, Pat Tebeau became so unnerved by one barrage of heckling that he threw a bat into the stands at the offender. The Baltimore police arrested Tebeau, who posted $2.45 bail and then left town. The league took no action against the Cleveland manager, since the Brush rules applied only to "villainously filthy" speech and not to bat throwing.

When the Spiders returned to Cleveland and swept a three-game set against the woeful Browns, Sockalexis remained on the bench behind the starting outfield trio of Burkett, McAleer, and Blake. Jesse Burkett was still one of the league's premier hitters with an average above .350. Harry Blake played unspectacular ball in right field, but his steadiness and all-around solidity appealed to Pat Tebeau. Jimmy McAleer, a notoriously weak hitter, provided no power at all to the lineup (84 of his 87 hits in 1898 were singles), but he was still the best-fielding center fielder in the game. Tebeau preferred to start McAleer and leave the better-hitting Sock on the bench.

The Indian did not see action again until he made an unsuccessful pinch-hitting appearance against the Phillies on July 14. This would be Sock's last game for the Spiders in 1898. His big left toe was bothering him, and a Cleveland doctor diagnosed the affliction as lumbago. The painful toe made running difficult, and in late July the club left Sock in Cleveland when they passed through on the way from Chicago to Pittsburgh. *The Sporting News* reported that Sock was "earning a part of his salary as a member of the Mansfield club of the Interstate League," so Tebeau must have sent Sockalexis to nearby Mansfield to keep the Penobscot in shape and occupy his time.[10]

The Spiders auditioned new outfielders in Sock's absence. A 23-year-old rookie named Emmett Heidrick, from the Atlantic League, joined the team on September 14 and belted four hits against the Senators in his first game. Heidrick didn't field well, but he batted .303 in 19 games for the Spiders and showed more speed than Sockalexis had recently displayed. Tebeau also gave brief tryouts to rookies Fred Frank and Ed Beecher and played pitcher Zeke Wilson in right field for a few games. The Spiders also drafted minor league slugger Ralph (Socks) Seybold, who, in the early 1900s, became an American League star. However, Seybold refused to report to the Spiders, not wanting to play for a team that spent months at a time on the road.

The Spiders played only four home games after July 9, and the national press called them the Exiles, the Wanderers, or, in an insult to the Irishmen on the team, the Wandering Micks. Tebeau's men spent two weeks in Philadelphia, playing not only the Phillies but also the Orioles and Senators, who drew more fans on the road than they did in their own home parks. The Philadelphia papers called the Spiders "our other hometown team," although the fans in the Eastern cities booed and heckled Tebeau's men at every opportunity. Robison also moved some Spider games to such towns as Rochester, New York, and Weehawken, New Jersey, where the crowds were not much larger than they would have been in Cleveland.

The never-ending road trip began to wear on the Cleveland team. They won only 17 of their last 42 games after their last home game on August 26. The Louisville paper reported that the Cleveland players stayed up all night playing cards, and subsequently lost a game to the Colonels the next afternoon. One unidentified Spider snarled to the reporter, "If the man who owns us doesn't give a damn whether we win or lose, why should we?"

"We haven't gotten a close call [from the umpires] in months," complained Jesse Burkett. "I never was as tired of a baseball season as I am of this one. Most of the time we have been without a home. Without morning practice, and with the umpires against you, what chance have you? I hope I'll never have to go through another season like this one."[11]

Ed McKean agreed. "Our chances for the pennant were fair when we left Cleveland," insisted the shortstop. "I don't say we would have won the flag, but I'm confident we would have finished in second place, and if we had been up there we would have drawn at least 2,500 people per game. That would have meant a good deal more money than was taken in out on the road."[12]

Without a home-field advantage or friendly home crowds, the Spiders fell back to fifth place as the Boston Beaneaters raced to the pennant with wins in 33 of their last 37 games. The Cleveland Spiders ended the season with a record of 81–68, 21 games behind the pennant-winning

Boston team. Most of the Spiders believed that their extended three-month road trip cost them a chance at first or second place. They played 114 of their 156 games, and 76 of their last 80, on the road.

Louis Sockalexis stayed out of trouble off the field in 1898 but batted only .224 in 21 games. He fielded well, making only one error in 16 outfield appearances, and threw as well as ever, but his batting average suffered from a lack of playing time. Only two of Sock's 15 hits went for extra bases, and he stole no bases, indicating that his once-excellent speed had diminished considerably. Tebeau still preferred to play Harry Blake, who hit only .245, and Jimmy McAleer, who hit .238, for their speed and dependability. The 34-year-old McAleer made noises about retirement again, but Emmett Heidrick waited in the wings for a shot at the right-field job. The Spiders included Sockalexis on their reserve list of players for 1899, but if Sock rejoined the team, he would face another uphill battle for a spot on the roster.

He did not know where that battle would take place. Already, rumors abounded that the Cleveland owner would sell or trade the team en masse to St. Louis or Brooklyn or that Robison would pull up stakes and move the franchise to Indianapolis or Milwaukee or Buffalo. The Cleveland team drew only 70,496 fans to League Park in the 1898 season,[13] the worst attendance in the league by far, and most observers expected that the Forest City would lose its baseball team. As the season ended, the papers filled many column inches speculating on where the Spiders might play their 1899 season, and Louis Sockalexis packed his gear not knowing where to report for spring training five months later.

By the end of 1898, the national sporting press treated Sockalexis as roughly as the fans in Chicago who threw firecrackers at him on the Fourth of July. Sportswriters openly discussed the Penobscot's battle with alcohol, and even the encouraging notices in the paper sounded condescending and insulting. "Sock swears by the feathers of his ancestors," remarked the *Pittsburgh Leader* in October of that year, "that he hasn't removed the scalp from even one glass of foamy beer since early last spring, when he whooped up a dance on Superior Street in Cleveland and was discovered the next morning by Tebeau in the act of fastening a half-Nelson to a lamppost ... the wiles and temptations of the big cities stimulate poor Lo's thirst and set him forth in search of the red paint."[14]

Sporting Life went further, hinting that Sock's downfall might be blamed on "his dalliance with grape juice and his trysts with pale-faced maidens."[15] The magazine offered no evidence to support the second charge, but other papers called Louis the "Red Romeo," in addition to the usual insulting remarks about Indians and their alleged constitutional

10. Sitting the Bench

The combined Cleveland–St. Louis team at spring training in Hot Springs, 1899. Pat Tebeau (center row, fifth from left) refused to allow Sockalexis to join the team in Arkansas. Note the varied collection of uniforms. (National Baseball Hall of Fame Library, Cooperstown, NY)

inability to control their liquor intake. Louis was an enthusiastic reader of the newspapers, and he certainly read all this speculation for himself. He must have noticed that few writers mentioned the name "Sockalexis" without the word "firewater" nearby.

Perhaps Louis, after two difficult seasons in the major leagues, simply tired of serving as a convenient object of ridicule and abuse from the fans and sportswriters. The enthusiasm that greeted him upon his arrival in the major leagues had turned into scorn after he displayed human failings. Sockalexis discovered, as have many athletes past and present, that fame is a two-edged weapon that can cut a man down as easily as it can lift him up. Like so many other Native Americans, Louis tried, and failed, to find lasting success in the world of the whites. He had become a novelty, like a performer in a Wild West show, and an ill-treated one at that. Perhaps his father was correct in warning young Louis against leaving the reservation in the first place.

Louis Sockalexis spent most of the winter of 1898–99 in Cleveland. The newspapers reported that Sock had trouble getting around on his injured knee, and the soreness in his leg prevented him from working out in the off-season. Sock did not keep in contact with the club in those months, and no one knew exactly how the Penobscot passed the time, but the evidence showed itself in the spring. The formerly fit, muscular Sockalexis gained a surprising amount of weight over the winter. By early 1899 he weighed well over 200 pounds, and rumors abounded that Louis had spent the winter abusing alcohol as well as food. He also paid little, if any, attention to his lumbago problem, and by early 1899 Sock's once-prodigious speed was gone forever.

He may also have had personal reasons for his troubles. Louis had not returned to the Maine reservation for several years except to visit his sister Alice, her husband, and their children. He did not have much contact with his parents since his teen-age years, and he stayed away from Indian Island for much of the time that his father served as tribal governor. It's likely that Louis traveled to Maine in the early part of 1899, however, because his mother Frances became seriously ill. She died on February 25, 1899, and was buried in the reservation cemetery.

No one knows how his father and other family members accepted Louis upon his return to Indian Island. It is known that following his mother's funeral, the overweight Penobscot headed west in an attempt to revive his baseball career, though he was in no physical or mental state to do so.

CHAPTER 11

"The Sorriest Shell of a Team Ever Seen..."

> "When [Sockalexis] began to drink and stay out all night, finding that fines and threats were useless, I promised him $6,000 the next year and $10,000 the season following if he would stay sober and play ball. He promised, all right. But he couldn't let the strong stuff alone."
> — Pat Tebeau, 1914[1]

As an out-of-shape Louis Sockalexis prepared to reclaim his baseball career, the National League magnates turned their attention to the problems facing their sport. The cellar-dwelling St. Louis Browns teetered toward bankruptcy, with the eccentric German immigrant Chris von der Ahe finally losing control of the team. The Cleveland Spiders had lost the fight for Sunday ball, and with it any possibility of operating the club at a profit. The cities of Louisville and Washington had proven themselves unable to support their teams, and the Baltimore franchise, despite the Orioles' record of success, was bleeding money. The twelve-team League had proved unwieldy, and the obvious solution would have been to drop the bottom four clubs and continue as an eight-team circuit.

However, baseball operated as a monopoly, and the greed of the individual owners outweighed any concern for the financial health of the League as a whole. During the winter of 1898–99, several owners negotiated to buy pieces of other teams in the league. Charles Ebbets, the new Brooklyn Dodgers owner, openly coveted Baltimore stars Willie Keeler and Hugh Jennings and knew that the best way to obtain these star players was to buy controlling interest in the Orioles. Ebbets also cast a covetous eye on Cleveland, and rumors abounded that he would either buy Cleveland's best five players for cash or buy the entire team outright. Before long, four different teams owned stock in the New York Giants, and several magnates made offers to buy the bankrupt Browns. The wheeling and dealing grew so heated that the March meeting of the league magnates ended in fisticuffs between the Chicago and Philadelphia owners.

Even so important a personage as Cap Anson, the greatest player of the 19th century, fell victim to the owners' greed. He was forced out of his manager's position in Chicago when, apparently, the team management reneged on an agreement to sell Anson stock in the team. Anson spoke for many when he stated, "Baseball as at present conducted is a gigantic monopoly, intolerant of opposition, and run on a grab-all-that-there-is-in-sight basis that is alienating its friends and disgusting the very public that has so long and cheerfully given to it the support that it has withheld from other forms of amusement."[2]

Predictably, the team owners turned on each other in monopolistic fury. In early January 1899, the owners of the Brooklyn club purchased the controlling interest in the Baltimore Orioles. They changed the name of the Brooklyn team from the Dodgers to the Superbas and transferred the best Oriole players to Brooklyn. Ned Hanlon, therefore, became the manager of the Superbas and the president of the Orioles at the same time. The league magnates then pushed von der Ahe out of baseball by voiding the St. Louis franchise for nonpayment of league dues and prepared to auction off the ownership of the Browns to the highest bidder.

While all this was occurring, the Cleveland players became concerned that Frank Robison would buy the Browns and move the Spiders to St. Louis. It appeared, however, that the Cleveland club might remain intact and play in Cleveland in 1899. Robison patched up his differences with the local construction unions early that year, and the unions called off their boycott of the ballclub after they and the Cleveland club owner signed an agreement of understanding about future construction projects at the ballpark. This agreement appeared to remove the threat of the team moving elsewhere and boded well for the success of the Cleveland franchise. Several Cleveland players, including Louis Sockalexis, had already signed their contracts for 1899 with the understanding that they would play the season in Cleveland.

The players gathered in Cleveland in early March for their spring training trip to Hot Springs, Arkansas, and before they left, Robison promised the players that he had no interest in going to St. Louis to attend the league-sponsored auction of the Browns. Thus assured, Tebeau and his men boarded the train for Hot Springs.

However, mere minutes after the meeting between Robison and his players concluded, the Cleveland magnate boarded a southbound train for

Cincinnati — and St. Louis. Robison attended the auction, engineered the winning bid, and became the new owner of the St. Louis franchise.³

Robison wasted no time putting his grand plan into motion. The Cleveland Spiders were a successful team in a poor baseball town, while the St. Louis Browns were a poor team in a great baseball town. Robison proposed to shift the Cleveland Spiders, en masse, to St. Louis and send the hapless Browns to Cleveland, in effect trading one team for another. Since many of Robison's fellow magnates also owned parts of multiple teams, and none objected to the Brooklyn-Baltimore merger, none protested this arrangement either.

The Baltimore and Cleveland franchises were now virtual farm teams for Brooklyn and St. Louis, respectively. The newspapers called it "syndicate baseball," and the outcry was almost immediate. The *Cleveland Press* called it "a shameful travesty," and the *Plain Dealer* wondered aloud what would happen when Cleveland and St. Louis played each other. "Of course there is bound to be a whole lot of suspicion," said the paper, "as long as two clubs are controlled by the same management, with one at the top and the other at the bottom."⁴ Monopoly of the most greedy and rapacious kind had arrived in baseball, and competition gave way to profit grabbing, as it had in other industries around the nation in this pre-trust-busting era.

In mid–March, the switch of the two franchises became official. The 1898 Spiders would play the 1899 season in St. Louis, and the awful 1898 Browns came to Cleveland as the new Spiders. Frank Robison, owner of the Spiders, gained a controlling ownership in the St. Louis team in return for the transfer of the players from Cleveland, including Cy Young, Jesse Burkett, and other stars. Pat Tebeau, Cleveland's manager since the middle of the 1891 season, left Cleveland and became the new boss of the St. Louis team. The deal was a financial coup for Robison, who invested no money in the St. Louis franchise, but gained 51 percent of the stock in the team in exchange for the services of Young, Burkett, and the rest of the former Cleveland players.

Robison fairly salivated at the thought of a contending team in St. Louis, where Sunday baseball was not only legal, but also wildly popular. As one of his first official acts, Robison dropped the nickname "Browns" in an attempt to distance the new team from the memory of the cellar-dwelling previous one. Before long, the local sportswriters started calling the team "Perfectos," after a popular cigar. Robison made improvements in Sportsman's Park (which he renamed Robison Field), installing new bleachers and erecting a sun canopy over the grandstand in anticipation of large crowds. The new St. Louis owner also upgraded the condition of the playing field, which was rocky and uneven in 1898. Von der Ahe, the former owner, did not employ a groundskeeper, requiring that the players themselves tend to the upkeep of the field.

Robison left his brother Stanley in charge of the Cleveland branch of the two-team baseball operation. While the Perfectos trained in the sunshine of Hot Springs, Arkansas, the new Spiders practiced in Terre Haute, Indiana, a much cheaper and colder training site. The Robisons slashed budgets and expenditures to the bone for the Spiders, and the papers were outraged when Stanley Robison commented that the Spiders would be "operated as a sideshow." The Robisons did not even bother to print schedules, take a team photograph, or engage in any publicity for the Spiders. Already, the papers were referring to the Cleveland team as "Forsakens" or "Misfits," and some columnists predicted that the Spiders would play most of their 1899 games on the road.

One of the few 1898 Spiders who was not invited to make the trek to St. Louis was Louis Sockalexis. Sock surfaced in Cleveland in early March, but he was so overweight and out of shape that Pat Tebeau refused to take him to Hot Springs with the rest of the team. *Sporting Life* reported that Tebeau "considered it a useless expense to take [Sockalexis] to the training camp unless his promise to be good is more faithfully kept than similar assurances have been in the past."[5]

Sock, for his part, optimistically told the papers that he would join a gymnasium to get himself into shape and "surprise Patsy," but Tebeau had heard it all before. After two years of threatening, cajoling, and pleading with Sockalexis to remain in condition and keep away from the bottle, Pat Tebeau finally gave up the struggle.

As it turned out, the new St. Louis aggregation did not need Sockalexis. Tebeau could form a good outfield in St. Louis with Jesse Burkett, Emmett Heidrick, and hard-hitting rookie Mike Donlin, with Harry Blake in reserve. The Perfectos also elected to retain Jake Stenzel, a mediocre outfielder whose ancestry made him popular with the German fans of St. Louis, so the Perfectos had no room for Sock on the team. "So much for freaks in baseball," snarled the *Washington Post*, and most observers believed that Sock's career was finally, irretrievably over.

However, the franchise switch gave Sock one more chance to make it in the major leagues. Only eight Spiders showed up in chilly Terre Haute for spring training, and the new Cleveland team was desperate for warm bodies of almost any kind. In addition, Lave Cross, the new Cleveland manager, did not know Sockalexis and therefore did not have a negative history with the Indian. While the new Spiders trained in Terre Haute, Sock remained in Cleveland, working out and waiting for a face-to-face meeting with the new field boss of the Spiders.

11. "The Sorriest Shell of a Team Even Seen..."

Lafayette Napoleon Cross played third base for the 1898 Browns, batting .317 in 151 games, and although he was one of the team's few good players, he found himself exiled to Cleveland. The Spiders needed a manager, and the Perfectos already had a good third baseman in Bobby Wallace. Cross accepted the job, even though Robison offered it first to Bill Joyce, an old teammate and friend of Pat Tebeau who had managed the Giants a few years before. Joyce turned the job down flat, recognizing an impossible situation when he saw one.

It fell to Lave Cross to whip this motley collection of rejected players into a team, and it soon became apparent that few of his charges had any business playing in the National League. Aside from second baseman Joe Quinn and 38-year-old catcher Chief Zimmer, a Cleveland fixture for 10 years, the Spiders possessed no player with more than mediocre talent besides Cross himself. Cross soon discovered that he had no good pitchers, no decent outfielders, and not even a passable shortstop or first baseman on the roster.

Lafayette (Lave) Cross, manager of baseball's worst team, the 1899 Cleveland Spiders. (Author's collection)

Few talented players wanted to spend the 1899 season in Cleveland, even if they were assured of starting positions. Ed McKean and Harry Blake refused to play for the Spiders, asking instead to be assigned to St. Louis, although each man would probably ride the bench for the Perfectos. Jimmy McAleer, who was not needed in St. Louis, retired from the game rather than play for the sad-sack Cleveland club. The only other player who might make a difference for Cross' team, if he could be kept on the straight and narrow, was Sockalexis.

Louis Sockalexis, still working out in Cleveland, chanced upon *Sporting Life* correspondent Elmer Bates on the street near the ballpark. Sock took the opportunity to proclaim his new commitment to sobriety. "I expect to be back in the game for good within a week," said Sockalexis to Bates. "I have cut out the red stuff for good, and am feeling fine. With Zimmer and I back on the team, it will help out the boys who have been playing out of form."[6] Sock also boasted to the *Plain Dealer*, "I will be in right field when the bell tinkles Friday, and if I feel as I do today, I'll knock the ball over to Lexington Avenue."[7]

When Sockalexis took the pledge of abstinence yet again, Cross saw no alternative but to believe the Indian. If Louis could control his drinking, he would become the star of the Cleveland team almost by default. He might also put some fans in the seats, and perhaps a replay of the hysteria of 1897 might mask the fact that the team itself was, as the *Plain Dealer* stated, "a half-frozen collection of has-beens from an alleged training camp at Terre Haute."[8] Cross did not yet add the Indian to the official roster but instructed Sock to report to League Park every day and get himself into playing form.

Sockalexis, now 27 years old, practiced on his own in Cleveland as the Spiders opened the season in St. Louis and lost to Cy Young by a 12–1 score. Sock appeared to apply himself, but he was not the Sock of old. He had put on weight over the winter, swelling to well over 200 pounds. "He is as big as an alderman," said teammate Dick Harley, and the aged catcher Chief Zimmer remarked, "I can give him twenty yards and beat him in a hundred…. You would not know the big Indian if you saw him now."[9] The Penobscot no longer covered acres of ground in the outfield, nor ate up the dirt in huge chunks as he motored around the bases. In only two years, Sock had gone from the fastest player in the National League to one of the slowest, and the loss of his speed would sorely affect any chance of regaining his stardom.

Louis joined the team officially on May 1, the date of Cleveland's home opener. Louis and the rest of the Spiders (called "hopeful cripples" by *Sporting Life*) soon received the first indication that their club would be the junior partner in the St. Louis-Cleveland merger. Frank Robison bought brand-new uniforms, white trimmed with Cardinal red, for the Perfectos, but Cleveland's uniforms were the same ones worn by the Browns in the 1898 season. Louis and the other Spiders could clearly see the outline of the words "St. Louis" in stitching holes beneath the "Cleveland" lettering on their uniform shirts.[10]

The Spiders played their first seven games of the season on the road in St. Louis, Louisville, and Cincinnati, losing six of them, and as the club made its way back to Cleveland for the home opener, the papers already bemoaned the team's prospects for the 1899 season. The *Plain Dealer* suggested in a sub-headline that "the Cleveland players hope the fans will not throw things,"[11] and the Cleveland ballclub became the joke of the National League before they even played a home game.

The fans, too, knew that the Spiders were doomed to failure, and fewer than 500 people paid their way into League Park on opening day to see the team in a doubleheader with Louisville. Louis didn't play as the Spiders won the first game, a 14-inning marathon, and lost the second. Sock's first appearance of 1899 came on the next day, when Lave Cross sent Louis up to pinch-hit in the first game of a twin bill. As the Indian stepped up to the plate Chief Zimmer solemnly remarked, "This may be the turning point of your career, Lou." Sock, however, struck out to end a 3–2 loss to the Colonels.

The Spiders won the nightcap, leaving them with a 3–9 record. The Spiders could not even avoid embarrassment while winning, for as the eighth inning ended, both teams ran off the field, thinking that the game was over. The scoreboard boy, keeping track of the innings on a chalkboard, mistakenly added an inning somewhere along the line, but the whole mess was not straightened out until the official scorer notified the umpires. At least the Colonels and the umpires suffered some embarrassment as well.[12]

The Chicago Colts, called the Orphans ever since their long-time leader, Cap Anson, left the team the year before, arrived in Cleveland on May 3 and beat the Spiders three times in a row by lopsided scores. Cleveland's decimated roster simply could not compete with the better National League teams, and even middle-of-the-pack clubs like the Orphans found no difficulty in walloping the Spiders. In the third game of the series against Chicago, only 125 Cleveland fans bothered to attend. Louis managed one pinch-hitting appearance in the series, grounding out in the ninth inning of a 10–2 blowout.

Lave Cross was quickly running out of options. The Cleveland pitchers were little better than semipros, and most of the position players had already proven by now that they could not hit major league pitching. One report states that Cross paid a visit to team owner Frank Robison and begged for reinforcements. "I need about five players to have a pretty good team, Mr. Robison. A couple of pitchers and a shortstop would help. Give me those and even with the other misfits we'll win some games."

Robison, according to this account, merely shrugged. "I'm not interested in winning games here," said the owner as he dismissed Cross. "Play out the schedule. That's your job."[13] *The Sporting News* suggested that, despite the losses, Robison and his Spiders were turning a small profit with their shoestring operation, and Robison saw no need to make adjustments.

By this time, Cross was aware that the 1899 Spiders were destined to finish the season in the cellar of the National League and that no help would be forthcoming. In desperation, he offered a tryout to Tony Mullane, the famous switch-pitcher who had won 285 games in the major leagues. However, Mullane was now 40 years old and had not pitched in the National League since 1894. Mullane failed the tryout, though it's difficult to imagine how he could have pitched worse than the hurlers already on the Cleveland roster.

The Spiders then went on the road to Chicago. Cross, not fully trusting Sockalexis' pledge of abstinence, left the Indian home in Cleveland to avoid the temptation of the big city. Sock practiced at League Park while the Spiders suffered two more losses, the second of which turned out to be one of the most heartbreaking defeats of the season. The Spiders took a 7–5 lead in to the bottom of the ninth inning, but the Orphans put two men on base. Harry Wolverton then ended the game with a three-run homer off Willie Sudhoff to give the Chicagoans an 8–7 victory. After this defeat, the Spiders returned to Cleveland to face the St. Louis Perfectos in a four-game series. With a mixture of hope and desperation, Cross gave Louis Sockalexis his first start of the season. Louis would play right field in all four games against the Perfectos.

The Spider fans, what few of them were left, cheered the Perfectos louder than the home team, since the Perfectos ("expatriated Indians," according to the papers) were almost all ex–Spiders. Every member of the St. Louis starting lineup played for the Spiders in 1898, while only two Spiders— Sockalexis and Chief Zimmer — played for the club the year before. The biggest Cleveland crowd of the season, 1,500 fans strong, saw the Spiders battle hard against Cy Young. The score was tied 1–1 in the eighth inning, when the Perfectos scored five times off Jack Stivetts to blow the game open. St. Louis added two more in the ninth to give Young an easy 8–1 win.

Sockalexis managed a single, but Young allowed only three other safeties. Sockalexis wasn't back in playing shape yet, but at least he appeared to be applying himself. The *Plain Dealer*, sharply critical all year of the team and its management, held out hope that Sock could regain his stardom. The paper remarked, "Sockalexis was back in the game for the first time in many a day. The big Indian seems to have come to his senses at last, and is doing his best to get back to his old-time form."[14]

Unfortunately, the next day turned out even worse for the embattled Spiders. Not only did the Perfectos bomb them, 12–2, by scoring in seven of the nine innings, but only 300 patrons witnessed a poor exhibition of ballplaying by the Clevelanders, especially by Louis Sockalexis. Sock walked and worked his way around to third, but when the next batter drilled a single, Sockalexis seemed to be daydreaming. He got a late start from third and was thrown out at home — on a clean single to the outfield. Louis also covered very little ground in right field, and though the scorer charged him with no errors on this day, several balls fell to earth safely that the faster Sock of two years before would have caught easily. However, many of the Spiders were guilty of poor fielding in this game. The *Plain Dealer* acidly commented, "A wooden Indian might get through the season without an error, and so might some of the Cleveland players if they continue to keep away from the ball."[15]

The next day's game marked the last hurrah of Louis Sockalexis, at least at the plate. Louis banged out five hits against the Perfectos, with four singles and a double to his credit. Louis' hitting energized the Spiders, but unfortunately the Indian's fielding canceled out his effective batting. He made an outstanding throw to double up a runner at third on a fly ball but also dropped two other easy flies in right field. He failed as a base runner in a double steal, getting himself thrown out at the plate by a huge margin. Again, Louis followed a familiar pattern of play. He threw spectacularly and hit well, but his mental lapses on the base paths and slowness afoot in the outfield had become embarrassing and detrimental to the ballclub.

Despite Louis' outfield antics, the Spiders battled hard that day, and for the first time in nearly a week the Clevelanders entered the last inning with a chance to win the game. The Perfectos led 8–6 in the bottom of the ninth when the Spiders loaded the bases with one out on singles by Quinn, Sockalexis, and McAllister. Tommy Tucker then belted a sharp line drive over third that looked like a sure bases-clearing double, but former Spider Bobby Wallace made a leaping catch, stepping on third base to double up Quinn and end the game. This defeat left the Clevelanders with a 3–17 record, dropping them behind the inept Washington club into last place.

The next day, Sock went hitless as the Spiders suffered another heart-rending loss, their ninth defeat in a row. They carried the Perfectos into extra innings, but former Spider Ed McKean belted an inside-the-park homer in the 10th to give St. Louis a 5–4 win and a four-game sweep of Cleveland.

The Spiders showed few flashes of good play in the four games, and it was painfully obvious by now that only third baseman Cross and second baseman Quinn were real National League ballplayers ("pearls among swine," said one newspaper). The Perfectos exposed the ineptitude of the Cleveland pitching staff, outscoring the Spiders 33–13, and the Spider outfielders played atrocious ball both at the bat and in the field. The Spiders held a 3–5 record against Louisville but were 0–13 against the rest of the National League. Most importantly, the Spiders won only two of their first eleven games at home, and the fans stayed away in droves.

The Cleveland team's poor performance against their St. Louis fellows raised eyebrows, since the same man owned the two clubs. Some papers gossiped that Pat Tebeau, the St. Louis manager, ordered Lave Cross to pitch Willie Sudhoff against Chicago on short rest and also dictated the presence of the obviously impaired Sockalexis in right field. "When the poor old Indian, Sockalexis, was put in the game against St. Louis," reported the *Plain Dealer*, "merely, as it appeared, to muff easy flies, there was another yell let loose all over the country."[16] No evidence to support these charges turned up, but the air was ripe with suspicions in the era of syndicate baseball.

Since Louis Sockalexis was batting over .300 in limited action, Lave Cross decided to take him on the road to Pittsburgh and give him another start in right field. If Sock failed, said the newspapers, he would probably be released in the next few days, since Cleveland was carrying 20 players under contract, and most teams kept only 13 or 14 after the first few weeks of the season.[17] The Spiders—called "Remnants," "Misfits," and "Expendables" by the newspapers—arrived in the Steel City on May 13 for two games against the Pirates.

The first contest of the series turned out to be Louis Sockalexis' final game in the major leagues. Louis looked lost at the plate, going 0 for 4, and humiliated himself when he fell down twice in the outfield. Both times he fielded a bouncing ball cleanly but tumbled to the turf with a thud as he straightened up to throw. The official scorer didn't know what to make of the embarrassing display and finally elected not to charge Louis with any errors.

After the second gaffe, Louis returned to the bench as the Pittsburgh fans cheered derisively. Louis tipped his cap and gave his "funny little nod," not realizing that the cheers were meant in jest. The Pirates cruised to an easy 6–0 win. Sock was "nothing more or less than a tobacco sign in right field," jeered the *Pittsburgh Post*. "In fact, a tobacco sign could not have done the damage he did."[18]

It appeared that Louis, who revealed his serious ankle injury in Pittsburgh two years before, had once more fallen off the wagon in the Steel City. Sockalexis was either drunk or hung over on the field again, and even the threat of release did not stop him from imbibing. Lave Cross, like Pat Tebeau before him, finally realized that Sock's career was beyond salvage. It was certainly no coincidence that the team lost all seven of the games it played with Louis in the lineup.

Although Sock was not the only Spider performing poorly, his ineptitude stood out among all the others. "Standing out in bold relief all by his lonesome, among the offenders on the visiting team, was Sockalexis,

11. "The Sorriest Shell of a Team Even Seen..."

the Indian," said the *Pittsburgh Dispatch* on May 15. "His Socklets must have been heap full of dope, for his efforts to take care of things that wandered into right field were as funny as a cage of monkeys. He was about as fast on his feet as a cow, didn't get within a mile of the drives in his garden and seemed to be dreaming of better days."

Still, it took one more incident to force Sock's release from the Spiders. The second game at Pittsburgh was rained out, and the team returned to Cleveland for one outing against the Reds, which the Spiders lost by a 3–0 score as Sock watched from the bench. That evening, Sock attended the theater to see a sketch called "A New Year's Dream" at the Lyceum but fell asleep noisily in his seat. His snoring disturbed the other patrons, and when Louis could not be roused awake, the manager of the theater called a policeman. The police hustled Louis to the central police station and booked him for public intoxication.

The papers reported that the lieutenant at the booking desk asked the Indian, "Ball player by trade?"

"A sort of one," replied Louis. He spent the night in the lockup, sleeping off the alcohol.[19]

Sockalexis, weak and shaking, appeared before a magistrate the next morning. The ballplayer was in no condition to put up a defense, so the judge decided to return Louis to jail for another day. In the meantime, Lave Cross, angered by this latest incident, released the Indian from his contract. "The judge would not release him, but Lave Cross did," said the *Plain Dealer*. Louis was appropriately remorseful the next day as the judge fined him for disorderly conduct, but his career with the Spiders, and in the major leagues, was truly over.

Newspapers across the nation expressed regret over the ruination of a once-promising career. Louis was "a grand specimen of manhood some seasons back," reported the *Washington Star*, "and gave indications of being a wonderful player. For the past two years it has apparently been the ambition of the Indian to see how much firewater he could get away with."[20]

"Just to think," chimed in the *Plain Dealer*, "that only a few days ago Sox made five hits out of as many times at bat, and promised by the love of his tribe to continue to be a real ball player."[21]

Incredibly, the release of Sockalexis sparked the Spiders on a modest winning streak. They won four of their next six games, but a 12–0 drubbing at the hands of the Baltimore Orioles brought the Clevelanders back to earth. By early June, they were buried in the cellar with an 8–30 record, and Frank Robison dispatched manager Lave Cross to St. Louis to play third base. The Perfectos were struggling, and this move allowed Perfectos manager Pat Tebeau to move Bobby Wallace to shortstop, where

Wallace began a career that would land him one day in the Baseball Hall of Fame.[22] Robison appointed Joe Quinn, the Spiders' only remaining good player, as manager for the balance of the season.

The St. Louis Perfectos became a hit at the box office, more than doubling their attendance of 1898, but played listlessly and fell to the middle of the standings despite another fine pitching season from Cy Young. In contrast, the awful Spiders averaged only about 150 fans per game in League Park. Ignored by the fans and mercilessly roasted in the press, the Spiders lost 15 of their next 18 games and sank even deeper into the basement of the 12-team National League. Robison abandoned all pretense of putting a competitive team on the field when he released the popular catcher Chief Zimmer, who was batting .342 at the time, in a salary-cutting move. Soon other higher-salaried Spiders were let go and replaced with minor-leaguers and collegians. The Spiders lost many of their games by football-sized scores.

To make matters worse, the other National League teams worked extra hard to beat the Spiders, not wanting to suffer the rank indignity of losing to the worst team in the history of baseball. In June, Baltimore pitcher Jerry Nops was hung over when he pitched the first game of a doubleheader against the Spiders, who battered him for a rare win. Orioles' manager John McGraw was so outraged by Nops' performance that he fined and suspended the pitcher, and the Orioles then walloped the Spiders in the second game by a score of 21 to 6. In mid-July the Spiders performed the rare feat of playing a doubleheader without scoring a run, losing to the Orioles by 10–0 and 5–0 scores.

The Spiders—no longer called "Indians" with the embarrassing end of Sockalexis—became a national joke among baseball enthusiasts. *Sporting Life* columnist Elmer Bates wrote half of a prehistoric Top Ten list to describe the good points of following such a terrible team:

- There is everything to hope for and nothing to fear.
- Defeats do not disturb one's sleep.
- An occasional victory is a surprise and a delight.
- There is no danger of any club passing you.
- You are not asked 50 times a day, "What was the score?" People take it for granted that you lost.[23]

Soon no more than 100 or so fans bothered to show up for games at League Park to see the team that historian Lee Allen called "the sorriest shell of a team ever seen in the major leagues." The crowds were so small that the ticket sales for some games totaled only about $25 or so, and visiting teams could not meet their expenses in Cleveland. In late June, responding to pressure from other club owners, the Spiders moved the rest of their home games to other cities and spent the last two months of the season on an extended road trip. The demoralized "Remnants," now the "Exiles" and the "Wanderers," lost a record 24 games in a row at one point and finished the season with 40 losses in their last 41 contests. The awful Spiders ended the campaign with 20 wins and 134 losses, by far the worst record in major league history. They finished a stunning 84 games behind the Brooklyn pennant winners.[24]

Louis batted .273 for the Spiders in his seven-game stint, but the other Spiders compiled some of the worst statistics ever seen in the game. Pitcher Jim Hughey led the staff in wins with 4 while losing 30 games, 16 of them in a row. Charlie Knepper also won 4 and lost 22, Harry Colliflower won 1 and lost 11, and Fred (Crazy) Schmitt was 2–17. Willie Sudhoff won 3 of his 11 games for the Spiders, good enough to earn his ticket to St. Louis, where he won 13 more games before the season ended. His replacement, Frank Bates, lost 4, won 1, and then lost 14 in a row. The Spiders hit only 12 home runs all season, while Washington's Buck Freeman belted a near-record 25 round-trippers all by himself.

Despite the team's rank ineptitude, the 1899 season represented a lost opportunity for Louis Sockalexis, perhaps the last chance he had to turn his life in a positive direction. The 1899 Spiders probably played under less pressure than any team in major league history, since no one ever expected them to win a game. They played no home games after July 1, so the usual hometown fan pressure was nonexistent. Sock could have cemented a credible comeback with a good, or even a fair, season. His washout, after only seven games, is a clear indication of the pernicious and apparently permanent hold of alcoholism on the life of Louis Sockalexis.

The sad example of the Cleveland Spiders exposed syndicate baseball as an artistic and competitive sham, and in the off-season the National League dropped Cleveland, Louisville, Baltimore, and Washington from its ranks. The resulting eight-team league operated in the same eight cities, without any franchise shifts, for the next half-century, an unprecedented era of stability. Most importantly, the magnates outlawed the practice of multiple team ownership, and syndicate baseball died a well-deserved and unlamented death.

CHAPTER 12

"A Sorrowful Spectacle..."

> I see that Sockalexis must forego frescoing his tonsils with the cardinal brush; it is so nominated in the contract of the aborigine.
> — Orator Jim O'Rourke,
> talkative New York Giants outfielder[1]

After a reasonably sober 1898 season, Louis Sockalexis fell completely off the wagon in early 1899. It is not known what started Sockalexis on the road to oblivion; perhaps the uncertainty of the St. Louis–Cleveland franchise shuttle, the ineptitude of the new Cleveland team, or the constant razzing from the fans and the newspapers hastened the downfall of the sensitive Indian. Whatever the reason, no other major league team showed even the slightest interest in the man who brought excitement to Cleveland baseball only two years before. Sock appeared to be the latest in a long line of ballplayers lost to alcoholism.

Drunken behavior appeared in baseball long before Louis Sockalexis ran into trouble in the summer of 1897. Alcoholism was one of the biggest issues plaguing 19th century baseball. "One of the prominent evils of the season of 1883," stated the 1884 *Spalding Guide*, "...was the drunkenness which prevailed in the ranks of many of the club teams. The number of League and American matches that were lost last season by dissipation of players would surprise the fraternity were they enumerated ... there was scarcely one team in the arena that did not have at least one 'weak brother' among its players."[2]

Baseball annals abound with stories of drunken ballplayers. Many of those are meant to be amusing, as was the case of Bobby Mathews, a star pitcher during the 1870s and 1880s. Mathews won 42 games in the National Association in 1874, then after a few down years he won 30 games three years in a row for the Philadelphia Athletics from 1883 to 1885. While pitching for Philadelphia, an inebriated Mathews once staggered out onto the field, past the pitcher's mound, and out to second base before his infielders stopped him. "Turn around, Bobby, the mound's that way!" called out the shortstop.

Mathews turned around and started back across the diamond. "Just whistle when I get to the box," requested the pitcher, "and I'll stop there." His teammates whistled, Mathews found the pitching rubber with his feet, and the game began. He was drunk, but sobered up as the game progressed, and he pitched a complete game that day.

Mike "King" Kelly may have been baseball's first matinee idol. A handsome, personable Irishman, Kelly starred for Cap Anson's Chicago Colts in the 1880s, winning two batting titles and helping the Colts to five pennants in seven seasons. The fans nearly rioted when the Colts sold him to the Boston team for the then-amazing sum of $10,000 in 1887, but Anson had taken his fill of Kelly's wild behavior. Anson once hired a private detective to tail Kelly, and the gumshoe reported that Kelly was in a bar at three in the morning, drinking lemonade.

Anson confronted Kelly with the detective's report. "That was straight whiskey!" Kelly exploded. "I never drank lemonade at that hour in my life!"

Another hard-drinking Chicago Colt was Ned Williamson, the shortstop. Williamson belted 27 home runs in 1884, a total that stood as a major league record until Babe Ruth hit 29 in 1919. Williamson, like Kelly, was a major thorn in Cap Anson's side, but the shortstop anchored the Chicago infield for 12 seasons.

One day, a drunken Williamson and an equally inebriated teammate, center fielder Billy Sunday, sat with a few other Colts on a curb after a wild bender. A bandwagon rolled by, and the musicians played hymns that Sunday recognized from his childhood. Sunday stood and addressed his teammates. "Goodbye, boys," said the future evangelist. "I am done with this way of life." Sunday never took another drink, but Williamson and the others merely shrugged and walked into another bar.

Bobby Mathews, Mike Kelly, and Ned Williamson had two things in common. They were all heavy drinkers, and none lived to see the turn of the century. By 1898 all three were dead, Mathews at age 46 and the other two at age 36.

Perhaps the most tragic story of all belonged to one of baseball's most feared sluggers. Ed Delahanty, a Cleveland native, is still the only man to have won a batting title in both the National and American Leagues. He batted over .400 three times for the Phillies, winning a title with a mark of .410 in 1899, then jumped to the new American League and led the circuit with a .376 mark for Washington in 1902.

Delahanty, too, was a prodigious drinker, and in July of 1903 he was put off a train at Niagara Falls, New York, for disorderly behavior. No one knows exactly what happened next, but it appears that the drunken Delahanty ran after the train across a railroad bridge and somehow fell off the bridge into the Niagara River. He was swept to his death over the falls at the age of 36.

Through the decades, baseball, as well as society, developed a great deal of tolerance for drinkers and their escapades. Paul Waner, the Pittsburgh Pirate hitting star of the 1920s and 1930s, once counseled his fellow players that when they were hung over and seeing three baseballs come out of the pitcher's hand, they should swing at the middle one. Mickey Mantle, who received a transplant to replace his cirrhosis-scarred liver before he died in 1995, once went to the plate as a pinch-hitter while suffering the effects of the previous night's bender. Mantle could barely see through his bloodshot eyes, but he smashed a home run and tottered around the bases. The fans cheered wildly. "They'll never know," mumbled the Yankee star to his teammates, "just how difficult that was."

Bill Veeck, the former owner of the Cleveland Indians, St. Louis Browns, and Chicago White Sox, neatly summed up the prevailing attitude about alcoholism in baseball. Veeck related that his father, William Veeck, the president of the Chicago Cubs in the 1920s, employed many legendary drinking men like Hall of Famers Rabbit Maranville, Hack Wilson, and Grover Cleveland Alexander. "If a player is ready to play when he puts on his uniform," the elder Veeck told his son, "and if he doesn't bring any adverse publicity to the club, it's none of our business what he does away from the park."[3]

Two of the elder Veeck's three Chicago Cub stars drank themselves into early graves. Hack Wilson, who held the National League record for home runs in a season until Mark McGwire broke it in 1998, died of alcohol-related liver disease at the age of 48. The former slugger earned one of baseball's highest salaries during the Depression, but at the time of his death he was so destitute that the National League paid for his funeral. Grover Cleveland Alexander, one of baseball's greatest pitchers, drank himself out of the major leagues by 1930. He wound up performing in a flea circus in New York's Times Square, telling stories of his baseball career to earn enough money for a few drinks. Alexander died in 1950, alone in a rooming house in Nebraska, of alcohol-induced liver failure.

The Cleveland Spiders released Louis Sockalexis, not because he drank, but because he displayed the effects of alcohol on the field and brought negative publicity to the team. His major league career was finished, and it remained to be seen if the remainder of Sock's life would follow the same course as many of baseball's most celebrated and tragic drinking men.

12. "A Sorrowful Spectacle..."

One man was not yet ready to give up on Louis Sockalexis.

Bald Billy Barnie was one of baseball's greatest 19th century entrepreneurs. Born in 1853, Barnie played briefly in the early 1870s as a good-field, no-hit catcher. His lifetime batting average stood at a less than mediocre .171, but Barnie soon found that his talent lay in promoting the game, rather than playing in it. In January of 1875 Barnie organized a baseball game in Brooklyn played on ice, which his team won by a score of 20–7. Ice baseball never caught on, but Bald Billy wasn't discouraged and plowed ahead with more plans and schemes.

By 1886, Barnie managed the Baltimore Orioles, a mediocre American Association team that moved into the National League in 1891. Barnie didn't move with it, as a result of a falling-out with the team's main owners, but Bald Billy gave the Orioles one important part of the future Baltimore pennant winners. Barnie signed a scatter-armed teen-aged third baseman named John McGraw, who eventually became the leadoff batter and captain of the legendary Orioles of the 1890s.

After his Baltimore sojourn, Barnie bounced to Washington, then Louisville, and finally to Brooklyn, where he was fired as manager in 1898 after another falling-out with his bosses. While managing Brooklyn in 1897, Barnie saw firsthand how Louis Sockalexis energized the crowds with his play and his charisma. Barnie also noticed that 17,000 fans filled the Brooklyn ballpark on Memorial Day 1897 to see the sensational Indian. Bald Billy, always accessible to the print media, lavishly praised the Penobscot's ability in the *Sporting News* that week and mentally filed Sock's name away for future reference.

He tried to put together a new circuit, called the Union League, with teams based in New York and New England, for the 1899 season. Barnie, with his usual optimism, announced that his league would become another major league and compete with the National League. Barnie's circuit never came to fruition, but in early 1899, Billy Barnie bought his way back into baseball, as manager of the new Hartford franchise in the eight-team Eastern League.

Barnie made a significant investment to fix up the downtrodden Hartford ballpark and then set out to sign players to make the team competitive. Despite the new manager's efforts, the Hartford nine got off to a poor start in 1899 with a rash of injuries to key players, and by mid–May the team had fallen all the way to seventh place. What's more, the attendance was poor in Hartford, and Billy Barnie cast about for ways to increase the fan support and improve the team's performance on the field. The recent release of Sockalexis by the Cleveland Spiders appeared to provide the answer to both of Barnie's problems.

Billy Barnie was nothing if not optimistic. Perhaps he believed that Sockalexis needed to get away from Cleveland to stop drinking, and perhaps he thought that familiar New England surroundings would help Sock regain his past stardom. Whatever the reasons, within days of Sock's release from jail in Cleveland, the Indian found himself on a train to Hartford for one more chance in organized baseball.

The Eastern League of 1899 was comprised of two teams in Canada (Montreal and Toronto), two in New York State (Syracuse and Rochester), and four in New England (Providence, Worcester, Springfield, and Hartford). The level of play was considered to be one step below the National League, sharing that distinction with the Western (soon to be the American) League. In those days, minor league operators made money by developing players and selling their contracts to higher leagues, and if Sock could reclaim his stardom in Hartford, Barnie would reap the rewards at the end of the season by selling his services back to a team in the National League.

The entrepreneurial Barnie welcomed Sockalexis with open arms, apparently hoping for a replay of the excitement the Indian brought to Cleveland in early 1897. He also hoped that Sock would hit well enough to add a charge to his weak-hitting lineup. Since the beginning of the season, Hartford batters had failed to produce at the plate. "Our left and center fielders," said Hartford's "Special Correspondent" to *The Sporting News*, "do not get to first base often enough to become familiar with the relative location of the other bases."[4]

Barnie had not decided on a nickname for his new team, but now the manager proudly informed the local reporters that the team would henceforth be called the Indians and that the talented but troubled Sockalexis would overcome his problems and lift the team in the standings. The publicity gained from the signing of Sockalexis seemed to have an effect, as Hartford's largest crowd of the season showed up for the Indian's first home game. Hartford defeated the Worcester Farmers by a 4–3 score, though Sock went 0 for 4 at the plate.

Sock struggled with the bat in his first week at Hartford, but he fielded passably and threw well. Sadly, though, Sock's speed was gone, and his added weight slowed him down on the field and the bases. Sockalexis belted a triple in his second game for Hartford, but his batting average hovered at the .200 mark. Barnie, having few other options with his injury-riddled team, kept his fingers crossed for Sock to start producing at the plate.

The Hartford team began winning after Sock joined the club, taking two out of three at Worcester and three out of four at Providence before returning to Hartford for 17 games at home. They started the long home stand by beating Providence three games in a row, all by identical 4–3 scores, and by early June Hartford moved all the way up to fourth place with a 27–27 record.

Unfortunately, Sock quickly reverted to his old habits. Not only did he stop hitting, but his fielding fell by the wayside after only a few games. He began committing errors as he had done in Cleveland, and many balls that fell safely in Sock's outfield territory could not be counted as errors because the Indian was too slow (or too inattentive) to reach them. At the bat, Sock put together a string of 0 for 4 and 1 for 5 days, and almost all of his hits were weak singles. The only positive attribute Sock retained was his powerful throwing arm, but his speed on the bases and his power at the bat were long gone. Sockalexis was only 27 years old, but he played like a man 20 years older.

Billy Barnie, who signed Sockalexis for his Hartford team after the Penobscot was released by Cleveland. (Library of Congress)

The Indian did show a few occasional flashes of his old form. He played his best two games in a Hartford uniform just before Memorial Day, going 2 for 3 in a 7–3 win over Rochester on May 23 and 2 for 4 with a triple in a 7–2 win over Syracuse the next day. Unfortunately, Sock's streak did not last. He went hitless in eight trips to the plate in the next two games and went 0 for 9 in two more losses on June 1 and 2. Sock hit three singles in a 4–3 win on June 10 before a season-high crowd of 2,500 in Hartford but went hitless in his next three outings. Also, according to the *Sporting News*, "his fielding for the past week has been below the amateur standard."[5]

By mid–June it was painfully obvious that Sock's drinking, which seemed under control for a few weeks, was worse than ever. "After all his promises of reform," harrumphed *The Sporting News*, "he has not recently taken care of himself nights, and consequently during the day he has been too lazy and slow for use. Sox certainly had a splendid opportunity here [in Hartford] and threw it away." Sock's poor play and the mounting injuries dropped Barnie's team down the standings again, and after three straight home losses to Worcester, the Hartford club reclaimed seventh place.

On June 17, Sockalexis made an embarrassing error, dropping an easy fly ball in a 4–3 loss against the last-place Syracuse Stars before a large Saturday crowd. The home fans booed mercilessly, and even the most optimistic manager now had to accept that the Indian's day was long past. Barnie reluctantly admitted defeat and released Sockalexis following the game.

In all, Sock batted .222 for the Hartford Indians in 26 games, though the *Spalding Guide* for 1900 gives Sock's average as .198 in 24 games. He managed to belt only three extra base hits in his 99 trips to the plate. He also fielded at a poor .918 percentage, which would have been much worse if mental lapses in the outfield counted as errors. *The Sporting News* summed up Sock's three-week stay in Hartford:

> No man ever appeared here who received so much applause when nothing had been done to deserve it as the Indian[,] yet the encouragement did him no good. It seemed to have the opposite effect, and the people became disgusted with a man who wants to do nothing but pose before an audience. He will now have time to reduce the swelling in his head and think it all over; and it is hoped that he may profit by the experience.[6]

Sporting Life agreed with that assessment. "The red man's days as a ball player are drawing rapidly to a close," wrote correspondent Tim O'Keeffe, "unless there is a decided improvement in his work. He did little or nothing while he was here to warrant his holding a job in a State league team, and he acted as though the effort to go to and from his position in left field caused him a heap of pain."[7]

The Hartford club, which kept the name "Indians" for the remainder of the season, rallied briefly after Sockalexis left. They began a new charge up the standings but sank a few weeks later and finished the season in sixth place, five games under the .500 mark and fifteen and a half games behind pennant-winning Rochester.[8]

Amazingly, the baseball career of Louis Sockalexis was not yet finished. He drank himself out of two leagues, but another lower league managed to give the troubled Indian another chance.

The Connecticut State League began its inaugural season in 1899, placing teams in the six largest cities (besides Hartford) in the state of Connecticut. The franchises were assembled with the backing of several well-known baseball personalities of the time. Tim Murnane, the respected

Boston player-turned-sportswriter, helped organize the new circuit and served as its first president. The league played in Class F, organized baseball's lowest classification, but before long it gained acceptance as one of the best-run minor leagues in the nation. The new circuit also designated a trophy, the Nutmeg Cup, for its pennant-winning team.

"Orator Jim" O'Rourke, the voluble former New York Giant outfield star, owned and managed the Bridgeport team, which he called the Bridgeport Orators, and also served as secretary of the league. Another former Giant, Roger Connor, played first base for his hometown Waterbury Rough Riders and served as manager of the team as well. Connor, who held the major league career record for home runs before Babe Ruth broke it in 1921, owned part of the Waterbury team and, at the age of 42, led the league in batting in the early part of the season.

The six teams in the circuit, unofficially dubbed the "Nutmeg League," were always looking for players. The Bristol Bellmakers, battling for the pennant, acquired a pitcher and an outfielder on loan from Billy Barnie's Hartford team in late June, and then manager John Gunshannon signed Louis Sockalexis almost immediately following his release by Hartford. Once again, someone must have believed that Louis would someday, somehow, quit drinking and return to his rookie form. Within a few days of Sock's release by Hartford, he was playing left field for the Bristol ballclub.

About three weeks later, Sock was released by Bristol and picked up by Roger Connor's Waterbury Rough Riders club. Neither *The Sporting News* nor *Sporting Life* mentioned why Bristol let the Indian go, but it appears that the teams of the league may have had an arrangement whereby clubs would loan players to each other on a temporary basis. Sockalexis was only one of many players who changed uniforms in the Connecticut State League that year.

In Connecticut, at an admittedly much lower level of competition, Louis played better baseball. He managed to stay out of trouble in Waterbury, and by September *Sporting Life* praised the Penobscot's performance in the field. "The work of Louis Sockalexis with the Waterbury team," stated the magazine, "has been of late about as fine as that of any fielder in the league."[9] Waterbury, stuck at the .500 mark when Louis joined the team, played excellent ball the rest of the way and challenged for the pennant, eventually finishing second in the league with a 52–43 record, four games behind the pennant-winning New Haven Blues.

The league statistics say that Louis batted a credible .320, the second-best average on the Waterbury team next to manager Connor's league-leading .392 mark. Sockalexis tallied 85 hits and 35 runs scored in 61 games, and the *Reach Guide* for 1900 gave the Penobscot credit for 14 doubles, five

triples, and one home run, which computes to a slugging percentage of .421. His defensive work must have been atrocious, notwithstanding the praise of *Sporting Life*, because his fielding percentage of .808 reveals that he erred on almost one of every five chances. The once-speedy Sock stole only four bases. However, Connor was pleased with the Indian's play, and the Waterbury Rough Riders included Sockalexis on its reserve list for the 1900 season.

Unfortunately, something happened to Louis during the winter months of late 1899 and early 1900. He was nowhere to be found when the spring of 1900 rolled around, and the Waterbury team played the season without him.

Where was Sockalexis? The 28-year-old ballplayer was living as a vagrant, sleeping in parks and abandoned buildings and, apparently, begging for money with which to buy liquor. It is not known how or why the Penobscot fell so spectacularly off the wagon once again, but the former baseball star spent the early months of 1900 tramping from one city to the next in a haze. He may have hitched rides in boxcars, begged rides from strangers, or simply walked from town to town. No one knows how Louis supported his alcohol habit; he may have played ball, performed odd jobs, or panhandled for money in those lost months on the road.

On August 24, 1900, Sockalexis was given a 30-day jail sentence in Holyoke, Massachusetts. "Louis Sockalexis, the once famous National League baseball player, appeared in court this morning on a charge of vagrancy and was given 30 days in the county jail," said a news item in the Holyoke paper. "He was arrested last night by Patrolman Greany, who found him sleeping in a tumble-down barn in Ward One. At the police station Sockalexis presented a sorry appearance. His clothing indicated that it had been worn for weeks without change. His hair was unkempt, his face gaunt and bristly with several weeks growth of beard, and his shoes so badly broken that his toes were protruding.

"In court this morning he attributed his downfall to firewater. He said, 'they like me on the baseball field, and I liked firewater'.... For the last year or so, Sockalexis has been a hanger-on around the cheap saloons in Hartford and other New England cities."[10] Sock served his 30 days then disappeared again.

On October 17, 24 days after his release from the Holyoke jail, Sockalexis was arrested in Pittsburgh as a vagrant. He was "brought up before Magistrate Kirby, and was a sorrowful spectacle ... suffering from an

Opposite: Waterbury Rough Riders manager and star slugger Roger Connor. He was major league baseball's premier home run hitter before Babe Ruth. (Author's collection)

extreme case of nerves."[11] The paper didn't report what sentence Louis received from the magistrate, but it is probable that the ex-ballplayer served another 30 days or so in the slammer.

Sometime in 1901, Louis Sockalexis returned to the Penobscot reservation on Indian Island. He was nearing his 30th birthday and was ready to put his life back in order after three solid years of abusing his body with drink. He was no longer the great athlete he had once been, but Sock decided to give baseball one more try. In early 1902 he tried out for, and won, a place on the Lowell baseball team in the rejuvenated New England League. Somehow it seemed fitting that he would return to the league in which he played one game in 1895 before he began his Cleveland career. Managed by Fred Lake, a former Boston Beaneaters catcher against whom Louis had played in 1897, the Lowell Tigers finished in sixth place in the 1902 season with a 52–59 record.

In Lowell, Sockalexis played in all but six of the team's scheduled games, batting a passable .288, but he still experienced problems in the field. The 30-year-old former major league star committed 29 errors in the outfield, and his .800 fielding percentage was one of the very worst in all of organized ball that year. Nevertheless, he lasted the entire season for Lowell, and it appeared that his drinking days were finally behind him. He didn't return to Lowell for 1903, preferring to stay closer to his home in Maine, but at least Louis cemented a moderately successful return to the professional ranks.

Louis played for Bangor in the Maine League in 1903. Since the Maine League was not a part of organized baseball at the time, no statistics for that league exist today, and almost nothing is known about the Indian's performance. After the 1903 season, Sockalexis never again participated in the ranks of organized baseball. He returned to the reservation on Indian Island and spent the rest of his life among his Penobscot tribesmen.

When the public discovered in mid–1897 that Louis Sockalexis had been suspended for alcohol abuse, one of the oldest racial myths about Native Americans gained new currency. Many people believed then, as some still do today, that Indians are racially susceptible to intoxication and drunkenness. Many people subscribe to the idea that the Native American is constitutionally unable to handle liquor and becomes drunker in a shorter amount of time than the white man does. This is called the "firewater myth" or the "drunken Indian myth" and is soundly rejected by most modern researchers.

No Native American tribes distilled alcohol before the Europeans arrived on the North American continent, save for some Southwestern tribes who concocted alcoholic beverages from fermented cactus. However, when

Sockalexis with the Lowell (Massachusetts) Tigers, 1902. (National Baseball Hall of Fame Library, Cooperstown, NY)

the whites arrived they brought the knowledge of distillery and fermentation with them and introduced the Indians to alcohol. No one knows if the name "firewater" came from the Indians or the whites, but before long barrels and bottles of rum and whiskey were being used as bartering objects in treaties between the colonists and the tribes.

The American colonists consumed large quantities of alcohol, and the Indians soon followed their example. Before long, alcohol abuse became a source of severe social disruption to the tribes, which were already decimated by disease and warfare. The problem was so acute that several Indian leaders began a temperance movement in the late 1700s and insisted that treaties with the whites include a ban on sales of alcohol to their tribesmen.

There was a great deal of alcoholism among white settlers during the 1700s as well, but when Indians caused disruptions they were looked upon as "savages" who could not "hold their liquor." As the Native Americans lost their land and found themselves forced to live on barren reservations, alcoholism became more pervasive among many of the tribes. They gained an undeserved reputation as "drunken Indians" when any ethnic group treated in such a way would also fall prey to crime, violence, and alcoholism.

Few researchers today believe that Indians are more prone to alcoholism than any other race of people. Alcohol use and abuse varies widely among Native American populations and appears to be more closely linked to poverty and hopelessness than to racial identification. Native Americans, from Louis Sockalexis' day to the present, have suffered from economic hardships and disadvantages, and these probably are responsible for the higher rate of Indian alcohol abuse than merely racial factors.

However, the long-standing assumption that the Indian "cannot handle firewater" unfortunately lives on. Some people point to statistics that show that chronic liver disease, often induced by alcohol abuse, is the fourth-highest cause of death among Native Americans (and only the sixth-highest cause in the rest of the population). Fetal alcohol syndrome, too, occurs with greater frequency among Indians than among non–Indian people. Other researchers make the opposing point that the rates of alcohol use and abuse vary widely among North American tribes and that poverty and a lack of education also play a part in high rates of alcoholism in many ethnic communities.

Many researchers have grappled with the questions raised by the phenomenon of Indian alcoholism. One leading researcher, Dr. Amir Rezvani of the University of North Carolina, describes the phenomenon this way:

> The American Indian population comprises many abstainers and many heavy drinkers, but relatively few moderate drinkers. Among Native Americans who drink, there are significantly fewer infrequent, light and moderate drinkers, and over twice the rate of heavy drinkers. The stereotypic "Indian" pattern of alcohol abuse includes relatively rapid drinking over a prolonged period of time, as drunkenness as the aim. This drunkenness has an aspect of "time out" from cultural rules, so that the drinker may behave in ways that ordinary be considered taboo by the community.[12]

The pattern described above seems to fit the drinking profile of Louis Sockalexis. He was a young man from a reservation suddenly thrust into a highly charged environment in the largest cities of the nation surrounded by the "sports" of Cleveland and other cities. The predominant white culture, 100 years ago, put a premium on drinking as a social activity, and buying a drink for someone was a socially acceptable way of being hospitable to a new acquaintance. Buying a baseball player a drink was also a way for a fan to congratulate the athlete for a job well done or a game well played. Sockalexis, Cleveland's newest star, was invited to receive many more drinks than he could handle, and he did not have the social confidence to turn anyone down.

Sockalexis was 25 years old at the start of the 1897 season, but he was not particularly mature. He had behaved well in the strict environment of Holy Cross but had failed miserably in the less restrictive atmosphere at Notre Dame. He then joined the Cleveland team, where manager Pat Tebeau ran the loosest ship in baseball. The Cleveland team had no curfews or bed checks on the road, and the tales of wild behavior on the part of Cleveland players are so numerous that it appears that such antics were expected of Spider players. It is apparent that Louis Sockalexis was the kind of young man who needed a highly structured and controlled environment, which neither Notre Dame nor Cleveland supplied, in which to thrive.

Perhaps Sockalexis drank because he enjoyed the attention he received from the fans, but perhaps he did so as a reaction to the difficulty of living as an Indian in a white-dominated society. He tried his best to fit into the white world, but he was an intelligent and somewhat educated individual and did not mesh well with his two-fisted, hard-driving teammates. Sockalexis, unlike so many of his fellow Spiders, did not curse the umpires, throw bats at hecklers in the stands, or beat up newspaper reporters. Sock was a likable young man, but his teammates left him alone with his admirers most of the time, in Cleveland and on the road.

Sockalexis was not really part of the Indian world, either. He had removed himself from life on the reservation, having left Indian Island in his early teen-aged years, and by the time he was in his early 20s his personality had undergone a transformation. He was no longer the stoic Penobscot, but, as *Sporting Life* put it, Louis was "for all intents and purposes, a down east Yankee" adopting the personal attributes and habits of the whites around him. By 1897 Sockalexis had almost completely separated himself from his former home in Maine, and he returned to the reservation only infrequently to visit his sister and other family members. He no longer lived there, and the rootless Penobscot found himself emotionally homeless.

One must also consider that the fans around the National League showered baseball's first Native American with insults and razzing that few onlookers had ever before witnessed. The fans, in Cleveland and elsewhere, looked upon Sockalexis as a mere novelty, like a performer in the Wild West shows of the period. He was one of the greatest athletes in America, but the fans threw firecrackers at him, taunted him about "firewater," and shouted out demeaning and ethnically offensive insults from the bleacher seats.

Some athletes perform better under pressure, but Sockalexis experienced pressure unlike any that any other major league player had to endure up to that time. If Sock's drinking was a "time out," as suggested above, it might have served as a respite from the stress Sock felt in performing a balancing act between the white and the Indian worlds. It also may have functioned as an escape from the mockery and harassment he encountered in the big cities of the nation.

CHAPTER 13

Bender, Meyers, and Andrew Sockalexis

> *The dominant fact in each Indian athlete's success, aside from his natural physical adaptability to the sport, has been a coolness under fire that amounts almost to carelessness, a quick, unerring eye, craftiness, cool, calculating judgment under the most trying conditions, an absolute lack of nervous system, and a stoicism that refuses to be shaken in the most crucial situations.*
> — Sporting Life, *attempting to explain the success of Native Americans in athletics, 1922*[1]

In the years immediately following the turn of the century, Louis Sockalexis made his home on Indian Island, within the boundaries of the reservation that he had left so many years before. His sister Alice still lived there, and Louis often visited her, her husband, and their children. Francis Sockalexis, Louis' father and the former tribal governor, died on Indian Island in February of 1905, and from that day forward Alice was the only surviving member of his immediate family.

Francis always wanted Louis to serve his people, and Louis found a way to do so. He taught baseball to the young Penobscot men on Indian Island, showing them how he threw, batted, and ran. In addition, Louis advised his younger tribesmen on the challenges and pitfalls of a professional baseball career. He spoke with pride in later years about the five Penobscot athletes who learned his lessons well enough to earn positions in the New England League.

Sockalexis no longer played baseball, though many sources indicate that he gave occasional exhibitions in throwing and hitting for the entertainment of his tribesmen. He could no longer effectively run, but his arm never lost its power, and he could still heave the baseball a long way.

However, he wanted to be connected to the game in an organized way, and so he pursued a career as an umpire.

The semiprofessional leagues of early 20th century Maine were nearly as wild and undisciplined as the National League had been in the 1890s. Factory owners, land barons, and mill owners controlled the teams, and they encouraged intense rivalries between their ballclubs, which usually involved heavy wagering and a generous amount of community pride. The leagues found it difficult to keep good umpires under contract, since unpopular decisions were often answered with brawls and near-rioting. Sometimes, the fans reacted to an umpire's ruling by swarming the field and chasing the unlucky arbiter into the Maine woods.

Sockalexis used his popularity and celebrity status to head off problems. Sources say that the former major league star became one of the best umpires in the Maine leagues, becoming known for his fairness and command. He had observed many other umpires in the National League, both good and bad, and Sockalexis knew the rules as well as any of them. "He is an absolute authority on rules," stated a Philadelphia newspaper, "and has hundreds of decisions by big league umpires in his head."[2] Many fans came out to the games, not to cheer for either team, but to see the great Sockalexis umpire.

Sock's first appearance as an umpire in the Northern Maine League, which included teams in Houlton, Caribou, Presque Isle, and Millinocket, came in a game between the league's two bitterest rivals. Sockalexis, according to a clipping on file at the National Baseball Hall of Fame, won the confidence of both teams for his "unerring judgment on balls and strikes, and was on top of every base play. He insisted on major league discipline of players saying little but when he had occasion to express himself to a player he let fly a single bolt of sarcasm that was as withering as it was unanswerable.... Even the most rabid kicker is somewhat at a loss as how to 'get to' Sockalexis."[3]

Some contemporary reports (probably exaggerated) stated that Sockalexis could have become a major league umpire. However, he had finally come to terms with life on the reservation and had no desire to leave Indian Island. Louis was comfortable in the Indian world once again, and he settled down with his Penobscot tribesmen, in an embrace that would last for the rest of his life.

In the two decades that followed Louis Sockalexis' departure from the major leagues, three other Native Americans, "Chief" Bender, "Chief" Meyers, and Jim Thorpe, made their mark on the national game.

Charles Albert Bender, called "Chief" as were almost all Native American ballplayers, was born on a reservation in Minnesota in 1883. The product of a Chippewa mother and a German father, Bender spent much of his childhood bouncing back and forth between the worlds of the whites and the Indians. Like Louis Sockalexis, Charles Bender found no enjoyment in life on the reservation, and at age 13 he left Minnesota and enrolled at Carlisle Indian School in Pennsylvania.

Carlisle was closer to a technical high school than a modern-day college, but the school gained renown in the 1890s through its participation in intercollegiate athletics. Carlisle regularly defeated the nation's most powerful college teams in football and track, as well as other sports. Charles Bender, an intelligent and temperate young man who performed well in the classroom, became one of Carlisle's premier athletes. He starred in baseball, football, and track, all of which were coached by the legendary Glenn "Pop" Warner. When Bender graduated from Carlisle at age 19, he briefly attended Dickinson College in Carlisle, Pennsylvania, and then entered professional baseball. By 1903 Bender was pitching in the American League for the Philadelphia Athletics.

Bender, like Sockalexis, was "jollied" about his Indian ancestry but refused to make an issue of it. He smiled and doffed his cap at the war whoops that emanated from the stands, though a sportswriter once quoted him as suggesting that the fans should "go back to their home countries" if they didn't like the way he pitched. Bender happily accommodated autograph-seeking fans, but he always signed his name as Charley Bender, never as Chief. Philadelphia manager Connie Mack, who called him Albert, called Bender his best clutch pitcher. "If I had all the men I've ever handled," said Mack, "and they were in their prime and there was one game I wanted to win above all others—Albert would be my man. He was my greatest 'money pitcher.'"[4]

Bender, a curve ball specialist, pitched for Mack until 1914. He won 210 games in his major league career and six more in World Series play. He did not possess the stamina of Eddie Plank or other Philadelphia starting pitchers, and he started 20 to 27 games in most seasons when Mack's other hurlers started 35 to 40 games. However, Bender found a niche as both a starter and a reliever. He turned in a sensational 23–5 record in 1910 and led the league in winning percentage three times. In 1913 Bender helped the A's to their third pennant in four seasons, with a win-loss mark of 21–10 and a then-record 13 saves, and followed that in 1914 with a 17–3 log and seven shutouts.

Bender was businesslike on the mound and quickly became one of the most important players on the pennant-winning Philadelphia teams. He was a fine athlete, who often played the field or pinch-hit when needed, as well as an expert coach and sign-stealer. Like Sockalexis, Bender excelled at many sports. He was an expert billiards player, golfer, and swimmer. At one time, Bender was rated as one of the top ten trap shooters in the country, touring the nation in shooting exhibitions for the Winchester Arms Company. After leaving the major leagues, he worked in a shipyard during World War I and then became the pitcher-manager of the minor league team in Richmond, Virginia. At the age of 36, Bender turned in a sensational 29–2 record and led his team to a second-place finish.

Fortunately, Charles Bender managed to steer clear of the temptations that ruined Sockalexis' career. The levelheaded Bender, who spent part of his childhood with a Quaker family, adopted their moderate habits and led a stable family life. When his playing days were ended, he remained in baseball as a manager, coach, and scout for the rest of his life. He was elected to the Baseball Hall of Fame in 1953, a year before his death at the age of 71.

While Charles Bender pitched in the American League, John Tortes Meyers caught in the National. Meyers' mother was a California Mission Indian of the Cahuilla band, and his father was a Union Army veteran who died when John was seven years old. John Meyers grew up near Riverside, California, and in 1905 entered Dartmouth College in New Hampshire on a special Indian scholarship. Meyers dropped out of Dartmouth in 1906 due to the illness of his mother and entered professional ball to help support his family. His first manager, at Harrisburg in the Tri-State League, was former Boston Beaneaters star and future Hall of Famer Billy Hamilton.

He later joined the New York Giants, and when catcher Roger Bresnahan left the team after the 1908 season, Meyers became the starting catcher for John McGraw's ballclub. Meyers caught almost all the games that star pitcher Christy Mathewson pitched from 1909 to 1916, and in that period the Giants won three consecutive pennants from 1911 to 1913. Meyers finished third in the Most Valuable Player balloting in 1912, when he batted .358, and fifth in 1913 when he batted .312 for the Giants. Traded to the Brooklyn Dodgers in 1916, he helped that team to the pennant that same year. By the time he left the major leagues in 1918, he had compiled a lifetime average of .291 and played in four World Series.

Meyers, who greatly disliked the nickname "Chief," was not an all-time great player but a steady, reliable performer, moderate in his personal habits and respected by players on other teams as well as his own. He, too, avoided the pitfalls that plagued Sockalexis, although Meyers expressed bitterness in later life for the abuse he received from the fans. Meyers was managing a minor league team in 1920 when his hometown fans viciously booed him. The proud Meyers became disgusted, resigned his position, and never returned to the game. He became a police chief for the Mission Indian agency in his native California, where he died in 1971 at the age of 91.

Meyers returned to the public eye later in life with the publication of Lawrence Ritter's *The Glory of Their Times*, an oral history of baseball's early days. Ritter interviewed many old-time baseball stars who were still living in the 1960s, and John Meyers was one of them. In their discussion, Meyers mentioned the treatment he received from the older players when he entered professional baseball 60 years before. "I don't like to say this," said Meyers, "but in those days, when I was young, I was considered a foreigner. I didn't belong. I was an Indian."[5]

The third of these Native American baseball stars, Jim Thorpe, was both the greatest athlete and the least accomplished baseball player of the three. Thorpe, whose Indian name was "Bright Path," was born on a Sac and Fox reservation in Oklahoma in 1888 and became a legendary athlete at Carlisle Indian School a few years after Charles Bender played there. Under the direction of Pop Warner, Thorpe became one of the greatest college football and track stars in the country. He cemented his status as the greatest athlete in the world when he won both the decathlon and the pentathlon at the 1912 Olympic Games in Stockholm, Sweden. Thorpe is still the only man ever to win Olympic gold medals in both events.

Thorpe lost his medals and trophies when it was revealed that he had earned a small amount of money playing semiprofessional baseball during his summer vacations from Carlisle. Many observers believed that a white athlete would not have been so harshly treated, but Thorpe was obliged to return his two gold medals to the International Olympic Committee. In the meantime, New York Giants manager John McGraw was not deterred by the controversy surrounding the great Indian athlete. In 1913 McGraw signed Thorpe to a contract to play the outfield for the Giants. Some say that McGraw, cognizant of the publicity value of the famous Indian athlete and its positive effect on ticket sales in New York, signed Thorpe sight unseen, without so much as a tryout.

Thorpe played in the National League for six seasons and was a teammate of John Meyers for the first three of those campaigns. Although Thorpe was one of the strongest and fastest men in the game, his athletic ability did not translate into baseball stardom. He was a right-handed batter who had trouble hitting a curve ball from a right-handed pitcher, just as Louis Sockalexis was a left-handed batter who could not handle the curves from lefties. Despite his great speed, he stole only 29 bases in his career. Thorpe, regarded as the world's greatest athlete, was only a part-time player for the Giants, Reds, and Braves, and in his first two seasons for the Giants he batted .143 and .194. He hit .327 in a part-time role in

Three Indian athletes who excelled at the 1912 Olympic Games. From left: Andrew Sockalexis, Jim Thorpe, and Lewis Tewanima. (Author's collection)

1919, but his career batting average of .252 fell far below the .313 mark of Louis Sockalexis and the .291 average of John Meyers. The 1919 campaign was his last in the major leagues, though he continued to play minor league ball into the early 1920s.

Thorpe played professional football each fall after the close of the baseball season. In 1920 his team, the Canton Bulldogs, joined the new National Football League, and the Indian served as ceremonial president of the new league in its first season. Thorpe, by now in his 30s, became the biggest star of the new league as a running back, punter, and place kicker. He played in the NFL until he was 41 years old and in 1963 was elected as a charter member of the Pro Football Hall of Fame in Canton, Ohio. In 1950, three years before Thorpe died at age 64, the Associated Press named him the nation's greatest athlete of the first half of the twentieth century. In 1983, the International Olympic Committee reinstated Thorpe as the decathlon and pentathlon champion of the 1912 Olympic Games and returned his medals and trophies to his family.

Strangely enough, there have been no comparable Native American baseball stars since Bender, Meyers, and Thorpe, and Bender remains the only Native American in the Baseball Hall of Fame. Several Hall of Fame players claim partial Indian ancestry, including former Pittsburgh slugger Willie Stargell (part Seminole) and Cincinnati catching great Johnny Bench (part Cherokee), but there have been no self-identified Native American stars in the game since Thorpe played his last season for the Boston Braves in 1919.

Native Americans did not disappear completely from the game. Moses Yellowhorse, also called "Chief," was the first full-blooded Indian major leaguer. A Pawnee from Oklahoma who pitched for the Pittsburgh Pirates in 1921 and 1922, Yellowhorse compiled a win-loss record of 8–4 in 38 games. Gene Locklear, a Lumbee Indian from North Carolina, batted .274 as a National League outfielder from 1973 to 1977. New York Yankee pitching star Allie Reynolds was only one-fourth Indian, but identified closely with that part of his heritage. His teammates and fans called him "Superchief" for his Cree ancestry.

One part–Indian star, Rudy York, was a half–Cherokee from a poor community who found success in the baseball world, but fought his own battle with the bottle. In 1954, six years after he left the major leagues, York wrote, along with Furman Bisher, an article in *Sport* magazine titled "A Letter to My Son." It contained advice for his teen-age son, who wanted to become a ballplayer:

> Son, there are some things about my baseball career I'm proud of, and some I'm so not proud of. They gave me a reputation for boozing, but

you can take any story about ballplayers and drinking with several grains of salt. Sure, I had my drink when I wanted it. So did a lot of other fellows. But remember this—I'm an Indian, so that means you're part Indian, too. All an Indian's got to do is be seen drinking a beer and he's drunk. Any time an Indian puts on a baseball uniform he becomes about six times as much of a character as any other player.

We're Cherokee and I'm proud of it. I've run into some pretty good Indian ballplayers in my time, like Bob and Roy Johnson, Ben Tincup, Chief Bender and Elon Hogsett, who was my roommate at Detroit for a while.... You've noticed that scar on my left cheek. I got it when I was nine years old. I ran into an axe my brother was swinging while he chopped wood. It makes me look tough, I guess, so I didn't have to do much to be called a bad boy.

But son, leave that liquor alone. I can tell you it never helped anybody, and if I had to do it over again that's one thing I'd use a lot less. I'd have had a couple more years of baseball left in me if I'd stayed away from it.[6]

York, who played first base for pennant-winning teams in Detroit in 1940 and in Boston in 1946, made good salaries in his heyday but never managed to save any of it. By 1949, when he was 36 years old, he was batting .233 for Union City in the Kitty League. When he related his story to Furman Bisher, he was broke and earning $150 a month as a firefighter for the Georgia Forestry Commission. Fortunately, his story ended on a happier note than that of Louis Sockalexis. York re-entered the baseball world and returned to the majors as a coach for the Red Sox for several years before he died in 1970. He was the only part–Indian coach in the game at the time.

Many people believed, in those less-enlightened times, that Native Americans were naturally gifted athletes by virtue of their race but that they lacked certain mental attributes that would improve them and carry them farther. Although it may be difficult to understand how anyone could be disappointed in the athletic accomplishments of a Jim Thorpe or a Charles Bender, some writers suggested that the Native American lacked the inner drive of white athletes. As *Sporting Life* put it in 1922:

> What the Indian athlete is he always was. His is not a story of gradual development, arriving at his highest efficiency through a steadfast application of industry and careful training that improved on his past efforts such as the paleface athlete, but rather a story of gradual retrogression from the point of highest efficiency that marked his natural ability.
>
> Hook up the natural adaptability of the Indian with the industry, mental poise, and capacity for overcoming difficulty of his paleface brother and you would probably give the world an athlete that would

boost marks so high that the present existing athlete couldn't see them with the aid of the Lick telescope.[7]

Sporting Life reported the widely held belief that the Native American athlete was "handicapped by ... racial traits of character." It seems more likely that the Native American athlete, from the Civil War–era marathon runner Lewis "Deerfoot" Bennett to the present day, is more handicapped by the attitudes and expectations of the prevailing majority culture. Still, no matter what the explanation may be, the fact remains that the Native American presence in major league baseball began with Louis Sockalexis in 1897 and, with few exceptions, ended with Jim Thorpe only 22 years later. Since the retirement in 1917 of Charles Bender, no self-identified Native American baseball player has put together a Hall of Fame–caliber career, though a case for enshrinement might be made for the part–Indian Allie Reynolds.[8]

In the last few years of Louis Sockalexis' life, his second cousin Andrew Sockalexis made a name for himself in athletics and emerged from the shadow of his more famous tribesman and relative. Andrew Sockalexis, born on the Penobscot reservation in 1894, attended the Carlisle Indian School in Pennsylvania and ran track every bit as enthusiastically as Louis had played baseball a decade before. Andrew, a lithe six-footer, emerged from Carlisle as one of the best long distance runners in the United States, and soon became the star of the North Dorchester Athletic Club in Massachusetts. He was only 17 years old when he ran his first major race, the 1911 Boston Marathon, in which he turned in a credible 17th-place finish.

The Penobscot were renowned for their running prowess, but Andrew Sockalexis rapidly became the most famous runner in the tribe's long history. Legends and stories grew up around his feats, just as the athletic achievements of Louis Sockalexis had become the stuff of legend a generation before. One story relates how two other native runners challenged Andrew to a one-mile race on Indian Island in which Andrew would be required to run the entire mile and his challengers would cover half the distance apiece. Despite the handicap, Andrew won the race hands down.

Andrew Sockalexis made national headlines in the 1912 Boston Marathon, one of the most exciting marathon races ever. The young Penobscot zoomed out to the front of the pack on a rainy day, splashing through the mud and slush as one challenger after another tired and fell back. The Indian grabbed the lead at the 22-mile marker, but Michael Ryan, running for the Irish-American Athletic Club of New York, stayed on Andrew's heels. Unfortunately, the Penobscot spent his energy too quickly. Ryan passed Sockalexis two miles from the finish line and held off the Indian's

Charles Albert (Chief) Bender, the only recognized Native American player in the Baseball Hall of Fame. (Author's collection)

furious charge, winning with a new Boston Marathon record time of 2 hours, 21 minutes, and 18 seconds. Andrew Sockalexis finished in second place, 34 seconds behind the winner, for the best finish by a native runner since Tom Longboat, an Onandaga Indian from Ontario, won the race in 1907.[9]

On the strength of this performance, Andrew Sockalexis earned a spot on the United States national team and sailed to Sweden to compete in the 1912 Olympic Games. On July 14, 1912, a brutally hot, humid day in Stockholm, the 18-year-old Sockalexis faced off against 63 of the greatest marathon runners in the world. The young Penobscot acquitted himself well. He overcame the elements and finished fourth on a day that saw a Portuguese runner collapse and die of sunstroke after the race. Sockalexis fell out of medal contention early but took fourth position in the late stages of the race, withstanding a stiff challenge from the Canadian star Jimmy Duffy. Sockalexis crossed the finish line in fourth place, beating the charging Duffy by 11 seconds. When Andrew returned to Maine, the city of Bangor celebrated his performance with a parade in his honor, one of the biggest ever held in that city.

Two other Native Americans from Carlisle performed spectacularly well in Stockholm. Lewis Tewanima, a Hopi, won a silver medal in the 10,000-meter race. Carlisle's most famous export, Jim Thorpe of the Sac and Fox tribe, won gold medals in both the decathlon and the pentathlon and was proclaimed "the greatest athlete in the world" by the King of Sweden.

Sockalexis entered the Boston Marathon again in 1913 and provided the spectators with another exciting contest. The Penobscot decided to keep his strength in reserve this time, so he held back as a Swedish-born Minnesotan, Fritz Carlson, took the lead and pulled away from Sockalexis and the rest of the field. Sockalexis held back too long, the Swede got too far ahead, and Sockalexis found himself four minutes behind Carlson with only four miles to go. The Penobscot made one of his patented charges to the finish, but he finished second again, one minute and 58 seconds behind Carlson.

No one knew it at the time, but Andrew Sockalexis was suffering from a serious lung infection when he ran that day in Boston. He had tried to overcome it with training, running as many as 50 miles in a single day and ending his daily workouts by paddling a canoe for an hour or more. His lungs grew weaker, but he decided to ignore the searing pain in his chest and run the race anyway.

After the 1913 Boston Marathon, Andrew married his longtime girlfriend Pauline Shea and listed his profession as "athlete and maker of baskets" on his marriage license. Needing to make money to support his new wife, Andrew Sockalexis turned professional and ran races for money in New England and Canada for the next year or so. However, his lungs weakened even further, and soon he was diagnosed with tuberculosis and forced to retire from the sport. Andrew returned to the reservation but became unable to work. His friends from the North Dorchester Athletic Club raised money to help Sockalexis pay his medical bills. In 1919 Andrew Sockalexis, the second-greatest athlete ever produced by the Penobscot Indian Nation, died in Old Town at the age of 25.

Andrew Sockalexis was buried in the cemetery on Indian Island, and his deeds were quickly forgotten. His memory languished in obscurity for more than six decades, until another great runner from Maine, Joan Benoit Samuelson, won the gold medal in the first women's marathon at the 1984 Olympic Games in Los Angeles. Samuelson's win brought new attention to the story of Andrew Sockalexis, Maine's first great Olympic athlete. Today, the Penobscot Indian Nation honors Andrew's memory with a five-kilometer race, the Andrew Sockalexis Memorial 5K Run, contested each August on Indian Island.

CHAPTER 14

The End of the Line

> *He had many years of success and fortune ahead of him, but the firewater proved too much; he lost his skill, fell from one league to another, sinking every season, and at last went home to the Island to emerge no more.*
> —*Baseball Digest,* March 1914

In the early part of the 20th century, Louis Sockalexis, formerly one of baseball's most famous stars, was engaged in manual labor in and around the Penobscot reservation where he grew up. During the fall and winter months he worked as a logger, cutting down massive pine trees and hauling them to the river for delivery downstream. Spring and summer found Sockalexis piloting a ferryboat from Indian Island to Old Town and back again. There was no bridge connecting Indian Island to the mainland at the time, and the ferry was the only mode of transportation across the Penobscot River, save for Indians who paddled their own canoes. As a Cleveland paper put it, "Few passed over on the little ferry and fewer still knew that the great, melancholy, full-chested Indian was the once-famous Sockalexis."[1]

Sockalexis umpired baseball games in the summer, but his playing days were long past. However, he still appeared in the newspapers every now and then. A Philadelphia reporter ventured to Old Town and filed an article in August of 1912 titled "Sockalexis, Fat and Lazy, Takes Ease in His Tribe." Sockalexis, according to the writer, "is just a fat, smokey, lazy Indian, who lives with the tribe on the Indian land reservation of the Penobscots which is virtually a part of the city of Old Town, being but a few rods from the mainland. He doesn't work much because he doesn't have to. He couldn't die in poverty because poverty is unknown in the tribe. While there are times when the people are not living in luxury, the tribe is, in a way, the ward of the state of Maine, and has tribal income enough to provide for the necessities.

14. The End of the Line

"As for being a ghost he weighs close to 200 pounds. When he takes a notion he picks up odd jobs and sometimes works or a ferryman, but for the most part spends his time reading the sporting news of which he never misses a line, and devours every big league game with great gusto."[2]

Sockalexis, according to the article, had lost none of his volubility. Sock was "always ready to fan with anyone," stated the writer. "...A peculiar trait of his is that he is about the only Indian ever known here [in Old Town] that would talk. Four words is the extent of the conversation of the average Penobscot, but Sockalexis has a great command of language and plenty of it."[3]

Indeed, Louis still followed major league baseball, avidly devouring newspapers and magazines that his ferry passengers saved for him. Louis paid especially close attention to men he had played with and against more than a decade before. In the fall of 1912 Sockalexis gave a newspaper interview in which he was asked if he still followed the game. Sockalexis replied, "I was just reading the account of the double-header between Jimmy Callahan's White Sox and the Boston team. I was sorry to see Jimmy lose the two games. I remember when I played with Holy Cross we met the Springfield team. At that time Callahan was the pitcher for Springfield, and my real start in baseball was in that game. I made three two-baggers off his delivery, and Jimmy was some pitcher, too. I like to read the baseball news. This is about all I do in my idle moments. I think I will try to go to the World's Series if the Giants and Red Sox win the pennant."[4]

The Giants and Red Sox met in the Series that year (the Red Sox won in eight games), but it is not known if Louis witnessed any of the contests at Fenway Park. He was not healthy; though he no longer drank, he suffered from attacks of rheumatism and caught colds and fevers easily. His dissipations of 10 years before had compromised his physical well-being, and he was no longer able to play baseball for recreation on the reservation. Sockalexis looked and felt like a man much older than his 41 years.

In the fall of 1913, Sockalexis went into the Maine woods as part of a logging crew, whose task was to fell large trees with two-handled saws and haul them to the river. It is possible that the weakened Sockalexis attempted more of this demanding work than he could safely handle. Louis, chatting amiably with his fellow loggers, was engaged in cutting down a massive pine tree in the forest near Burlington, Maine, on December 24, 1913, when he suffered chest pains. He sat down, turned pale, and almost immediately stopped breathing. In a few short moments, Louis Sockalexis was dead of heart failure at the age of 42. His fellow loggers brought his body back to Old Town for burial, and some say that the morticians found a wad of newspaper clippings from the 1897 season inside his jacket.

Three of the four Cleveland papers paid little attention to the passing of the player who caused a sensation only 16 years before. The *Cleveland Press* didn't even report his death, and the *News* gave it only one paragraph. The *Plain Dealer* printed only a short item from the wire services, but the *Leader* published a melodramatic article that recounted many of the myths surrounding the late Penobscot. The *Leader* reporter spiced his copy with an emotional account, probably apocryphal, of Sock's last hours. According to the article, about one hour before he died, the former baseball hero said to his companions, "Like me, the sun has gone home to rest. Soon will come the shadows."[5]

The *Leader* also went to the trouble of seeking out Sock's old teammate Ed McKean for an interview. McKean, nearly 50-years-old and retired from baseball since 1899, recalled the great Penobscot. "He was a wild bird," said the old shortstop. "He couldn't lose his taste for firewater. His periodical departures became such a habit [that] he finally slipped out of the majors.

"He had more natural ability," said McKean, "than any player I have ever seen, past or present."[6]

Baseball Magazine was less charitable about the memory of the great Indian ballplayer. In the same issue in which the magazine reported Sockalexis' death, this item appeared:

> Whenever a big league ball player drops out through long association with John Barleycorn there are always numerous paragraphs about how the "lure of the big cities" and "the associations of the bright lights" led the poor fellow to temptation. And it's 100 to 1 if you could go back upon the trail that every one of these unlucky athletes was a rounder in his little village or a leader of the joy gang at college. They had their thirsts long before they ever wore a uniform — but you can't make it half as pathetic if you tell the honest truth about them. Anybody who "falls" in the big league usually got tripped up before he signed his first contract.[7]

Louis Sockalexis, the most famous Penobscot Indian of all, was laid to rest in the reservation cemetery. His tribesmen marked the grave with a wooden cross with his name and birth and death dates burned into it. The grave remained undisturbed, neglected and overgrown by weeds, until 1934. In that year, an Old Town newspaper editor named Thomas Wadsworth spotted the neglected grave and began a campaign to raise funds for a proper marker. Contributors included Maine residents, Holy Cross alumni, members of the Penobscot tribe, and Cleveland baseball fans who wished to honor the first Cleveland Indian.

In the summer of 1934, the Penobscot Nation hosted a ceremony to

The grave of Louis Sockalexis in Old Town, Maine. (Author's collection)

unveil the new marble grave marker. A brass plate was affixed to the front of the stone and featured a baseball on the top with two crossed bats beneath. Underneath the crossed bats reads the inscription, "In memory of Louis Sockalexis whose athletic achievements at Holy Cross College and later with the Cleveland major league baseball team won for him national fame. Born Oct. 24, 1871—Died Dec. 24, 1913. Erected by his friends."

Even in death, Louis inspired one more piece of poetry. John A. Fitz-Gerald, who attended Holy Cross during Sock's career as a Crusader, wrote a poem for the occasion:

> Louis, we've gathered here today
> Tribesmen and sportsmen, we all attend
> To mark the spot where your mortal clay
> Came to our universal end.
> More than one epitaph's been penned
> Of the player that never had a peer
> But here's your deed, from an old-time friend:
> "He was loyal, and brave, and his heart sincere."[8]

Shortly after the death of Louis Sockalexis, a reporter ventured to the Irish district of St. Louis for a meeting with the man who brought Sock to the major leagues.

Pat Tebeau, Sock's former Cleveland manager, had been absent from the game of baseball for 13 years. Tebeau managed the St. Louis Perfectos to a disappointing fifth-place finish in 1899 and returned to the job in 1900 after the team dropped its arrogant nickname and became known as the Cardinals. Tebeau immediately ran into conflict, because St. Louis team owner Frank Robison decided to improve his club by importing several of the stars from the defunct Baltimore Orioles and mixing them in with their sworn enemies from Cleveland. Tebeau appointed John McGraw as captain of the new Cardinals, a move that angered ex–Spiders like Jesse Burkett, who wanted their Cleveland teammate Jack O'Connor to have the job.

This new St. Louis aggregation may have possessed more talent than any other National League team, but they also led the league in squabbling and arguments. McGraw, who didn't want to play for the Cardinals, performed no favors for Tebeau that season. He and catcher Wilbert Robinson contrived to have themselves thrown out of games so they could spend their afternoons at the racetrack, conveniently located across the street from the St. Louis ballpark. After months of clubhouse turmoil between the former Spiders and former Orioles, Tebeau resigned his managerial position in August 1900. He never returned to the game; instead, he opened a bar on the St. Louis waterfront and spent the next few years there, in the Kerry Patch neighborhood from which he came.

Tebeau reflected on the late Indian ballplayer. "No other player, to my knowledge, ever sacrificed as much on the altar of his appetite as did the red man," lamented Tebeau. The old manager then recounted the events of July 3–4, 1897, when Sockalexis injured his leg in a drunken fall from a second-story window. Sock's drinking bout that weekend started the Indian on the road that ended with the demise of his career in the major leagues.

Close-up of Louis Sockalexis' grave marker. (Author's collection)

"Poor Sox!" exclaimed the former manager. "He could have made $10,000 or $12,000 a year. He was worth that for playing alone, but also as an attraction. Nobody ever heard of Cy Young, Bobby Wallace, or any of us when Sox was with us."[9]

Tebeau himself was no stranger to bad times. He was not yet 50 years old in 1913, but he suffered from poor health. His financial fortunes ebbed and flowed, and a few years later he became seriously ill. Estranged from his wife and unable to tolerate the constant pain, Pat Tebeau died in 1918 by his own hand.

Some of Sock's other teammates lived shortened lives as well. Cupid Childs died of Bright's disease in 1912 at age 45, and Harry Blake, who beat Sockalexis out for a starting position in 1898, was only 45 when he perished in a fire in 1919. Ed McKean, who made his home in Cleveland after his playing days ended, died of kidney failure in 1919 at 55. Jimmy McAleer spent a long and productive career in baseball as a manager and part-owner of the Senators and Red Sox, but in 1931 he developed cancer and killed himself with a handgun, as Pat Tebeau had done 13 years earlier.

Perhaps most tragic of all was Mike Powers, the man who brought Sock to Holy Cross and then to Notre Dame. Powers, who played for Notre

Dame for only one year, graduated from that institution and joined the Louisville Colonels in the National League. He then jumped to the new American League and wound up with Connie Mack's Philadelphia Athletics in 1901. Powers served as a backup catcher for nine seasons, while attending medical school in the off-season and eventually earning his medical degree. On April 12, 1909, Powers slammed into a railing while chasing a pop-up in the Athletics' home opener. He suffered a serious abdominal injury and two weeks later died of gangrene at age 38.[10]

However, the three Spiders who earned election to the Baseball Hall of Fame (Cy Young, Jesse Burkett, and Bobby Wallace) all lived into their 80s. Burkett returned to his adopted hometown of Worcester, managed the local minor league team, and coached baseball from 1917 to 1920 at Sock's old school, the College of the Holy Cross. The Crab remained as irascible as ever. In 1921 he accepted a position as coach for the New York Giants, managed by his old Oriole nemesis, John McGraw. The Giants won the pennant that year, but the New York players refused to vote the difficult Burkett a share of the World Series money. McGraw paid a full share to Burkett out of his own pocket.

Wallace, who played in the major leagues until 1918, became a popular figure in St. Louis as a respected manager, coach, and scout and stayed employed in baseball until his death in 1960. Young spent his days farming in rural Ohio, taking in games every now and then at Cleveland's Municipal Stadium and appearing regularly at old-timers events in Cleveland and other major league cities.

Late in life, Cy Young offered a reporter five rules for success on the baseball field. He didn't mention anyone in particular, but Young was a tee-totaling Methodist, and he had seen too many of his teammates lose their careers because of their taste for alcohol. He warned young ballplayers to stay away from the strong stuff. "Let liquor severely alone," advised the old pitcher. "A player should try to get along without any stimulants at all. Water, pure cool water is good enough for any man."

The legend of Sockalexis grew to immense proportions after his death.

Hugh Jennings, star shortstop for the Baltimore Orioles in the 1890s, played against Louis Sockalexis many times in the 1897 and 1898 seasons. Jennings then became one of baseball's greatest managers, winning three pennants as manager of the Detroit Tigers from 1907 to 1920. He left baseball in 1926 and wrote a series of syndicated newspaper articles about his long career, titled "Rounding Third," in which he declared that Sockalexis "had the most brilliant career of any man who ever played the game. At no time has a player crowded so many remarkable accomplishments into such a short period. He should have been the greatest player of all time—

greater than Cobb, Wagner, Lajoie, Hornsby, and any of the other men who made history for the game of baseball."[11]

Jennings is also responsible for one of the most enduring myths concerning the Penobscot. In one article, Jennings recounted a mythical tale of Sock's grand-slam homer winning a game against Chicago, after which the Indian supposedly celebrated by tasting alcohol for the first time. "After the game," wrote Jennings, "the Spiders celebrated their unusual victory. Sockalexis, the hero of the occasion, was finally induced to take a drink by the jibes of his more or less intoxicated teammates. It was the first taste he ever had of liquor, and he liked it. He liked the effects even better, and from that time on Sockalexis was a slave to whiskey."[12] Though demonstrably false, this tale has become an enduring part of the lore of the great Indian ballplayer.

Another respected baseball figure to sing the Indian's praises was Holy Cross graduate Bill Carrigan, who managed the Boston Red Sox to World Series victories in 1915 and 1916. Carrigan was born in Maine in 1883, so he must have been a teenager when he saw Sockalexis, but in the 1930s he said, "I don't remember ever seeing a quicker bat or a stronger arm. Among the moderns, possibly the one player worthy of a comparison is that young man, Joe DiMaggio. He has a trace of Sockalexis's stuff, but I don't believe he can run or throw with the Indian."[13]

Andy Coakley was a fine major league pitcher from 1902 to 1911. He played for the Holy Cross Crusaders in 1901 and 1902 when their coach was John Pappalau, who was Sock's teammate at Holy Cross and, briefly, in Cleveland. Pappalau kept the memory of Sock's talent alive for his Crusader players, and it is unclear whether Coakley actually saw the Indian play or not. Nonetheless, Coakley, who later became the baseball coach at Columbia University, remarked that Sockalexis belonged on any "all time, all-star baseball team. He had a gorgeous left-hand swing. He hit the ball as far as Babe Ruth, and like Ruth, was a left-handed batter. He was faster than Ty Cobb and as good a base runner. He was as good a fielder as Tris Speaker, and he threw with the speed of Bob Meusel."[14]

Perhaps the most succinct assessment of Sock's talent came from Ed Barrow, the long-time baseball executive and member of the Baseball Hall of Fame. Barrow discovered the greatest shortstop of all time, Honus Wagner, and later managed Babe Ruth with the Boston Red Sox. Barrow was the man who moved Ruth from the pitching mound to right field, where the Babe became the most famous home run hitter in the history of the game.

Nevertheless, Barrow opined one day to a group of sportswriters that Louis Sockalexis, not Babe Ruth, was the greatest outfielder of all time. The writers couldn't believe that Barrow was serious and asked him if he really meant what he said. "Of course I mean it," replied Barrow. "Sockalexis was the greatest outfielder in history—the best hitter, the best thrower, the best fielder, and also the best drinker, and he was the most brilliant gardener."[15]

How talented was Sockalexis, and would he have earned a place in the Baseball Hall of Fame if he had managed to control his drinking? Since he played more than 100 years ago, long before the existence of motion pictures and television, it is difficult today to evaluate his performance. Baseball historians rate players through the voluminous statistical records of the game, but Sockalexis played at peak efficiency for only the first three months of the 1897 season and participated in only 94 major league games in all. The legend of Sockalexis became inflated by the very lack of information about him. As Detroit sportswriter H. G. Salsinger once wrote, "While they [later writers] spoke in superlatives when his name was mentioned, none seemed to know a great deal about him ... the legends about him are often vague and contradictory. At times he appears to have been a mythical, rather than a legendary, figure."[16]

Baseball research, as a popular pastime, began in earnest in the 1970s with the foundation of SABR, the Society for American Baseball Research. One of the most prominent baseball researchers is Bill James, who developed landmark statistical formulae in a series of books called the *Bill James Baseball Abstract*. In his 1987 edition of the *Abstract*, James spent a great deal of effort in classifying rookies based upon their age. James pointed out that younger rookies have a much greater chance to develop into stars than older ones, and that even a difference of a year or two is critical in determining the future development and production of ballplayers.

Applying this analysis to Louis Sockalexis, we find that the Penobscot was 25 years old when he began playing for Cleveland in April 1897. Most of the greatest players of the game entered the majors at age 22 or less, and all-stars such as Ty Cobb, Babe Ruth, Bob Feller, and others were teenagers when they began their major league careers. The number of all-time greats of the game who entered the majors at age 25 or older can be counted on the fingers of one hand, with the exception of pitchers.

James stated his findings as follows:

> In trying to figure out how much a player will develop, probably the one most important factor to consider, other than the player's ability, is his age. Every year is important. If you compare a 20-year-old rookie and a 25-year-old rookie of exactly the same ability, the 20-year-old rookie can be expected to play almost three times as many games in the major leagues. A 20-year-old rookie can be expected to hit about four times as many home runs as a 25-year-old rookie of the same ability.[17]

14. The End of the Line

Some of the 20-year-old rookies covered in James' study were Willie Mays, Johnny Bench, and Hank Aaron, all of whom reached the Baseball Hall of Fame, as well as other fine players like Joe Torre and Buddy Bell. Similar rookie seasons of 25-year-olds belonged to players such as Randy Jackson, Gene Green, Clint Courtney, and Sam Bowens, none of whom played in the majors for very long. If Sockalexis had developed from a 25-year-old rookie into a Hall of Famer, he would have been a rare exception to the general rule as espoused by James.

Some of the Indian's admirers like to compare him to two other great players who burst upon the major league scene in 1897. Napoleon Lajoie and Honus Wagner entered the National League for Philadelphia and Louisville respectively, and they concluded their careers with over 6,900 hits and 11 batting titles between them. Some insist that Sockalexis, who gained more newspaper attention for his feats in 1897 than Lajoie and Wagner combined, could have equaled or surpassed these two great players. However, Lajoie was 22 years old and Wagner 23 at the start of the 1897 campaign.[18] The 25-year-old Sockalexis, by James' reasoning, would probably not have blossomed into another Lajoie or Wagner, because he got a later start on his career.

Lajoie, like Sockalexis, battled alcohol problems in 1897, though it appears that Lajoie quickly changed his behavior before his career was threatened by his drinking. The statistical record shows that Lajoie finished the 1897 season far ahead of Sockalexis, despite being three years younger.

	Sockalexis	Lajoie
Games	66	127
At-Bats	278	545
Runs	43	107
Hits	94	197
Doubles	9	40
Triples	8	23
Home Runs	3	9
Runs Batted In	42	127
Stolen Bases	16	20
Batting Average	.338	.361
On-Base Average	.385	.392
Slugging Average	.460	.569

Lajoie developed into a consistent .300 hitter with power, and within three years people already considered him to be the best player in the game. It stands to reason that Sock, due to his later start, would never have equaled Lajoie as a batter even if he had managed to conquer his alcoholism. Sock also may not have caught up to Wagner, who played in 61 games (five fewer than Sockalexis) in 1897, matching Sock's .338 average and stealing more bases. Three years later, Wagner won the first of his National League record eight batting titles.

James illustrated his thesis by examining the winners of the Rookie of the Year award, which was instituted in 1947. Players such as Willie Mays (1951), Pete Rose (1963), Johnny Bench (1968) and Tom Seaver (1967) won the award at age 22 or less, while 25-years-or-older winners included Ron Kittle (1983), Chris Sabo (1988), Pat Listach (1992) and Bob Hamelin (1994). Several of the younger rookie award winners since 1950 have earned places in the Baseball Hall of Fame, but none of the older ones have managed the feat. The best of the older Rookies of the Year (since 1950) was probably Lou Piniella, who was 26 when he won the prize in 1969. Piniella put together a solid career but is more likely to make the Hall of Fame as a manager rather than as a player.

There are exceptions to every rule, as James readily admitted. Another hard-hitting Cleveland outfielder, Earl Averill, arrived in the majors at age 27 in 1929 and battered American League pitchers for the next 12 seasons. By the time Averill left the game, he held the Cleveland career record for homers and owned a lifetime batting average of .318, enough to earn future enshrinement in the Hall of Fame. If Sockalexis had managed to remain sober, he could as easily been another Earl Averill as another Bob Hamelin.

However, Sockalexis may also have become another Walt Dropo. This muscular 27-year-old first baseman was Rookie of the Year in 1950 when he belted 34 homers with 144 runs batted in and a .322 average for the Red Sox. Unfortunately, Dropo never scaled these heights again in the remaining 11 seasons of his career. He never hit 30 homers, drove in 100 runs, or batted .300 ever again, and in 1952 he returned to the minor leagues for a short time.

Dropo, a big, slow-footed, right-handed hitter with an unexceptional throwing arm, did not physically resemble Sockalexis, so perhaps this comparison is not apt. Averill, a left-handed batter, was closer to Sock; he had good speed and a good throwing arm, though he was not as physically talented as Sockalexis. Averill batted .331 as a rookie with 13 stolen bases, while Sockalexis hit .338 with 16 steals.

Perhaps the best comparison to Louis Sockalexis is the first Rookie of the Year award winner, Jackie Robinson, who was the most notable exception to James' rule. Born in 1919, Robinson joined the Brooklyn Dodgers in 1947 at the age of 28 and immediately became one of the dominant stars of the National League. Unlike other older rookie stars, Robinson maintained and improved his production, winning the batting title and Most Valuable Player award in 1949 and leading the Dodgers to six pennants in the 10 seasons he played for them. He was elected to the Baseball Hall of Fame in 1962, his first year of eligibility.

Sockalexis resembles Robinson in many ways. Each man was the first recognized member of his race to play in the major leagues. Each took abuse from fans and opponents, though Robinson undoubtedly received a great deal more. Like Sockalexis, Robinson was an all-around athlete, excelling in basketball, football, and track as well as baseball.[19] Robinson, like Sockalexis, was a college man, having attended the University of California at Los Angeles. They were the same height, both muscular in build, and each was recognized as intelligent, though Robinson was probably better educated than Sockalexis. Sadly, both men died young; Robinson died of diabetes in 1972 at the age of 53.

The main difference between the two men lies in the way they handled the highly charged environment of major league baseball. Jackie Robinson, unlike Sock, was a fiery competitor who seemed to thrive on pressure. He was one of those rare players who performed better under stress, and the more the fans and opponents abused him, the better he played. Before Robinson joined the Dodgers, he had gained a great deal of maturity during his World War II service, where he fought for his rights against the racism that proliferated in the Army. Sockalexis experienced racism as well, but he was not a fighter. Perhaps his personality type explains why he crumbled under the strain and turned to drink after only three months, leaving his career and life in a shambles.

In one respect, the stories of Louis Sockalexis and Jackie Robinson ended differently. The 1997 season marked the 50th anniversary of Robinson's entrance into the major leagues and the lifting of the barrier against African American players. The same season also marked the 100th anniversary of the arrival of Sockalexis with the Cleveland Spiders. Robinson's feats were celebrated throughout the nation in 1997, with the issuance of a postage stamp in his honor and, most impressive of all, the retirement of Robinson's uniform number by all 30 major league teams. Sockalexis, on the other hand, was virtually ignored that year. Only a handful of newspapers bothered to mention the centennial of the first recognized Native American in the majors and the first minority player of any kind in the National League.

If Sock had been able to handle the pressure, his career would probably have lasted much longer, and his final statistics might have resembled those of Jackie Robinson. If the Penobscot had managed to conquer his drinking problem, he might have, despite his late start in the major leagues, wound up with a plaque on the wall in the Baseball Hall of Fame.

CHAPTER 15

Louis Sockalexis and the Cleveland Indians

> *In the fraction of one season, which was the extent of his major league appearances, [Sockalexis] attracted more fame, more adventure, and more publicity in his work than most moderns do in a lifetime. He changed the name of a big league ball team before he wore its uniform.*
> —Holy Cross Alumni Magazine, 1951[1]

In January 1915, a little more than a year after the death of Louis Sockalexis, Cleveland baseball was on the ropes once again.

The Spiders folded after their disastrous 1899 campaign, but in 1900 the new American League placed one of its eight teams in Cleveland, with Sockalexis' ex-teammate Jimmy McAleer as manager. The new owner, a millionaire real estate and coal magnate named Charles Somers, wanted to distance his new team from the memory of the National League Spiders, so in 1901 he named them the Blues.[2] This designation stirred no great excitement, so in 1902 the Cleveland team became the Broncos. Again, the new name was tepidly received, so most writers and fans usually referred to the team as the Clevelands.

In mid–1902, Charles Somers managed to acquire one of the biggest stars in baseball for his team. Napoleon Lajoie, who like Sockalexis burst upon the National League as a star in 1897, jumped to the American League's Philadelphia Athletics in 1901 and batted an incredible .422 with 145 runs batted in. However, Lajoie's old team, the National League Phillies, obtained a court order preventing him from playing for the Athletics in 1902, so Somers stepped in and obtained the hard-hitting infielder for his Cleveland nine.

With this deal, Somers gave his new team a legitimate star, as well as a new identity. The outgoing, personable Lajoie quickly became as popular with the Cleveland fans as the Penobscot from Maine had been, though Lajoie's stardom lasted a longer time. So popular was this French-Canadian second baseman that soon after his arrival in 1902, the writers started calling the team the Naps in his honor, much as they renamed the Spiders the Indians when Sockalexis joined.

The well-respected Lajoie became the playing manager of the team in 1905 and drove the Naps up the standings with future Hall of Fame members Elmer Flick, Addie Joss, and Lajoie himself leading the charge. The Naps reached their high-water mark in 1908, when they lost the pennant to Detroit by half a game when the Tigers were not required to make up a rainout. Lajoie stepped down as manager in 1909 but continued to play second base for the team that was named for him.

The team began to falter after 1908, though Charles Somers imported new players in an attempt to keep the team in pennant contention. One of the new arrivals was Sockalexis' old Spiders teammate, pitcher Cy Young, whom Somers acquired from the Red Sox in 1909. The 42-year-old Young had, by this time, won more games than any other pitcher in the history of baseball, but he gave the Naps only one good season before fading in 1910. Somers also received one of baseball's best young hitters, Shoeless Joe Jackson, from Philadelphia in a trade. Jackson batted .408 in 1911 and .395 in 1912, but the rest of the team aged quickly, and the Naps fell in the standings under a succession of managers.

By 1914, the Cleveland team had hit rock bottom. The 39-year-old Lajoie slowed down noticeably, batting only .258, and could no longer cover much ground on the infield. Despite the hot bat of Shoeless Joe Jackson, the Naps finished in last place with a 51–102 record. Attendance fell to disastrously low levels, and Somers could no longer afford the $9,000 salary of his aging star. Lajoie's tenure in Cleveland was finished, and in January 1915 Charles Somers reluctantly released his most popular player to his old team, the Athletics.

The Cleveland team could no longer be called the Naps with Lajoie gone to Philadelphia, so Somers asked the Cleveland sportswriters for ideas on a new nickname. He also wanted the writers to choose a new name for his minor league squad, the Bearcats, who played their games in League Park when the Naps were on the road. Some of the local writers solicited suggestions from the public in their columns, and the *Cleveland Press* reported that the fans had sent in 57 different nicknames for consideration.[3]

The *Cleveland Plain Dealer* of January 17, 1915, explained what happened next:

With the going of Nap Lajoie to the Athletics, a new name had to be selected for the Cleveland American league club. President Somers invited the Cleveland baseball writers to make the selection. The title of Indians was their choice, it having been one of the names applied to the old National league club of Cleveland many years ago.

The nickname, however, is but temporarily bestowed, as the club may so conduct itself during the present season as to earn some other cognomen, which may be more appropriate. The choice of a name that would be significant just now was rather difficult with the club itself anchored in last place.

While picking a name for the Cleveland A.L. team, the committee also agreed that the Cleveland A.A. team owned too many names, and that while they were at it, it might be well to agree on just one name for the erstwhile Bearcats. Consequently, the other old nickname of the Cleveland National leaguers was adopted and henceforth all the local papers will call the A.A. club the Spiders.

So there you are — Indians and Spiders.

The name "Indians" recalled the most exciting period of Cleveland baseball — the first few months of 1897, when League Park shook with war whoops and Indian yells when an Indian from Maine lined out hits and made incredible throws. This news report did not establish a direct link to Sockalexis, though the late Penobscot appeared to be indirectly responsible for the new name of the American League club. The excitement of 1897 didn't last long, but in 1915 the older writers on the Cleveland papers well remembered the electricity in League Park 18 years before and hoped that the name "Indians" would rekindle the spark of baseball interest in Cleveland.

The *Plain Dealer*, on January 18, 1915, printed an editorial that tied the memory of Sockalexis to the new name.

> Many years ago there was an Indian named Sockalexis who was the star player of the Cleveland baseball club. As batter, fielder, and base runner he was a marvel. Sockalexis so far outshone his teammates that he naturally came to be regarded as the whole team. The "fans" throughout the country began to call the Clevelanders the "Indians." It was an honorable name, and while it stuck the team made an excellent record.
>
> It has now been decided to revive this name. The Clevelands of 1915 will be the "Indians." There will be no real red Indians on the roster, but the name will recall fine traditions. It is looking backward to a time when Cleveland had one of the most popular teams in the United States. It also serves to revive the memory of a single great player who has been gathered to his fathers in the happy hunting grounds of the Abenakis.

This editorial established a connection between the new Indians nickname and the Penobscot. Whether that connection is direct or not has

15. Louis Sockalexis and the Cleveland Indians

Cartoon from the *Cleveland Plain Dealer*, January 17, 1915, celebrating the selection of "Indians" as the new team nickname. (Author's collection)

been the subject of controversy for many years, but it appears that the "Indians" name is, at the very least, indirectly inspired by the short-lived stardom of Louis Sockalexis. His recent death had put his memory back into the minds of the writers and perhaps made them fondly recall the excitement that he brought to baseball in Cleveland.

There was one other explanation for the new name. The Boston National League club, dubbed the Beaneaters in the 1890s, changed its nickname several times during the 1900–1910 period. When the cellar-dwelling Boston team became the Braves, they pulled off the most amazing pennant charge in baseball history in 1914. Last in the standings on July 4 of that year, the new Braves stampeded to the pennant and swept the Philadelphia Athletics in the World Series that fall. Some of the Cleveland writers opined that a Native American nickname would revitalize the Cleveland team in the same fashion.

It didn't happen all at once. The new Indians got off to a poor start in 1915 and prompted Charles Somers to fire manager Joe Birmingham; this was the fifth managerial change for the team in only six seasons. The ballclub dropped to seventh place and remained there, while fewer fans passed through the turnstiles at League Park than had seen the team the year before. To make matters worse, Cleveland's biggest star, Joe Jackson, actively entertained offers from the rival Federal League, a short-lived competitor to the established American and National circuits. Somers, deeply in debt and fearing the loss of Jackson, traded the popular Shoeless Joe to the Chicago White Sox in August 1915 for three players and $31,500. Less than a year later, the near-bankrupt Somers was forced to sell the Indians.

The new owners quickly came up with another star player when they bought the services of Tris Speaker, baseball's best center fielder, and in 1920 Speaker led the Indians to Cleveland's first major league pennant. The Indians became world champions when they defeated the Brooklyn Dodgers in the World Series that fall.

The name Indians, originally thought to be a temporary appellation, lasted and became an integral part of the team's identity through success (four more pennants and a 1948 World Series title) and failure (a 41-season drought between flags before 1995). Writers and broadcasters referred to the team as the Tribe, for short, and sometimes called them the Sons of Geronimo. The manager was called the Chief, the organization itself was the Wigwam, and fans showed up for games wearing feathers and war paint, pounding tom-toms and emitting Indian yells much like the ones that Sockalexis heard in 1897.

In 1968, in preparations for the observance of professional baseball's centennial, major league teams dug into their histories and focused new attention to their long-forgotten stars. In that year, the Cleveland ballclub included a brief biography of Louis Sockalexis in its media guide. Most Cleveland fans had never heard of Sockalexis prior to 1968, but from that point on, the memory of Sockalexis as the "Original Cleveland Indian" took its place as an important facet of the team's history. A biography of Sockalexis has appeared prominently in the media guide every year since.

However, the team made sure that the life of Sockalexis was sanitized for public consumption. Each year, the biographical sketch in the media guide each year omitted all details of his alcoholism, and his eventual release by the team after a series of embarrassing incidents. In addition, the biography got some of the facts wrong. This bit of information appeared in the team's media guide in 1996:

> After Lajoie was released in 1914 a Cleveland newspaper held a contest to rename the team. The winning entry in the contest was

"Indians." The fan who sent it in explained that it would be a testament to the game's first American Indian. The memory of Louis M. Sockalexis was not forgotten then, and today, 78 years later, he is still remembered.

The Cleveland writers of 1915 solicited fan opinions, but there was never any contest in any of the four major papers in the city in the 11 days between Lajoie's release and the choice of the new name. No mention of Sockalexis turned up in print, not even in the *Cleveland Press* article of January 12, 1915, which listed 57 different suggested nicknames for the team. The editions of January 1915 made it clear that the new team name was chosen by a committee of sportswriters and approved by Charles Somers.

In addition, the media guide misreported Sockalexis' name, since his middle name was Francis, and 78 years back from 1996 was 1918, not 1915. Nevertheless, the team's assertion that the name was chosen by the fans in a newspaper contest, though demonstrably incorrect, lived on for several more years and still appears in most explanations of the Indians nickname. An article by Ithaca College professor Ellen Staurowsky, published in the *Sociology of Sport Journal* in 1998, convincingly debunked the idea that the fans chose the team name and called into question the team's assertion that the name was chosen to "honor" Sockalexis.[4] In 2000, the team finally changed the text in the media guide and removed the part about a newspaper contest; however, the team still celebrates Louis Sockalexis as the "original Cleveland Indian" and as the inspiration for the name "Indians" as applied to the Cleveland ballclub.

The most popular, and controversial, aspect of the team's Indian identification is a grinning character with red skin and large teeth that carries the name Chief Wahoo. In the 1910s and 1920s the team occasionally employed symbolic representations of Indians with feathered headdresses but did very little else in the way of Indian identity. In 1946 noted baseball showman Bill Veeck bought the club. The previous Cleveland team ownership had virtually ignored the value of positive public relations,[5] and Veeck immediately decided to capitalize on the team nickname for publicity purposes.

In 1947, at Veeck's behest, the first cartoon character of the "Chief," designed by a 17-year-old local artist named Walter Goldbach, appeared. Called "the Smiling Indian," this stereotypical orange-skinned, big-nosed, pony-tailed Indian appeared on the team's uniform sleeves in the 1948 world championship season. The Smiling Indian turned up in the team yearbook and game programs, and the team also distributed Smiling Indian patches to young fans, along with coloring books that featured the character.

Veeck sold the team in 1949, and the new owners changed the Smiling Indian's name and appearance. In 1950 Chief Wahoo assumed his present form. His skin is fire-engine red, he wears a huge, buck-toothed grin, and a single feather sticks out from behind his head. In 1951 the grinning Chief took his place inside the "C" on the players' caps, where it remained until 1958. The character also appeared in different places on the uniform through the years, and although the Indians lost many more games than they won in the 1960s, Chief Wahoo became a fondly remembered symbol for the Baby Boomers generation of Cleveland baseball fans.[6]

For many years, fans and sportswriters uncritically enjoyed the Indian identification of their baseball team. When the Indians won, the writers said that the team "scalped the opposition"; when they lost, they were "sent back to the reservation." Players held out from spring training because they wanted "heap big wampum," and a late-inning rally was "an Indian uprising." The team management erected a large teepee behind the outfield fence at Municipal Stadium, though tribes east of the Mississippi did not build teepees, and a huge figure of a batter with Chief Wahoo's head greeted fans as they entered the stadium.

The local newspapers also utilized the caricature of the Chief. In the 1950s, if the Indians won, a picture of a happy Chief Wahoo appeared on the front page of the *Plain Dealer* with a finger upraised. If the team lost, the Chief looked battered, with missing teeth and his feather broken.

Perhaps the most ethnically insensitive moment came in the early 1970s when a Cleveland soft-drink company filmed a television commercial featuring all-star catcher Ray Fosse. In the spot, Fosse, decked out in a headdress and war paint, intoned, "Me Ray Fosse. Me dodging the posse. Me like wampum and me like Big Red." In this simpler time, few people concerned themselves with what later critics would label as "appropriation" of pseudo–Native American imagery for commercial purposes.

The National League Braves, who moved from Milwaukee to Atlanta in 1966, also enjoyed their use of Indian symbols. They erected a teepee in their left field area, inside which was a character named Chief Noc-a-Homa wearing a feathered headdress. When a Braves player hit a home run, Chief Noc-a-Homa emerged from the teepee and performed a dance. With sluggers like Henry Aaron and Eddie Mathews playing for the Braves, the Chief performed his dance quite often in the 1960s and 1970s. The Braves also placed an image of an Indian brave, a "Screaming Mohawk," on their uniform sleeves and put a decorated tomahawk symbol on the shirts of their players.[7] The tomahawk disappeared in the late 1960s but reappeared in 1989 and remains to this day.

The Indians and Braves received a public relations jolt in 1972 when a Native American advocacy group filed a lawsuit concerning their use of Indian symbolism. The American Indian Center of Cleveland, headed by activist Russell Means, sued the two baseball teams, as well as football's Kansas City Chiefs and Washington Redskins, for more than nine million dollars apiece. The suit charged that the use of Chief Wahoo and other "Indian" images created a "mocking and scornful" attitude in the community toward real Native American people. The suit dragged on for several years and eventually went nowhere, but the Indian identification of the Cleveland baseball team came under challenge for the first time.

When Cleveland businessman Nick Mileti bought the team in 1973, he decided to change the image of Chief Wahoo in order to mollify some of the more vocal protesters. Mileti hired Leonard Benner, an artist with a Cleveland graphics firm, to redesign Chief Wahoo. Benner made Wahoo's nose smaller, turned the figure of Wahoo from a left-handed batter (like Sockalexis) to a right-handed one, and made the Chief's body much thinner. He also designed a logo that featured the full body of the character, which made the character's head less prominent. However, the general image of Wahoo was largely unchanged, and many people failed to see much of a difference in the new character.

Over the next few years, the Cleveland Indians toned down their outward identification with pop-cultural Indian images. They removed the teepee from the outfield area, and when they moved into the new Jacobs field in 1994 they did not transport the huge, grinning Chief Wahoo sign from the old stadium to the new one. Many high schools and colleges in this era changed the names of their sports teams from Indian-the med names to non–Indian ones, but the Cleveland team resisted this radical move. However, Chief Wahoo remained popular, and the full face of Wahoo returned to the uniform in 1983. In 1986 the team, at the suggestion of the Cleveland players, placed Chief Wahoo on the players' caps once again.

The Chief Wahoo character became even more popular with the fans when the team finally started winning in the early 1990s. By then, the character had been part of the Cleveland baseball scene for more than 40 years, spanning two or three generations of baseball fans. Rather than change or eliminate the Chief Wahoo character, the Cleveland team embraced it and sought to deflect criticism by invoking the memory of Louis Sockalexis, the "original Cleveland Indian."

The popularity of the character was proven by the boost in sales of Chief Wahoo paraphernalia, especially the team caps, after 1986. When the Indians won two American League pennants and five Central Division titles in the 1990s, the Chief became almost ubiquitous on caps, T-shirts, bumper stickers, and other such souvenirs all over northeastern Ohio. Today, the Indians sell more merchandise than almost every other team in major league baseball, and most of that merchandise is adorned with the grinning image of Chief Wahoo.

Since Louis Sockalexis was established as the "original Cleveland Indian," Chief Wahoo and Sockalexis became linked in the minds of Indian fans. Some assume that Chief Wahoo is, in fact, a representation of Sockalexis himself or was at least inspired by the Penobscot's own facial features. Chief Wahoo is not Louis Sockalexis, but the Chief remains the outward representation of the identification of the ballclub with Native American imagery, for good or ill.

The Braves, for their part, insisted that since they hired a real Native American to portray Chief Noc-a-Homa, they could not be accused of insensitivity. Still, the character disappeared in the 1970s, and the Braves removed the teepee from the outfield area and took the Screaming Mohawk patch off the sleeve of the uniform. At the same time, the Atlanta fans spontaneously adopted a group cheer called the "tomahawk chop," which probably began at Florida State University as a way to cheer the FSU football team, the Seminoles. The popularity of this cheer caused the Braves to embrace the tomahawk as a symbol, much as the Cleveland club embraces Chief Wahoo. Activists were upset in the 1990s when they watched team owner Ted Turner and former President Jimmy Carter doing the tomahawk chop at post season Braves games in Atlanta.

The Braves receive significant criticism for employing the tomahawk chop, much as the Indians do for the continued use of Chief Wahoo. However, both teams make money and sell merchandise by their use of these symbols. The Braves have sold hundreds of thousands of foam-rubber tomahawks, which people wave at games and attach to the radio antennae of their cars so that the tomahawk waves in the breeze, doing the "chop" all by itself in traffic. The Indians, as noted before, have found a veritable gold mine from the sale of items adorned with the visage of Chief Wahoo. Still, they do so in the face of protests; activists demonstrated in Cleveland during the 1995 World Series, in which the Indians and Braves faced each other. Two years later, three protesters were arrested when they burned Chief Wahoo in effigy outside Jacobs Field before another World Series contest.

At the outset of the 21st century, the controversy over Chief Wahoo and the appropriation by sports entities of Indian or pseudo–Indian symbols, such as feathers, war paint, and dancing, shows no signs of abating. Many critics insist that the club's ongoing use of the Wahoo character, though probably not intended to give offense, nevertheless demeans those very people that it claims to honor. "False images of the 'Indian,'" stated writer Laurence Hauptman in 1995, "whether demeaning or not, are usually simplistic and generally classify the great diversity of Native America into a single entity, obscuring the textures as well as the complexities of the past or present, whether because of convenience, economics, or other reasons."[8] Others disagree, and a "Save the Chief" movement has sprung up in Cleveland and attracted media attention.

In December of 2000, the Penobscot Nation weighed in on the Chief Wahoo controversy. The tribal council passed a resolution, supported by tribal Governor Barry Dana, which opposed the team's use of Native American cultural symbols and images. The resolution asked that the Cleveland Indians "recognize, accept and honor the rich legacy of Louis Sockalexis and Native American cultures" and also requested that the ballclub "advocate for the elimination of racist images of Indians" and "strengthen the spirit of tolerance and justice in your community and our country."

The resolution explained that the Penobscot Nation "finds the red-faced American Indian cartoon/mascot, 'Chief Wahoo,' to be an offensive, degrading and racist stereotype that firmly places Indian people in the past, separate from our contemporary cultural experience. This depiction, further, emphasizes a tragic part of our history—focusing on wartime survival while ignoring the strength and beauty of Indian cultures during times of peace."[9]

In these culturally sensitive times, it seems anachronistic that a professional sports entity would prominently display a team-defining symbol that a significant number of people, fans or otherwise, find offensive. While people may disagree over the degree of insensitivity involved, the fact remains that the Cleveland baseball team, which claims to honor Native Americans in general and Louis Sockalexis in particular, does nothing of the sort in its embrace of the Chief Wahoo character. Perhaps it is time, more than 100 years after Sockalexis played in the major leagues, for the team that claims him as its inspiration to rid itself of the outdated, faintly embarrassing visage of Chief Wahoo. The time has come for the Cleveland ballclub to design a new symbol that truly honors the talent of Sockalexis and stirs the pride of all Native Americans.

It's interesting to note that throughout its long history, the Cleveland Indians have produced many young stars who, in imitation of Sockalexis, burn brightly and flame out quickly. Joe Charboneau was the 1980 Rookie of the Year, but back problems ended his career only three years later. Pitcher Herb Score, the 1955 rookie award winner, was struck by a line drive on the mound in 1957, virtually ending his promising career. Shoeless Joe Jackson joined the team in 1910 and batted .375 in five seasons but was traded for economic reasons, while Hal Trosky and Al Rosen saw their paths to the Hall of Fame blocked due to injuries. Ray Fosse was run over by Pete Rose in the 1970 All-Star Game and was never the same afterwards, while Ray Chapman and Addie Joss died young.

Only four years after Sockalexis' memorable 1897 campaign, a new player joined the Cleveland American League team and brought another dash of excitement to town. His name was Ervin (Zaza) Harvey, and he hit the Forest City with a bang. Like Sock, Harvey was a left-handed-hitting outfielder with speed and an excellent throwing arm. His arm was so powerful that he pitched 17 games in the major leagues, in addition to playing the outfield.

Harvey, a 22-year-old Californian, batted .353 in 1901 and stole 15 bases in 45 games, and his numbers were even better than Sock's four years earlier. The city of Cleveland fell in love with Zaza Harvey, but he flamed out as well. In 1902 he retired from baseball due to illness, leaving a lifetime batting average of .332, 19 points higher than the Penobscot's. Unlike Louis Sockalexis, Zaza Harvey is almost totally forgotten today.

Why is Sockalexis remembered a century after his career ended, while Zaza Harvey and so many others are not? Sockalexis was, indeed, an exceptional physical talent, and though many of the tales told about him are exaggerations, they seem to have a basis in fact. Of all the thousands of players in the long history of baseball, few — Jim Thorpe, Jackie Robinson, and perhaps a handful of others — could match the great Penobscot in terms of sheer athletic ability. Despite his incredible physical gifts, Sock's career ended tragically, and after his fall, his feats took on an almost mythical aura. Baseball history, after all, is a form of mythology, with towering heroes like Babe Ruth and Jackie Robinson and tragic figures like Shoeless Joe Jackson and Louis Sockalexis.

In addition, the handsome Sockalexis was an exotic sight in a uniform as baseball's first recognized Native American. Sockalexis arrived in the National League in 1897, 21 years after Little Big Horn and seven years after Wounded Knee, when the Indian was no longer the active enemy of the white man. With the conclusion of the Indian wars, the popular culture was ready to celebrate, rather than fear, the physical prowess of the Native Americans. The success of the Carlisle Indian School football team and the fame of native track stars such as Lewis "Deerfoot" Bennett encouraged the public to embrace the idea of the Indian as a talented athlete, a role that the college-educated Sockalexis was able to fill for a few short months.

However, the main reason that Sockalexis is remembered today seems to be that he arrived in Cleveland at exactly the right time for maximum attention. In the middle of the 1890s, Pat Tebeau molded the Cleveland team into a fighting, battling unit, but the fans did not embrace this image. Sockalexis came when the fans and sportswriters of Cleveland were starved for positive news about their baseball team, and, for three months, he delivered it. Baseball suffered in Cleveland after he left, but Sockalexis gave the struggling team an identity, one that the present American League entry embraces to this day.

CHAPTER 16

Epilogue

> *What a place to live, what a place to die and be buried in! There certainly men would live forever, and laugh at death and the grave.*
> — Henry David Thoreau, visiting the Maine woods in the company of Penobscot guides, 1846

In the years following the death of its most famous member, Louis Sockalexis, the Penobscot Indian Nation has tried its best to adapt to the modern world. In the late 1800s, the encroachment of white settlement and the building of factories along the Penobscot River severely reduced the supply of fish and game upon which the tribe depended. Nonnative commercial fishermen monopolized the area where the Penobscot River empties into the Atlantic, and hunters and sportsmen filled the pine forests where the Penobscot families once lived. Even Katahdin, the "Great Mountain" and spiritual and religious centerpiece of the Penobscot tribe, became "Mount Katahdin" on the maps and became just another tourist attraction, with hotels and knickknack shops springing up around it.

Tribal objections to the pervasive encroachment went unheeded, since the reservations were still considered "enclaves of disenfranchised citizens bereft of any special status" by law, and the Maine Indians did not yet have the right to vote in federal or state elections.[1] In 1906, the huge Milford dam, built in the river a few hundred feet below Indian Island, virtually destroyed the remaining available supply of eel, salmon, and shad.

Robbed of their traditional avenues of earning a living, the tribe turned to the production of handmade items such as canoes, baskets, axe handles, and wooden buckets, but before long other companies found ways to mass-produce such items at a much cheaper price. With few jobs to be found on the reservation, many young Penobscot left Indian Island and moved to Bangor and other cities to find work, while those who remained coped with difficult circumstances. The tribe even seemed to lose its traditional interest in athletics. Since the death of Andrew Sockalexis in 1919, the Penobscot have produced no more nationally recognized athletes.

The conveniences of modern life were slow in coming to Indian Island; there was no running water until 1939 and no electricity until 1940. There was no bridge connecting the reservation to the mainland until 1950. Before then, people crossed the river in their own canoes or on a ferryboat like the one that Louis Sockalexis operated after his baseball career ended. In the winter, the tribe laid down a path of sawdust over the ice to mark the way to the mainland.

The fortunes of the Penobscot tribe changed dramatically in the last half of the 20th century. In the 1950s, a Passamaquoddy Indian named John Peters found a copy of the 1794 treaty that the Maine Indians signed with the federal government. Tribal lawyers discovered that the government failed to live up to the terms spelled out in the document, and they also found that the treaty was never ratified by Congress. This discovery led to a lawsuit, filed by the Penobscot and Passamaquoddy tribes in 1972, which accused the federal government of illegally taking 12.5 million acres from the tribes. The land in question represented the ancient homelands of the two tribes and comprised more than two-thirds of the state of Maine.

This legal battle ended with the passage of the Maine Indian Land Claims Settlement Act, which was approved by Congress and signed by President Jimmy Carter in 1980. By the terms of the settlement, the two tribes forfeited their claims to the land in Maine in exchange for a $27-million trust fund and $51 million to be used to purchase up to 300,000 acres of land. This settlement gave the Penobscot and the Passamaquoddy tribes a large fund to help improve the lives of their members, and many observers watched closely to see if the tribes would use the money wisely.[2]

The Penobscot Nation made several investments with its share of the settlement. The Penobscot built a factory to manufacture audiocassette tapes, bought a business that created and sold mobile homes, and purchased thousands of acres of timberland to lease to logging companies. The Penobscot made these investments with an eye toward building tribal-owned businesses to provide jobs for tribal members. These investments proved a mixed bag; the cassette factory still operates today, but the mobile-home venture lost money and closed after a few years, and the Penobscot failed to attain their goal of providing jobs in significant numbers for its members.

The tribe's other major investment proved a failure. The Penobscot constructed a huge ice rink on Indian Island, hoping to make money from high school teams renting the arena for practice and for games. They also anticipated that the public on the mainland would cross over the two-lane bridge to Indian Island for skating, ice shows, and the like. The tribe named the arena after its greatest athletic hero, and in 1982 the Sockalexis Ice Arena opened for business on Indian Island. However, the arena struggled financially, and within a few years the tribe closed the Sockalexis Ice Arena. The arena did not draw enough paying customers, probably because people on the mainland resisted traveling to the economically depressed reservation for hockey games and public skating. The building stood unused for several years as a physical representation of the difficulty encountered by the tribe in turning the promise of the 1980 settlement into reality.

Unfortunately for the Penobscot, the tribe may have missed out on an even greater economic opportunity when it accepted the land claims settlement. The Penobscot opened the nation's first large-scale Indian bingo parlor on the reservation in 1973, but the state government objected to gambling in such a form, and a series of legal challenges led the tribe to close the bingo parlor in 1982. A clause in the 1980 settlement, little noticed at the time, forbade the Maine Indians from opening gambling facilities on their reservations without the approval of the state legislature. In 1988, Congress passed a new federal law allowing Indian tribes to build spacious gambling casinos, but the Maine tribes were excluded from that law by virtue of their agreement of eight years before. The Penobscot could only watch with envy as other New England tribes, such as the Pequot in Connecticut, made huge profits from casino gambling. The Foxwoods casino in Connecticut, operated by the Pequot, brings in more money per month than the Penobscot received in the 1980 land claims settlement.

In the early 1990s the Penobscot Nation petitioned the state legislature to allow the tribe to reopen its bingo operation, and after much discussion, the legislature granted its approval in 1993. The tribe rebuilt the Sockalexis Ice Arena and turned it into the Sockalexis Bingo Palace, one of the largest in the nation. It doesn't bring in as much money as casino gambling, but the high-stakes bingo operation employs tribal members and puts money into the tribal coffers. It also helps pay for educational scholarships for Penobscot youth, and today some 77 percent of Penobscot high school students graduate from high school and about 15 percent earn college degrees. These figures compare favorably with the population of Maine as a whole, but about one fourth of households on the reservation live below the poverty line and receive assistance from the federal government.

Like most Indian tribes across the nation, the Penobscot have struggled with alcoholism, unemployment, poverty and crime. Still, their traditional pride shows in their efforts to preserve what is left of their culture. Few people spoke the Penobscot language by 1950, but ethnologists came to the reservation and recorded the voices of the tribe's older members for posterity. Frank G. Speck, a leading cultural anthropologist and professor from the University of Pennsylvania, wrote books and articles about the Penobscot and brought attention to the idea that Penobscot culture, and by extension those of other tribes, was well worth saving.

Today, the tribe is engaged in full-scale efforts to preserve its culture and resurrect the long-dormant Penobscot language. Traditional skills such as canoe making and basketry are cultivated, and native instructors at the school on Indian Island teach Penobscot history and language to children on the reservation. "Before I die," said tribal governor Barry Dana in 2000, "I would like to hear people speaking fluent Penobscot."[3] Since tribal history and culture are inexorably linked to the Penobscot River, the tribe has also taken a leading role in fighting water pollution and has involved itself in a legal and environmental battle against the paper mills that foul the river.

Many of the cultural and environmental events sponsored by the tribe are held at the Sockalexis Bingo Palace, which also serves as the main meeting hall and convention center for the Penobscot. Perhaps it is fitting that the efforts to reinvigorate the culture and history of the Penobscot Indian Nation take place in the building that bears the name of the tribe's most famous and celebrated son.

Though he participated in only 94 major league games, Louis Sockalexis is remembered today while other great players of the 1890s are long forgotten. He is called "the father of the Cleveland Indians," though some critics insist that the Cleveland American League team is more interested in selling pennants and baseball caps than in honoring the contributions of Native Americans. Sockalexis, directly or indirectly, inspired the nickname of the Cleveland baseball team. His athletic feats have been honored by many different organizations. The great Penobscot athlete was elected to the Holy Cross Athletic Hall of Fame in 1956, the Maine Baseball Hall of Fame in 1969, and the Maine Sports Hall of Fame in 1985. In April 2000, he and his second cousin Andrew Sockalexis were inducted into the American Indian Athletic Hall of Fame.

He is not eligible for induction into the National Baseball Hall of Fame in Cooperstown, New York; although he has been nominated in the past, Sockalexis played in the National League for only three seasons, and Hall of Fame candidates are required to have played in all or part of 10 major league campaigns.[4] If he had managed to stay away from alcohol, Louis Sockalexis might well have joined his Cleveland teammates Cy Young, Bobby Wallace, and Jesse Burkett in Cooperstown. Nonetheless, he has earned his place in baseball history. He is remembered not only as the original Cleveland Indian and as the first recognized Native American to play in the major leagues but also as one of the greatest "might-have-beens" in the annals of the game.

Appendix 1

William J. Fox Letter

This letter (from the College of the Holy Cross Archives) was written by Louis Sockalexis' Holy Cross classmate William J. Fox more than 50 years after the two men played together on the Crusader baseball nine. Fox went into the priesthood after graduating from Holy Cross in 1900, and at the time of this letter he was the Right Reverend Monsignor Fox, serving at a church in Connecticut.

> St. Aloysius' Church
> Box 578
> New Canaan, Conn.
>
> July 20, 1949

Dear Friend John:

I received your letter and I was very sorry to hear of the false statement that Sockalexis was expelled from Holy Cross for drinking. That cannot be true. Sock, when at the Cross and a member of the baseball team, was not addicted to drink; in fact I can truthfully say that I never saw Sock take an intoxicating drink while a student at the Cross. Furthermore, I heard at the time he left and from a reliable source, that the members of the faculty were very much displeased at Sock leaving college. Sock was a good, sober, likable fellow and very popular with all the boys on the team with him.

Best wishes to you John for happiness and success.

> Sincerely yours,
> William J. Fox

APPENDIX 2
Sockalexis Statistics

Sockalexis, Louis F.
Born: October 24, 1871, Old Town, Maine
Died: December 24, 1913, Burlington, Maine

Professional record:

Year	Team	League	G	AB	R	H	2B	3B	HR	RBI	Batting Avg	Errors	Field Avg
1895	Lewiston	NE	1	4	1	1	1	0	0		.250	0	1.000
1897	Cleveland	Nat.	66	278	243	94	9	8	3	42	.338	16	.888
1898	Cleveland	Nat.	21	67	11	15	2	0	0	10	.224	1	.964
1899	Cleveland	Nat.	7	22	0	6	1	0	0	3	.273	2	.818
1899	Hartford	East.	26	99	8	22	2	0	0		.222		.918
1899	Water-Bristol	Conn.	61	266	35	85	14	5	1		.320		.808
1900–1901		Out of baseball											
1902	Lowell	NE	105	406	50	117					.288	29	.800
1903	Bangor	Maine	No statistics available										
Major League		Totals	94	367	54	115	12	8	3	55	.313	19	.896

College record:

Year	Team	G	AB	R	H	Batting Avg	Errors	Field Avg
1895	Holy Cross	24	94	31	41	.436	11	.784
1896	Holy Cross	26	126	38	56	.444	8	.888
College totals		50	220	69	97	.441	19	.838

Notes

Chapter 1

1. Paul Bisulca, "Penobscot: A People and Their River," Internet article found at http://www.clf.org/pubs/penob.htm.

2. "Wabenaki" is the generic term for all Maine Indians. The "Abenaki" are one of three groups within the Wabenaki and refers to those in the western and central parts of the state. The other Wabenaki groups were the Armouchiquois, who lived in the area from southern Maine to Cape Elizabeth, and the Etchemin, the modern-day Passamaquoddy and Maliseet, who made their home between the Kennebec and St. John rivers. Some historians also use the term Tarrantines, or Tarratines, to describe the Penobscot.

3. The white man calls it "Mount Katahdin," but the Penobscot know that the word "Mount" is superfluous when referring to the Great Mountain.

4. Frank G. Speck, *Penobscot Man: The Life History of a Forest Tribe in Maine* (Philadelphia: University of Pennsylvania Press, 1940), page 34.

5. Speck, page 186.

6. Joseph B. Oxendine, *American Indian Sports Heritage* (Champaign, Illinois: Human Kinetics Books, 1988), page 11.

7. Speck, page 312.

8. "A Timeline of Native American Culture," from Maine Public Broadcasting System Internet site, "Home: The Story of Maine," at http://www.mpbc.org.

9. This nearly 250-year-old proclamation now hangs on a wall in the tribal governor's office on the Penobscot reservation.

10. Bisulca, op. cit.

11. Frank G. Speck's book *Penobscot Man* lists Sockbeson as a Passamaquoddy name and details mixed marriages in the Sockalexis family between Penobscots and whites in the early to mid–1800s. However, the Penobscot Nation today lists Louis in its records as 100 percent Penobscot Indian, because both of his parents identified themselves as such.

12. Interview in *The Sporting News*, May 1, 1897.

13. *Ibid.*

Chapter 2

1. Anthony J. Kuzniewski, *Thy Honored Name: A History of the College of the Holy Cross, 1843–1994* (Washington, D.C.: Catholic University of America Press, 1999), page 166.
2. These game descriptions are found in "The Hill-Top," the newspaper of the Poland Spring resort, in the issues of July 22 to September 19, 1894.
3. Kuzniewski, page 194.
4. In 1909, Holy Cross Preparatory was separated from the college and designated as a "Classical High School."
5. Kuzniewski, page 164.
6. Kuzniewski, page 168.
7. Kuzniewski, page 168.
8. Kuzniewski, page 171.
9. See Appendix A for the text of this letter.
10. Author's correspondence with JoAnn Carr, archivist of the College of the Holy Cross, June 2001. Other writers have stated that Sockalexis was "reprimanded" for alcohol offenses while at Holy Cross, but such statements are not supported by entries in the discipline diary. Besides, Holy Cross at the time invariably expelled students for inebriation, even for a first offense.
11. "Sockalexis— The Greatest Crusader?" *Holy Cross Alumni Magazine*, May 1951, page 308.
12. Kuzniewski, page 166. Basketball and other sports were played at the O'Kane Gymnasium, which was built in the early 1890s.
13. Undated clipping in Louis Sockalexis file, National Baseball Library, Cooperstown, New York.
14. Sockalexis stole four of the six bases as a substitute runner for an injured teammate. The rules of college ball at the time allowed for one man to bat and another to run for him, if agreed to by both team captains.
15. *The New York Times*, May 16, 1895.
16. Robert L. Tiemann and Mark Rucker, editors. *Nineteenth Century Stars* (Kansas City, Missouri: Society for American Baseball Research, 1989), page 136. Louis had played in several games against Lewiston at Poland Springs in 1894.
17. Many sources state that Louis Sockalexis pitched several games for Holy Cross, and some even claim that he pitched three no-hitters while playing college ball. However, Holy Cross records and newspaper box scores do not list any games in which the Indian pitched.
18. Kuzniewski, page 173.
19. Jay Feldman, "The Rise and Fall of Louis Sockalexis," *The Baseball Research Journal #15 (1986)*, page 40.
20. Related in *Williams College Alumni Review Online*, Spring 2001.

Chapter 3

1. Anthony J. Kuzniewski, *Thy Honored Name: A History of the College of the Holy Cross, 1843–1994* (Washington, D.C.: Catholic University of America Press, 1999), page 170.

2. Many sources erroneously suggest that Frank Merriwell was based on Christy Mathewson, the great Bucknell athlete who became a widely admired pitching star for the New York Giants in the early 1900s. However, Merriwell made his first appearance in dime novels while Mathewson was still attending high school.

3. *New York Sun*, November 11, 1926.

4. Georgetown, like Holy Cross a Jesuit institution, banned football in 1893 after one of their players died from an injury incurred in a game. Georgetown did not play football again until 1898.

5. Kuzniewski, page 170.

6. Kuzniewski, pages 171–172.

7. Kuzniewski, page 172.

8. Kuzniewski, page 168.

9. Kuzniewski, page 172.

10. H. G. Salsinger, "The Facts About Sockalexis," *Baseball Digest*, June 1954, pages 54–56.

11. *Cleveland Plain Dealer*, May 6, 1897.

12. Salsinger, op. cit.

13. *South Bend (Indiana) Tribune*, March 19, 1897.

14. Ibid.

15. *South Bend (Indiana) Tribune*, March 20, 1897. Two days later, the paper seemed to soften its view of the departed Sockalexis, saying that his "loss will be keenly felt" by the baseball team.

Chapter 4

1. *Sporting Life*, May 1, 1897.

2. Robert L. Tiemann and Mark Rucker, editors. *Nineteenth Century Stars* (Kansas City, Missouri: Society for American Baseball Research, 1989), page 124.

3. Bill James, *The Bill James Historical Baseball Abstract* (New York: Villard Books, 1987), page 39.

4. David Nemec, *The Great Encyclopedia of 19th-Century Major League Baseball* (New York: Donald I. Fine Books, 1997), page 580.

5. The four attackers were Tebeau, Jesse Burkett, Ed McKean, and Jimmy McAleer. Tebeau and Jack O'Connor later beat up a Cleveland newspaper reporter, Elmer Pasco, for a story he wrote about the Louisville incident.

6. Charles Alexander, *John McGraw* (New York: Viking Penguin, 1988), page 39.

7. Ibid., page 41.

8. Dennis DeValeria and Jeanne Burke DeValeria, *Honus Wagner: A Biography* (New York: H. Holt, 1996), page 48. "Base ball" was written as two words until the 1920s.

9. *Toledo Blade*, August 11, 1883.

10. Ibid.

11. The Chicagoans won the game by a 7–6 score in ten innings behind their second-string pitcher, Fred Goldsmith. Walker played errorless ball in right field, but he was the only Toledo player to go hitless that day.

12. Labor unions, public transportation, and many other public entities also segregated themselves nationally in this period.

13. *Sporting Life*, September 24, 1884. The magazine investigated the source of the letter and determined that the names of the four men who signed it were fictitious.

14. Interview with Mullane in *New York Age*, January 11, 1919. Also referenced in Jules Tygiel's *Baseball's Great Experiment: Jackie Robinson and His Legacy* (New York: Oxford University Press, 1983), page 15. Mullane added, "One day he signaled me for a curve and I shot a fast ball at him. He caught it and walked down to me. 'Mr. Mullane,' he said, 'I'll catch you without signals, but I won't catch you if you are going to cross me when I give you a signal.' And all the rest of the season he caught everything I pitched without knowing what was coming."

15. Sol White, *The History of Colored Base Ball* (Lincoln: University of Nebraska Press, 1995), page 76. Originally published in 1907, White's book was the definitive history of minority baseball in the latter part of the 19th century; without it, many stories of Moses Walker and other stars would have been forgotten.

16. *Ibid.*, page 15.

17. Moses Walker turned to political pursuits, editing a newspaper with his brother Welday and writing a book in which he advocated black resettlement in Africa. He died in Cleveland in 1924 and was buried in an unmarked grave.

Chapter 5

1. *Cleveland Plain Dealer*, March 20, 1897.
2. Franklin Lewis, *The Cleveland Indians* (New York: G.P. Putnam's Sons, 1949), page 30.
3. *The Sporting News*, March 27, 1897.
4. *Cleveland Plain Dealer*, March 26, 1897.
5. *Cleveland Plain Dealer*, March 23, 1897.
6. *Cleveland Plain Dealer*, March 26, 1897.
7. *Cleveland Plain Dealer*, March 27, 1897.
8. From an undated clipping in the Louis Sockalexis file at the National Baseball Library, Cooperstown, New York.
9. *Sporting Life,* March 27, 1897.
10. The Cleveland Ministerial Association usually supported conservative Republican candidates for city and state office. The mayor of Cleveland, a man named McKisson, had his eye on higher office in 1897 and could not afford to give his approval to Sunday ball and thus offend the conservative elements of the local and state Republican party.
11. *The Sporting News*, March 13, 1897.
12. *Cleveland Plain Dealer*, March 8, 1897.
13. *Cleveland Plain Dealer*, April 1, 1897.
14. *Cleveland Plain Dealer*, March 15, 1897. This poem, by R. K. Munkittrick, was reprinted from the *New York Journal*.
15. *Cleveland Plain Dealer*, April 3, 1897.

16. *The Sporting News*, April 24, 1897.
17. Lewis "Deerfoot" Bennett (1828–97), the greatest marathon runner of the 19th century, was a Seneca Indian from New York who won many distance races in America just before the Civil War. In 1861 he traveled to England and won more races there and on the Continent. Some of the records that he set for 10-mile and 12-mile runs lasted into the 20th century.
18. *Cleveland Plain Dealer*, April 18, 1897.
19. *The Sporting News*, April 24, 1897.

Chapter 6

1. Jonathan Fraser Light, *The Cultural Encyclopedia of Baseball* (Jefferson, N.C.: McFarland, 1995), page 11. However, as noted before, the Penobscot Nation considers Louis to be 100 percent Penobscot Indian.
2. *Louisville Courier-Journal*, April 24, 1897.
3. *Cleveland Plain Dealer*, May 4, 1897.
4. John Phillips, *Chief Sockalexis and the 1897 Cleveland Indians* (Cabin John, Maryland: Capital Publishing, 1991).
5. *The Sporting News*, May 1, 1897.
6. *Cleveland Plain Dealer*, May 8, 1897.
7. Reprinted in the *Cleveland Plain Dealer*, May 13, 1897.
8. *The Sporting News*, February 27, 1897.
9. Reprinted in the *Cleveland Plain Dealer*, May 15, 1897.
10. *Washington Post*, June 9, 1897.
11. *Sporting Life*, April 24, 1897.
12. *Sporting Life*, July 24, 1897. Brown became the manager of the Senators later that year.
13. *Washington Post*, May 27, 1897.
14. Wallace took the starting position at third base away from Sock's Holy Cross coach, Chippy McGarr, who was released by Cleveland in May.
15. Phillips, op. cit.
16. *Cleveland Plain Dealer*, May 8, 1897.
17. *Washington Post*, May 18, 1897.
18. Reprinted in the *Cleveland Plain Dealer*, May 15, 1897.
19. *Sporting Life*, April 24, 1897.

Chapter 7

1. *Sporting Life*, June 19, 1897.
2. *The Sporting News*, August 7, 1897.
3. *Washington Post*, May 22, 1897.
4. *Cleveland Plain Dealer*, May 25, 1897
5. *Cleveland Plain Dealer*, May 24, 1897. The last verse of the poem applied to the Cleveland ministers:

> "Oh, give us rain," the preacher prayed,
> "And give us sunshine too," he said,

"And give us life, and health, and peace,
And make the good and true increase,
And keep us from all sins that come,
To wreck the life and mar the home,
Let us remember Adam's fall,
And keep away from Sunday ball."
Then the fans said,
"Sock-a-lex-is."

6. *Sporting Life*, May 15, 1897.
7. Reprinted in the *Bangor (Maine) Daily Commercial*, May 6, 1897.
8. *Sporting Life*, June 19, 1897.
9. *Sporting Life*, May 15, 1897.
10. This latest embarrassing loss by the Senators forced Washington manager Gus Schmelz to resign and leave the team. Captain Tom Brown took over as manager of the Senators for the remainder of the season.
11. *Cleveland Plain Dealer*, May 15, 1897.
12. *Ibid.*
13. *Cleveland Plain Dealer*, June 16, 1897.
14. *The New York Times*, June 17, 1897.
15. *The New York Herald*, June 17, 1897.
16. John Phillips, *Chief Sockalexis and the 1897 Cleveland Indians* (Cabin John, Maryland: Capital Publishing, 1991).
17. *Ibid.*

Chapter 8

1. *Sporting Life*, May 15, 1897.
2. Lee Allen, *The National League Story* (New York: Hill & Wang, 1961), page 74.
3. Washington Post, July 14, 1897. The papers said that Sock received more "mash notes" than Lee Viau, a former Cleveland pitcher once regarded as the most handsome player in the game.
4. *The Sporting News*, July 24, 1897.
5. *Ibid.*
6. *Cleveland Plain Dealer*, July 13, 1897.
7. *Ibid.*
8. *Cleveland Plain Dealer*, July 22, 1897.
9. *Ibid.*
10. *The Sporting News*, August 27, 1897. A few weeks later, the *Pittsburgh News* printed its own short poem about the Penobscot's troubled season:

For coining words to fit the case,
The season's been prolific.
The strain upon the lexicon
Has been something quite terrific.
The chaps who write about the fights
Have given us solar plexus,

> And a jag they call in Cleveland town
> A quiet Sockalexis.

11. *The Sporting News*, August 14, 1897.
12. *The Sporting News*, August 7, 1897.
13. *Ibid.*
14. Pickering was the inspiration for the term "Texas Leaguer," applied to a bloop hit over the infield. Pickering came to the majors from the Texas League and made several of those hits early in his career.
15. *Sporting Life*, August 21, 1897.
16. John Phillips, *Chief Sockalexis and the 1897 Cleveland Indians* (Cabin John, Maryland: Capital Publishing, 1991).
17. *Wheeling (West Virginia) Register*, August 5, 1897. Burkett was born in Wheeling, though he lived in Worcester most of his adult life, and the Wheeling papers closely followed his career.
18. *Cleveland Plain Dealer*, August 14, 1897.
19. *Washington Post*, August 4, 1897.
20. Phillips, op. cit.
21. *Washington Post*, August 8, 1897.
22. Young's no-hitter was the first one in the National League in four years and the first in all of Organized Baseball in three years.
23. Keith Hodgdon, "The Cleveland Indian," *Sports Illustrated*, June 25, 1973, page M4.
24. *The Sporting News*, October 9, 1897. Tebeau also had Bobby Gilks, an outfielder from Toledo, ready to challenge for the right-field job.

Chapter 9

1. David Voigt, *American Baseball: From Gentleman's Sport to the Commissioner System* (Norman: University of Oklahoma Press, 1966), page 277.
2. *The Sporting News*, January 8, 1898.
3. *Ibid.*
4. *Cleveland Plain Dealer*, March 22, 1898
5. *The Sporting News*, March 12, 1898.
6. *Cleveland Plain Dealer*, March 7, 1898.
7. *Cleveland Plain Dealer*, March 14, 1898.
8. *Cleveland Plain Dealer*, March 11, 1898.
9. *Cleveland Plain Dealer*, March 12, 1898.
10. *Cleveland Plain Dealer*, March 22, 1898.
11. *Cleveland Plain Dealer*, April 1, 1898. The paper also stated that Sock would only receive his salary as long as he "keeps away from the firewater."
12. *Cleveland Plain Dealer*, March 22, 1898.
13. *Cleveland Plain Dealer*, March 19, 1898.
14. *The Sporting News*, April 2, 1898.
15. Pond, who remained in the Army and lived in the Philippines for the remainder of his life, took part in campaigns to eradicate diseases such as leprosy

and malaria from the islands. He served under the governor-general of the Philippines, future President William Howard Taft.

16. *The Sporting News*, April 2, 1898.

17. The Penobscot did not gain the right to vote in national elections until 1954, or in Maine state elections until 1957.

18. Dennis DeValeria and Jeanne Burke DeValeria, *Honus Wagner: A Biography* (New York: H. Holt, 1996), page 56.

19. Pickering held the advantage over Sockalexis until Pickering suffered an injury in spring training when he cut his hand while opening a can of peaches. Pickering played no more for the Spiders but performed well for Cleveland's American League team in 1901 and 1902.

Chapter 10

1. *Sporting Life*, May 7, 1898; also mentioned by J. Thomas Hetrick, *Misfits! The Cleveland Spiders in 1899: A Day-by-Day Narrative of Baseball Futility* (Jefferson, N.C.: McFarland, 1991), page 194.

2. Robison also toyed with the idea of building a Sunday park at Cedar Point, the Lake Erie resort in Sandusky that drew visitors from Detroit and Toledo as well as Cleveland.

3. Robison was disappointed with the attendance in Collinwood. In Chicago that same Sunday, a record crowd of 22,400 saw the Colts defeat the Cincinnati Reds.

4. The city of Cleveland did not allow professional baseball to be played on Sundays in the city until 1911.

5. *Cleveland Plain Dealer*, March 23, 1897.

6. Von der Ahe's money problems caused the Browns franchise to be forced into receivership on August 10, 1898.

7. John Phillips, *The 1898 Cleveland Spiders* (Cabin John, Maryland: Capital Publishing, 1997), pages 66–67. "Pittsburg" was spelled without an ending H in the 19th century.

8. *Ibid.*

9. Phillips, page 67.

10. *The Sporting News*, September 10, 1898. Sockalexis' name does not show up in the statistics of the Interstate League in 1898, so Sock did not play in any official games for the Mansfield nine.

11. Phillips, page 119.

12. *Sporting Life*, November 5, 1898.

13. By contrast, 50 years later the Cleveland American League team drew more than 81,000 fans on a single day.

14. *Pittsburgh Leader*, October 21, 1898; Hetrick, page 25.

15. *Sporting Life*, July 24, 1897.

Chapter 11

1. Lee Allen, *The National League Story* (New York: Hill & Wang, 1961), page 74. Tebeau, speaking 17 years after Sockalexis' memorable 1897 season,

certainly exaggerated the salary figures, since the maximum salary in the league at the time was $2,400.

2. Daniel Okrent and Harris Lewine, editors, *The Ultimate Baseball Book* (Boston: Houghton Mifflin, 1981), page 28.

3. A St. Louis man named G. A. Gruner made the winning bid of $33,000. Edward Becker, Robison's St. Louis partner, then bought the club from Gruner for $40,000.

4. *Cleveland Plain Dealer*, May 18, 1899.

5. *Sporting Life*, March 18, 1899.

6. *Sporting Life*, April 29, 1899.

7. *Cleveland Plain Dealer*, April 25, 1899; J. Thomas Hetrick, *Misfits! The Cleveland Spiders in 1899: A Day-by-Day Narrative of Baseball Futility* (Jefferson, N.C.: McFarland, 1991), page 25.

8. *Cleveland Plain Dealer*, April 2, 1899.

9. *The Sporting News*, May 27, 1899.

10. Hetrick, page 26.

11. *Cleveland Plain Dealer*, April 29, 1899.

12. Hetrick, page 33.

13. Franklin Lewis, *The Cleveland Indians* (New York: G.P. Putnam's Sons, 1949), page 31.

14. *Cleveland Plain Dealer*, May 10, 1899.

15. *Cleveland Plain Dealer*, May 11, 1899.

16. *Cleveland Plain Dealer*, May 18, 1899.

17. Some of the papers also suggested that Cross might send Sockalexis to the Western League team in Detroit to get himself into playing shape.

18. *Pittsburgh Post*, May 14, 1899; Hetrick, page 40.

19. *Cleveland Plain Dealer*, May 17, 1899.

20. John Phillips, *The '99 Spiders* (Cabin John, Maryland: Capital Publishing, 1988).

21. *Cleveland Plain Dealer*, May 17, 1899.

22. Wallace moved to shortstop and took the place of 35-year-old Ed McKean, who was then released by the Perfectos.

23. Allen, pages 79–80.

24. After their last game—a 19–3 loss to the Cincinnati Reds—the Spiders presented their traveling secretary, George Muir, with a diamond locket. "You," said the players to Muir, "are the only person in the world who had the misfortune to watch us in all our games." *Ibid.*, page 80.

Chapter 12

1. Jonathan Fraser Light, *The Cultural Encyclopedia of Baseball* (Jefferson, N.C.: McFarland, 1995), page 11.

2. *1884 Spalding's Official Base Ball Guide.*

3. Bill Veeck with Ed Linn, *Veeck as in Wreck: The Autobiography of Bill Veeck* (New York: Bantam Books, 1963), page 22.

4. *The Sporting News*, June 24, 1899.

5. *Ibid.*
6. *Ibid.*
7. *Sporting Life*, June 24, 1899.
8. The Hartford team kept the Indians nickname in 1900 as well, but Billy Barnie's tenure as manager drew to an end when he resigned due to illness early in 1900. Barnie was only 47 years old when he died of pneumonia on June 16, 1900.
9. *Sporting Life*, September 2, 1899.
10. Undated clipping from Louis Sockalexis file, National Baseball Library, Cooperstown, New York.
11. *Ibid.*
12. Dr. Amir Rezvani, "Models of Addiction," from a course taught at the Bowles Center for Alcohol Studies at the University of North Carolina at Chapel Hill. The entire text can be found on the Internet at http://www.med.unc.edu/alcohol/.

Chapter 13

1. Reprinted in *Literary Digest*, May 27, 1922, pages 53–54.
2. *Philadelphia North American*, August 4, 1912.
3. *Ibid.*
4. Jonathan Fraser Light, *The Cultural Encyclopedia of Baseball* (Jefferson, N.C.: McFarland, 1995), page 11.
5. Lawrence S. Ritter, *The Glory of Their Times: The Story of the Early Days of Baseball Told by the Men Who Played It* (New York: Macmillan, 1966), page 233.
6. Rudy York and Furman Bisher, "A Letter to My Son," *Sport*, June 1954. Reprinted in Charles Einstein, *The Fireside Book of Baseball* (New York: Simon and Schuster, 1956), pages 479–80.
7. Reprinted in *Literary Digest*, May 27, 1922, pages 53–54.
8. Reynolds became active in Indian affairs in his native Oklahoma after he retired from baseball. He served as president of the American Indian Athletic Hall of Fame at the time of his death in 1994. Reynolds won 182 games and lost 107 in his career for the Indians and Yankees, with a 7–2 mark in World Series play.
9. Longboat's 1907 victory was something of a fluke. He was battling one other runner for the lead when he and his challenger crossed a train track at the 12-mile mark. A slow-moving train then came and held up all the other runners for 20 minutes.

Chapter 14

1. *Cleveland Leader*, January 4, 1914.
2. *Philadelphia North American*, August 4, 1912.
3. *Ibid.*
4. Newspaper clipping, dated September 21, 1912, from the Louis Sockalexis file, National Baseball Library, Cooperstown, New York.
5. *Cleveland Leader*, January 4, 1914.
6. *Cleveland Plain Dealer*, April 24, 2000.

7. *Baseball Magazine*, March 1914.

8. The entire poem appears in an article by Catherine Davids titled "A Season of Brilliance," which can be found on the Internet at http://earnestman.tripod.com/sockbio.htm.

9. Lee Allen, *The National League Story* (New York: Hill & Wang, 1961), page 74.

10. It's not clear if Powers was having abdominal problems before the accident on the field, but some insist that he, not Ray Chapman in 1920, was the first on-field fatality in major league baseball.

11. "Rounding Third," undated newspaper clipping in the Louis Sockalexis file, National Baseball Library, Cooperstown, New York.

12. *Ibid*.

13. Undated newspaper clipping from the Louis Sockalexis file, National Baseball Library, Cooperstown, New York. Also referenced by Catherine Davids in "A Season of Brilliance."

14. *Ibid*.

15. "Barrow Roots for Sockalexis," undated newspaper clipping from the Louis Sockalexis file, National Baseball Library.

16. H. G. Salsinger, "The Facts About Sockalexis," *Baseball Digest*, June 1954, pages 54–56.

17. Bill James, *The Bill James Baseball Abstract 1987* (New York: Ballantine Books, 1987), page 56.

18. Lajoie played in 39 games for the Phillies in 1896, but 1897 was his first full season. Also, most sources state that Lajoie was born on September 5, 1874, but his tombstone lists his date of birth as 1875.

19. In fact, Jackie Robinson was one of the greatest athletes in the nation in the 1940s. He led the Pacific Coast conference in scoring in basketball, starred as a running back in football, and, in track, won the 1940 NCAA title in the broad jump. He was also a fine tennis player, golfer, and swimmer.

Chapter 15

1. "Sockalexis—The Greatest Crusader?" *Holy Cross Alumni Magazine*, May 1951, page 308.

2. Some sources list the team name in 1901 as the Bluebirds. The 1900 team was called the Lake Shores.

3. Among the names submitted were Blues, Grays, Lions, and Barons. Cleveland team president Ernest S. Barnard was reportedly partial to Grays as a new name.

4. Ellen Staurowsky, "An Act of Honor or Exploitation?" *Sociology of Sport Journal*, December 1998, volume 15, pages 299–316.

5. For example, before 1946 the Cleveland management required stadium ushers to retrieve foul balls and home runs hit into the stands and did not let the fans keep them.

6. The name of Chief Wahoo probably came from a comic strip called "Big Chief Wahoo," created by Allen Saunders and Elmer Woggon, which made its

debut in the nation's newspapers in 1936. A few years later, the strip introduced the character of an adventurer named Steve Roper, who eventually supplanted Big Chief Wahoo as the main focus of the proceedings. The strip, now written by Allen Saunders' son John, still appears in newspapers today under the title "Steve Roper and Mike Nomad."

7. By coincidence, the Mohawk were the historic enemies of the Penobscot.

8. Laurence M. Hauptman, *Tribes and Tribulations: Misconceptions About American Indians and Their History* (Albuquerque: University of New Mexico Press, 1995), page 81.

9. *Bangor Daily News*, December 9, 2000.

Chapter 16

1. The two main tribes in Maine, the Penobscot and the Passamaquoddy, have each had a representative in the state legislature since the 1820s. That representative has a voice but no vote.

2. Separate settlements in the next few years covered the smaller Micmac and Maliseet tribes, bringing the number of tribes officially recognized by the State of Maine to four.

3. *Boston Globe*, February 20, 2000. Governor Dana uses the traditional term penawahpskewi-sagama, meaning tribal chief of the Penobscot, for his office.

4. Sockalexis could, conceivably, gain election to the Hall as a contributor or a builder of the game by the Committee on Veterans, which elects nonplayers such as managers, executives, and umpires.

Bibliography

Books

Alexander, Charles. *John McGraw* (New York: Viking Penguin, 1988).
Allen, Lee. *The National League Story* (New York: Hill & Wang, 1961).
Burns, Ken, and Geoffrey C. Ward. *Baseball: An Illustrated History* (New York: Alfred A. Knopf, 1994).
The Cleveland Indians 1996 Media Guide.
Danzig, Allison, and Joe Reichler. *The History of Baseball* (Englewood Cliffs, New Jersey: Prentice-Hall, 1959).
DeValeria, Dennis, and Jeanne Burke DeValeria. *Honus Wagner: A Biography* (New York: H. Holt, 1996).
Hauptman, Laurence M. *Tribes and Tribulations: Misconceptions About American Indians and Their History* (Albuquerque: University of New Mexico Press, 1995).
Hetrick, J. Thomas. *Misfits! The Cleveland Spiders in 1899: A Day-by-Day Narrative of Baseball Futility* (Jefferson, N.C.: McFarland, 1991).
James, Bill. *The Bill James Baseball Abstract 1987* (New York: Ballantine Books, 1987).
_____. *The Bill James Historical Baseball Abstract* (New York: Villard Books, 1987).
Johnson, Lloyd, editor. *The Encyclopedia of Minor League Baseball: The Official Record of Minor League Baseball* (Durham, N.C.: Baseball America, 1997).
Kuzniewski, Anthony J. *Thy Honored Name: A History of the College of the Holy Cross, 1843–1994* (Washington, D.C.: Catholic University of America Press, 1999).
Lewis, Franklin. *The Cleveland Indians* (New York: G.P. Putnam's Sons, 1949).
Light, Jonathan Fraser. *The Cultural Encyclopedia of Baseball* (Jefferson, N.C.: McFarland, 1995).
Nemec, David. *The Great Encyclopedia of 19th-Century Major League Baseball* (New York: Donald I. Fine Books, 1997).
Okrent, Daniel, and Harris Lewine, editors. *The Ultimate Baseball Book* (Boston: Houghton Mifflin, 1981).
Oxendine, Joseph B. *American Indian Sports Heritage* (Champaign, Illinois: Human Kinetics Books, 1988).

Phillips, John. *Chief Sockalexis and the 1897 Cleveland Indians* (Cabin John, Maryland: Capital Publishing, 1991).
_____. *The 1898 Cleveland Spiders* (Cabin John, Maryland: Capital Publishing, 1997).
_____. *The '99 Spiders* (Cabin John, Maryland: Capital Publishing, 1988).
Randall, Willard Sterne, and Nancy Nahra. *Forgotten Americans: Footnote Figures Who Changed American History* (Reading, Massachusetts: Addison-Wesley, 1998).
Ritter, Lawrence S. *The Glory of Their Times: The Story of the Early Days of Baseball Told by the Men Who Played It* (New York: Macmillan, 1966).
Seymour, Harold. *Baseball: The Golden Age* (New York: Oxford University Press, 1971).
Smith, Robert. *Baseball* (New York: Simon and Schuster, 1947).
Speck, Frank G. *Penobscot Man: The Life History of a Forest Tribe in Maine* (Philadelphia: University of Pennsylvania Press, 1940).
Tiemann, Robert L., and Mark Rucker, editors. *Nineteenth Century Stars* (Kansas City, Missouri: Society for American Baseball Research, 1989).
Tygiel, Jules. *Baseball's Great Experiment: Jackie Robinson and His Legacy* (New York: Oxford University Press, 1983).
Veeck, Bill, with Ed Linn. *Veeck as in Wreck: The Autobiography of Bill Veeck* (New York: Bantam Books, 1963).
Voigt, David. *American Baseball: From Gentleman's Sport to the Commissioner System* (Norman: University of Oklahoma Press, 1966).
White, Sol. *The History of Colored Base Ball* (Lincoln: University of Nebraska Press, 1995). Originally published in 1907.

Newspapers

Bangor Daily News
Boston Globe
Boston Record
Chicago Tribune
Cleveland Leader
Cleveland News
Cleveland Plain Dealer
Cleveland Press
Detroit News
New York Age
New York Herald
New York Sun
New York Times
South Bend (IN) Tribune
Toledo Blade
Washington Post
Wheeling (WV) Register
Worcester (MA) Telegraph

Magazines

Baseball Digest
Baseball Magazine
Baseball Research Journal
Literary Digest
The National Pastime
Sport
Sporting Life
The Sporting News
Sports Illustrated

Internet Sites

Baseball Reference (http://www.baseball-reference.com)
National Baseball Hall of Fame and Museum (http://www.baseballhalloname.org)
Society for American Baseball Research (SABR) (http://www.sabr.org)
The Sporting News (http://tsn.sportingnews.com)

Index

Aaron, Hank 177, 186
Abenaki 6–7, 110
alcoholism in baseball 142–144
Alexander, Grover C. 144
Allen, Lee 140
American Indian Center of Cleveland 187
Anson, Adrian (Cap) 51–52, 130, 135, 144
Averill, Earl 178

Bangor, Maine 5, 11
Barnie, Billy 145–149
Barrow, Ed 175–176
Bates, Elmer 60, 61–62, 77, 86, 133–134, 140
Bates, Frank 141
Beecher, Ed 125
Belden, Ira 107–108, 111, 114, 117
Bell, Buddy 177
Bench, Johnny 163, 177–178
Bender, Charles 158–160, 163–165
Benner, Leonard 187
Bennett, Lewis (Deerfoot) 66, 165, 190
Bergen, Marty 99
Birmingham, Joe 184
Bisher, Furman 163–164
Blake, Harry 58–59, 73, 78, 88, 96, 98, 100, 107–108, 111–112, 114, 117–118, 123–124, 126, 132–133, 173
Bowens, Sam 177
Breitenstein, Ted 70, 71
Bresnahan, Roger 160
Brown, Tom 77, 91

Brush, John T. 114
Brush Rules, 114–115
Burkett, Jesse 31,33, 41, 55, 58, 63, 71, 74–75, 77–78, 85, 87, 90, 92–93, 104–107, 112, 115, 117, 120, 124, 125, 131–132, 172, 174, 195

Callahan, Jimmy 28, 169
Campbell, Thomas 26
Carlisle Indian School 37, 159, 161, 165, 190
Carlson, Fritz 167
Carrigan, Bill 175
Carter, Jimmy 188, 193
Chalmers, A. B. 63
Chapman, Ray 190
Charboneau, Joe 189
Chief Noc-a-Homa 186, 188
Chief Wahoo 3, 185–189
Childs, Clarence (Cupid) 55, 57–58, 78, 90, 105, 120, 173
Clarke, Fred 70
Clarke, Henry 99–100
Cleveland, Grover 81
Cleveland Indians 2–4, 60–61, 64, 69, 104, 111, 182–189
Coakley, Andy 175
Cobb, Ty 176
Colliflower, Harry 141
Collins, Jimmy 99
Comiskey, Charles 49
Connecticut State League 148–151
Connor, Roger 149–151
Conrad, C. A. 60
Cooke, Fred 103–104
Courtney, Clint 177

Cousy, Bob 40
Criger, Lou 92, 96, 105
Cross, Lave 132–139
Crowfoot, Joe 35
Cuppy, George (Nig) 63, 78, 87, 107, 111, 120
Curley, Walter 26–27
Custer, Gen. George A. 80, 89

Damman, Willie 70
Dana, Barry 189, 195
Delahanty, Ed 76, 102, 106, 143–144
Donlin, Mike 132
Donnelly, Jimmy 102
Dropo, Walt 178
Duffy, Hugh 88, 99
Duffy, Jimmy 166

Ebbetts, Charles H. 129
Ewing, Buck 123

Feller, Bob 176
Finn, John 35
firewater myth 152–155
Flick, Elmer 102, 181
Fosse, Ray 186, 190
Fowler, Bud 53
Fox, William H. 26–27, 30
Fox, William J. 26
Frank, Fred 125
Fraser, Chick 69
Freeman, Buck 141
French and Indian War 11

Gardiner, James 38
George II 11
Goldbach, Walter 185

Index

Great Dying 10–11
Green, Gene 177
Gunshannon, John 149

Hamelin, Bob 178
Hamilton, Billy 160
Hanlon, Ned 49, 130
Harley, Dick 134
Harvey, Ervin (Zaza) 190
Hauptman, Laurence 189
Heidrick, Emmet 125–126, 132
Hill, Bill 117
Hindel, William 41–43
Holy Cross, College of the 21–40
Holy Cross, Congregation of the (Sanctus Christi) 40
Holy Cross Preparatory 24
Hopper, DeWolf 61
Houlton Academy 16–17, 89
Hughey, Jim 141
Hurst, Tim 76

Jackson, Joe 181, 184, 189–190
Jackson, Randy 177
James, Billl 176–178
Jennings, Hugh 129, 174–175
Jesuits (Society of Jesus) 23–24, 26
Joss, Addie 181, 190
Joyce, Bill 91, 133

Katahdin 6, 192
Keefe, Tim 76
Keeler, Willie 129
Kelley, Joe 102
Kelly, Mike (King) 143
Kennedy, Bill 80
Kerrigan, G. C. 22
Kittle, Ron 178
Klobedanz, Fred 75, 85
Knepper, Charlie 141

Lajoie, Napoleon 82–83, 102, 177, 180–182
Lake, Fred 152
Lehy, John 35, 38–39
Listach, Pat 178
Locklear, Gene 163
Longboat, Tom 166
Longfellow, Henry Wadsworth 9, 71, 84
Lowe, Bobby 99
Lynch, Tom 56
Mace, Harry 86

Mack, Connie 88, 99, 159, 174
Maine Indian Land Claims Settlement Act 193–194
Maliseet 7
Mantle, Mickey 144
Maranville, Rabbit 144
Maroney, William 26, 29, 31
Martin, Luis 38–39
Mathews, Bobby 142–143
Mathews, Ed 186
Mays, Willie 177–178
McAleer, Jimmy 58–59, 85, 92, 104, 107, 109, 111–112, 117–118, 120, 123–126, 133, 173, 180
McAllister, Lew 96, 98–100, 102, 104, 108, 120, 137
McBride, Pete 123
McDermott, Mike 87
McDermott, Sandy 74
McFarland, Eddie 71
McGarr, James (Chippy) 22, 31, 33, 41, 55
McGraw, John 49, 69, 140, 145, 160–161, 170, 174
McGurk, Edward 35
McGwire, Mark 144
McKean, Ed 55, 58, 75, 78, 85, 92, 96, 98, 105, 107, 125, 133, 137, 170, 173
McKinley, William 117
Means, Russell 187
Mears, Charles W. 66–67
Meekin, Jouett 91
Mercer, Win 83, 86
Merriwell, Frank 34–35
Meyers, John T. 158, 160–161, 163
Micmac 7
Mileti, Nick 187
minorities in baseball 50–53, 68–69, 158–165
Mohawk 6–8
Morton, Charles 51–52
Muir, George 112
Mullane, Tony 52, 136
Munkittrick, R. K. 84
Murnane, Tim 48, 148–149

Naismith, James 27
National Baseball Hall of Fame 83, 174, 179, 195
Nichols, Kid 74, 86, 99
Nops, Jerry 87, 140
Notre Dame University 39–44, 54

O'Connor, Jack 73, 74, 78, 92, 105, 120, 170
O'Day, Hank 91
O'Keeffe, Tim 148
Old Town, Maine 5, 7, 11–12, 17
O'Malley, Raymond 41
Orono, Joseph 8
O'Rourke, Jim 142, 149

Pappalau, John 26–29, 31, 63, 64, 87, 92, 175
Pardow, William 29
Passamaquoddy 7, 11, 14, 193
Patten, Gilbert (Burt L. Standish) 34–35
Payne, Harley 85
Penobscot Indian Nation 5–16, 110–111, 170, 192–195
Pequot 194
Peterson, A. C. N. 35
Pickering, Ollie 104, 106, 108–109, 111, 114, 117–118
Piniella, Lou 178
Plank, Eddie 159
poetry 2, 61, 64, 71–72, 80, 83–84, 101, 172
Poland Spring Hotel 19–21
Pond, Arlie 116
Powell, Jack 63, 76, 79, 92–93, 98, 100, 105, 107, 120
Powers, Mike 21–23, 26–29, 31–33, 39–40, 43, 50, 173–174
Purbrick, Edward 26, 39
"pure men" 13
Purinton 12

Quinn, Joe 133, 137, 140

Ratio Studiorum 23
Reilly, Charlie 77
Reynolds, Allie 163, 165
Rezvani, Dr. Amir 154
Richter, Francis 47–48
Ricker Classical Institute 16–17, 19
Ritter, Lawrence 161
Robinson, Jackie 4, 52–53, 178–179, 190
Robinson, Wilbert 49, 170
Robison, Frank 57–58, 61–63, 69, 75–76, 78–79, 82, 92–93, 98, 103–104, 107–108, 111–113, 116–122, 130–132, 134–135, 139–140

Index

Robison, Stanley 62, 122, 132
Rose, Pete 178
Rosen, Al 190
Rusie, Amos 89–91, 93, 108
Ruth, Babe 176, 190
Ryan, Michael 165

Sabo, Chris 178
St. Mary's College 17
Salsinger, H. G. 42, 176
Samuelson, Joan Benoit 167
Schmitt, Fred (Crazy) 141
Score, Herb 189
Seaver, Tom 178
Selbach, Kip 120
Seybold, Ralph (Socks) 125
Shea, Pauline 167
Shindle, Billy 85
Sockalexis, Andrew 165–167
Sockalexis, Frances 14, 128
Sockalexis, Francis Peol 14–19, 21, 31, 80–81, 157
Sockalexis, Joseph 14
Sockalexis, Louis: alcohol abuse 42–45, 47, 94–97, 100–104, 112–114, 138–139, 141–142, 147–148, 151–152, 155–156; and Chief Wahoo 3, 187–189; childhood 14–17; in Connecticut State League 148–151; death 169–172; education 16–17, 23–24; 1897 spring training 54–55, 59–66; 1898 spring training 111–114; 1899 spring training 132–134; family 12–14; football career 37–38; as gate attraction 58, 66–67, 84–85, 134, 146; at Hartford 145–148; hazing 64–65, 72, 86, 88, 123–124, 126–127; at Holy Cross 22–40; later life 168–169; at Notre Dame 39–44; at Poland Spring 19–21; relations with teammates 77–78, 105–106; relationship with father 14–19, 21, 31; signs with Cleveland 41–42; and sportswriters 79–80, 126–127; tall tales 80–81, 93–94, 174–176; throwing prowess 21, 30, 32, 66, 76–77; track career 27; umpiring career 158, 168
Sockalexis, Soluice 14
Sockalexis, Tellus (Alice) 14, 128, 157
Sockalexis, Tomar 14
Sockalexis family 12–14
Sockalexis Ice Arena (Bingo Palace) 193–194
Soden, Arthur 74
Somers, Charles 180–182, 184–185
South Bend, Indiana 39–44
Spanish-American War 116
Speaker, Tris 184
Speck, Frank G. 8, 10–11, 194–195
sports, Native American 8–10, 74, 158–165
Stahl, Chick 99
Stargell, Willie 163
Staurowsky, Ellen 185
Stenzel, Jake 69, 102, 132
Stivetts, Jack 136
Stovey, George 52
Sudhoff, Willie 136, 138, 141
Sunday, Billy 143
Sunday ball 57–58, 62–63, 75–76, 79, 92, 98–99, 108, 119–122
syndicate baseball 129–131, 141

Tebeau, George 65
Tebeau, Oliver (Patsy) 33, 41–42, 44, 47–48, 50, 54–61, 63–66, 70, 72–79, 82–83, 85–93, 95–102, 104–109, 111–114, 118, 120, 123–126, 129–132, 138–139, 155, 172–173, 191
Temple Cup series 55–56, 115
Tenney, Fred 29, 99
Tewanima, Lewis 167
Thayer, Ernest L. 80
Thorpe, Jim 37, 158, 161–165, 167, 190

Tiernan, Mike 90
Torre, Joe 177
Toy, James M. 68–69
Trenchard, Thomas 35
Trosky, Hal 190
Tucker, Tommy 137
Turner, Ted 188

umpires 48–50

Veeck, Bill 144, 185–186
Veeck, William 144
Vila, Joe 85
Von der Ahe, Chris 78, 122, 129–132

Wabenaki 6, 10
Wadsworth, Thomas 170
Wagner, John (Honus) 83, 117, 177–178
Walker, Moses F. 50–53
Wallace, Bobby 55, 63, 78, 86–87, 98, 105, 107, 117, 120, 137, 139–140, 173–174, 195
Waner, Paul 144
Ward, John M. 33, 52, 61
Warner, Glenn (Pop) 159, 161
Warren, Maine 30–31
Weidman, Stump 48
Williamson, Ned 143
Wilson, Hack 144
Wilson, Zeke 76, 86–87, 107, 120
Wolf, William 105
Wolverton, Harry 136

Yellowhorse, Moses 68–69, 163
York, Rudy 163–164
Young, Denton T. (Cy) 55, 58, 63, 71, 78, 85–88, 92–93, 102–104, 107, 118, 121, 131, 134, 136, 140, 173–174, 181, 195
Young, Nicholas 50, 79, 98–99, 108

Zimmer, Charles (Chief) 55, 58, 63, 73, 78, 86, 92, 102, 124, 133–136, 140

www.ingramcontent.com/pod-product-compliance
Ingram Content Group UK Ltd.
Pitfield, Milton Keynes, MK11 3LW, UK
UKHW041953140426
5217IPUK00015B/774